Conversations with God

Conversations with God

Two Centuries
of Prayers
by African
Americans

edited with an introduction by

James Melvin Washington, Ph.D.

HarperCollins*Publishers*

HarperCollins books may be purchased for educational, business, or sales promotional use. For information please write: Special Markets Department, HarperCollins Publishers, Inc., 10 East 53rd Street, New York, NY 10022.

FIRST EDITION

Designed by Nancy Singer

Library of Congress Cataloging-in-Publication Data

Conversations with God : two centuries of prayers by African Americans / edited with an introduction by James Melvin Washington. — 1st ed.
    p.   cm.
Includes bibliographical references and index.
ISBN 0-06-017161-8
1. Afro-Americans—Religion.   2. Prayers.   I. Washington, James Melvin.
BR563.N4C65   1994
242'.8'008996073—dc20   94-25327

94 95 96 97 98 PS/RRD   10 9 8 7 6 5 4 3 2 1

To my precious and dearly beloved
mother,
Annie Beatrice Moore Washington (1912–),
retired housekeeper, and a member of
the Mothers' Board of the Mount Olive Baptist Church
(Knoxville, Tennessee),
who taught me to pray,
and
Willie Charlease Gaines Crutcher (1920–),
my dearly beloved spiritual mother,
and the first lady emeritus (1951–1989) of
the Mount Olive Baptist Church,
and
in memory of my mother- and father-in-law,
Lula Cole Alexander (1908–1993) and
Clarence Edward Alexander (1906–1989),
whose prayers at the kitchen table renewed our faith

Contents

Part II. The Crucible of the Anglo-African Conscience, 1861–1893

Part V. The Civil Rights Ethos, 1956–1980

List of Illustrations

Frontispiece: Deaconess Rosa Williams prays before a women's meeting at the Progressive Baptist Church (Brooklyn, New York) in 1989. Used by permission of the photographer, Marilyn Nance.

Part I.   Sol Etyinge sketched this familiar scene of "A Negro Campmeeting in the South." It was published in *Harpers Weekly* (10 August 1872): 620. Courtesy the New York Public Library, Schomburg Center for Research in Black Culture.

Part II.   Joseph Becker sketched this intense moment of worship at an African-American church at Grafton, New Yorktown, Virginia, during the watch night service on New Year's Eve, 1879. This sketch was published in 1880. Courtesy the Bettmann Archive.

Part III.   An ex-slave kneels in prayer before the rural gravesite of his loved one. This photograph by Leigh Richmond Miner is entitled "The Memory." It was taken in 1900. Courtesy the Tuskegee Institute Archives.

Part IV.   These church women raise their hands in praise and personal prayer while their bishop is praying. Although the specifics of this photograph have been lost, it captures the fervency of the new urban African-American spirituality that developed during this period of the greatest African-American migration in American history. Courtesy the Bettmann Archive.

Part V.   On 21 July 1962 the Reverend Samuel B. Wells led some civil rights demonstrators in Albany, Georgia, in prayer. In an effort to fill jails beyond their capacities, the "Albany Movement" used several continuous waves of demonstrators. Wells and 112 others were jailed for parading without a permit after nearly 200 local, county, and state police stopped a larger march of approximately 500 demonstrators. Later, 48 African Americans who were participating in a second march were also arrested. Courtesy the Bettmann Archive.

Part VI. Heru Khuti (front left) and other young men who will mature in the twenty-first century use their own spiritual resources rather than those proffered by institutionalized religions to offer moving prayers of thanksgiving and homage to God for their ancestors who were buried in the recently discovered African Burial Ground in lower Manhattan. This picture was taken in 1992, and is used by permission of the photographer, Marilyn Nance.

Acknowledgments

Many debts have been accumulated in the course of producing this book. There will inevitably be persons whom I will forget to mention. This is one of the hidden taxations of a weary editor at the end of a very difficult project. But there are some friends and colleagues that it would simply be unforgivable not to acknowledge. I depended upon a core group to assist in producing the manuscript. The quarterback of the effort to convince me to edit this book was Quinton Hosford Dixie, my excellent research associate and Ph.D. student, whose constant but gentle nudging finally helped me to see the necessity for producing this collection. I also cannot possibly convey to both Tracey Sherrod, our precious friend, and Denise Stinson, my literary agent, the full extent of my gratitude. Denise's invaluable advice and deep spirituality helped me to weather many personal and professional trials. Her enthusiasm for this project arrested my attention and emboldened my spirit. I deeply appreciate her confidence in me and my work. Strong words of encouragement came at the right moment from my two pastors: the Reverend Dr. Gary V. Simpson of the Concord Baptist Church of Christ (Brooklyn), and the Reverend Dr. James A. Forbes, Jr., of the Riverside Church (New York). Although I thought about the possibility of doing a book like this over twenty years ago while a student at Harvard Divinity School, I never consciously pursued it until Richard Newman, a good friend and distinguished bibliographer of African Americana, rekindled my interest.

It would not have been possible to produce this book without the splendid assistance and cooperation of the staffs of three great libraries in the City of New York: the Walter Burke Library at the Union Theological Seminary, the largest theological library in the Western Hemisphere, the New York Public Library's Schomburg Center for Research in Black Culture, and the Libraries of Columbia University. I especially want to express my gratitude to Professor Milton McCormick Gatch, Jr. (Director), Betty Bolden, Drew Kadel, and Seth Kasten of the Burke Library, and my good friend, Howard Dodson, Chief of the Schomburg Center.

The Board of Directors and the Faculty of Union Theological Seminary supported production of this book by granting me a sabbatical leave during the 1993–94 academic year. The Lilly Endowment also indirectly supported this project through monies paid me to direct a major grant given to Union Theological Seminary to support my long-range research project on the religious history of the Civil Rights Movement. I am indebted beyond measure for the largess of these two grand institutions.

Along the way of completing this complex project, words of encouragement, insights, information, and other forms of assistance cheered me on. Those I feel particularly indebted to for such gifts include Lucas Bernard Wilson, Nathaniel Everett Deveaux, Obie Wright, Jr., Michael Eric Dyson, Genna Rae McNeil, Ann and Barry Ulanov, Richard Norris, Randall Burkett, David Daniels, Moses N. Moore, Irene Jackson-Brown, John Wright, Vera Balma, Patrick Minges, Martha Wiggins, and Eloria Gilbert. Numerous pastors across the nation have responded graciously and kindly to my requests for information and assistance. I especially appreciate the help of the Reverend Drs. J. Alfred Smith and Cecil Williams. Professor Cornel West of Harvard University, my precious friend and brother, knows the depth of my appreciation and love for all he means to me and to America. I dedicate my own prayer in commemoration of the nearly twenty years we have shared in the struggle for human decency, justice, and spiritual integrity in an unrighteous world.

Peternelle van Arsdale, my excellent, extraordinarily patient editor, endured my overburdened schedule and idiosyncrasies with graciousness far beyond the call of duty. I am particularly grateful that she did not try to suppress my distinctive, and maybe even peculiar, voice.

My beloved, lovely, and vivacious wife, Patricia Anne Alexander-Washington, and of course Ayanna Nicole, our daughter, provide sanity, structure, and sober joy for their obsessive-compulsive husband and father. Words are inadequate to express the depth of my appreciation and affection.

Alas, I must take responsibility for all the strengths and shortcomings of this book. But I trust that the prayers of the righteous will ask for mercy, and grant forgiveness for my faults.

Introduction

A strange irony haunts this book. I did not believe that it could or should be done. Others believed in it before I did. I am unsure of the mixture of motivations for their efforts to encourage me to edit this book, but my reasons for resisting their entreaties are now clearer to me. They constituted a threefold ensemble of fears. Rather than see this book as a presentation of acts of faith, profiles of spiritual intimacy and courage among an often despised people, and insights into the oratory and rhetoric of personal prayer, I feared unwittingly making a contribution to the grotesque profiteering, profanation, and cultural voyeurism that stalk our times.

I felt that such a book might be seen as another attempt to maraud the African-American past for the sake of profit and curiosity. My disdain for profiteers is matched only by my repugnance for eavesdroppers who have spawned what Stephen Carter rightly calls "the culture of disbelief." I did not want to participate in parading the spiritual healing processes of my wounded people before unempathetic consumers.

As a historian of African-American religion, I was quite aware of the cynicism that has often made the spiritual life of my people part of a cultural menagerie. This indecency callously subjects genuine spiritual struggles to ridicule, dismissing them as superstitious and escapist, or reducing them to various doctrinaire theories of group frustration.

The intellectual hegemony of the social sciences for most of the twentieth century accounts for how some descriptions profane African-American spirituality. Even William E. B. Du Bois, the great African-American social scientist and historian, was a captive of the objectivist language of his academic disciplines. On the one hand, he admonished those who observe "the frenzy of a Negro revival in the untouched backwoods of the South" to remember the limitations of the art of description. "As described," he opined, "such scenes appear grotesque and funny," but, on the other hand, "as seen they are awful."[1] Portrayals of the sublime usually defy the rationalistic assumptions of modernists. The sometimes violent churnings of religious experience strike its bourgeois analysts as vile precisely because such sacred wrenchings labor for rebirth oblivious to the canons of correct behavior.

The tools of intellectual analyses are actually a double-edged sword. They allow us to see into the entrails of human expressions of the divine. But they are rarely able to explain the meaning of what is seen, or how to re-create the corpora of divinity. The sublime, with its mixture of beauty and ugliness, is best acknowledged in its extremities. After his close documentation of the various macrocosms of religious experience, William James felt the necessity to explain why he chose the most graphic examples to illustrate his theories. He wrote, "I took these extreme examples as yielding the profounder information. To learn the secrets of any science, we go to expert specialists, even though they may be eccentric persons, and not to commonplace pupils. We combine what they tell us with the rest of our wisdom, and form our final judgement independently. Even so with religion."

From the standpoint of many believers, however, such procedures are fraught with sacrilege. Even some describers of black religious experience admit their feelings of embarrassment in revealing the details of spiritual intimacy. Those who report on their visits to black prayer meetings often feel compelled to apologize for their fascination. Eli N. Evans, a southern-born Jew, highlighted this ambivalence in how he remembered his attendance at black prayer meetings:

> We white boys went to black prayer meetings of the holy rollers just to watch them move, and clap hands, and sing out "Hallelujahs" and "Amen, brother." We bathed in the "Oh tell it . . . tell it" magic of hypnotic stimulation between preacher and congregation, each driving the other on to mounting excess of singsong sermonizing and jump-up conversions and twitching moments of "cain't-stand-it-no-more" spiritual release and liberation.

He went on to describe the cultural chasm separating the observer and the believer: "For us white boys clustered way back where we had to stand to see anything, it was more like going to a performance than to a religious service."

The necessity for such distancing is entirely understandable for a Jew who finds Christianity oppressive. Indeed, Evans quickly asserted that African-American religion posed no threat to his sense of Jewish identity. He reasoned that no black preacher would invite Jewish white boys to convert to Christianity. Moreover, "afterwards, all of us [white boys] together would imitate the Negro preacher, moaning and crying out the 'praise the Lawd' accents of the panting sermons." The problems and pains of African-Americans as evident in their religious expressions have been too often a source of humor, black or white.[2] Why I take religion so seriously can best be explained autobiographically.

If I do not add this parenthetical comment, what follows might be viewed as unwarranted vanity, if not spiritual arrogance. I must speak in this way, however, even though it makes me uneasy. Self-disclosure is fraught with pretension and unwitting, if not intentional, caricature. Nonetheless, an editor has an obligation to disclose the criteria, assumptions, and worldview that influenced the content and structure of his or her book. The ethics of authorship demand at least that modicum of respect for one's readers. Yet, encroachments of self-deception, those fleeting shadows of the unconscious, often disguise the layered masks of years of carefully crafted repressions. This of course cannot lead to the presentation of the real person. That is too ugly to see and too painful to share. Nevertheless, the servanthood of authorship, especially of a text that is so shamelessly about the spirituality of a despised people, must attempt to draw from the encrusted conventicles of the author's persona precisely because what the author sees is inevitably the hidden sinew of the book itself. And only the author is situated behind those eyes. An author must therefore choose an appropriate camera for the self-examination of his soul lest the enterprise fall prey to an embarrassing sentimentality.[3] With this confessional excursus out of the way, I can now explain why I strongly dislike caricatures of any people's or person's spirituality.

Unlike Evans's, my first experience in observing the prayers and rituals of another faith tradition and race struck me as poignant and holy. Like most kids, I definitely could be silly and frivolous—but not about religion. According to my mother, and many other adults in my neighborhood and at the Mount Olive Baptist Church, I had the mark of divine anointment on me. In fact, my mother often told me that Mr. Warren, our next-door neighbor in the Austin Homes Project, looked over in my crib when she and my father brought me home from the old Colored General Hospital in Knoxville, Tennessee, and yelled, "Annie! Will! That little rascal will either be a preacher or go crazy!" He told them that he saw the light of God's countenance shine upon my little face. Later, I indeed felt that some strange sunshine was beaming excruciatingly hot rays upon my soul. A crass materialist reading of my experience might conclude that it was the churning of hormones, or the whirlwinds of the Civil Rights Movement. I was in a state of profound angst, but I did not have the intellectual or social maturity to speculate about the source of my experience of God's presence. I only knew I felt the numinous clearly and powerfully.

The year was 1962, and I was 15 years old and in the tenth grade. The tumultuous public anxiety surrounding the student sit-ins beckoned me to join the fray. I tried. But Willie, one of my older brothers, threatened to beat me if he saw me embarrassing us by joining in with "those crazy students." I always took his threats seriously—perhaps because he made good on them with what I felt was rather malevolent precision. In order to keep me out of trouble, and encourage me to help ease our poor family's enormous financial burdens, he secured a job for me as his helper. He was the custodian of the Heska Amuna Synagogue, which belongs to the Orthodox branch of American Judaism.

After sundown on Fridays, the men of this congregation, usually led by Rabbi Max Zucker and the cantor, would have their prayer services. I found it enthralling and enchanting to hear the descendants of Jesus sing praises and utter prayers to the God of Abraham and Sarah in the Hebrew tongue. As I listened to their services, I thought about the lessons I was learning from Mr. Lorenzo Grant, my black world history teacher, about the evils of Christendom's pogroms against the Jews, and especially about what Hannah Arendt called "the banality of evil" that was shamelessly fomented by the Nazi Holocaust. I heard and felt the pain and suffering of the Jewish people remembered and surrendered to Yahweh.

I was not sure even then, however, that these affluent people understood and appreciated the terrors and pains of my people's history. I sensed that they were more sensitive than most other white people. But I felt their sensitivity was based more on pity than on personal knowledge or affection. Too many of them did not even see me. I was invisible until they needed a light switch turned on, a meat dish rather than a dairy dish, and so on. I did not feel the need to hold this against them. After all, they were white. I had been taught to expect to be treated like a "whatnot" by white people. But these Jews were a different sort of white people. They seemed to have real religion. I felt the presence of God as they prayed and sang. For me, no one's religion is a laughing matter, most certainly not my own.

In the summer of 1961, I had already arisen from my seat at a youth convocation sponsored by the National Baptist Young People's Union (BYPU) declaring that God had called me to be a preacher while the great Lucie Eddie Campbell Williams sang "It Pays to Serve Jesus." She died the following year. But my commitment did not wane.

I began my ministry as a teenage pastor in east Tennessee after I was ordained in 1967 by the Mount Olive Baptist Church at the request of the Riverview Missionary Baptist (Lenoir City, Tennessee). In the midst of the Black Power Revolt, I became my 126-member congregation's nineteen-year-old pastor. I underwent the traumas of confronting the need to change from a Negro to a black man. Then from black to Afro-American, and now to African American. These demands for identity changes bespoke a deep yearning for roots and continuity on the part of many baby boomers like myself. Those of my generation who were saved from the altars of infanticide in the service of the American war against Vietnam often found ourselves seeking messianic hope wherever we could find it. The American Dream, John Winthrop's City upon a Hill, collapsed under the weight of the shameful and macabre spectacle of the wanton destruction of Vietnamese villages, body bags containing our dead friends and neighbors, as well as pompous and unrepentant nationalism paraded daily on national television. That theater of the Cold War shattered the youthful idealism that was spawned by the Civil Rights Movement as well as the collapse of colonialism and the repressive comatose shadows of Victorian culture.

I escaped military experience because of severely fallen arches, conscientious objection to war, and a fervent call to ordained Christian ministry. My contemporary religious hero was Martin Luther King, Jr. When he was martyred on 4 April 1968, I reexamined my vocational commitments. Inspired partly by James Baldwin's *The Fire Next Time* (1962) and James H. Cone's *Black Theology and Black Power* (1969), I discovered in existentialism a certain secular celebration of the inevitability of marginality. I now have recovered what I repressed then: These intellectually respectable endorsements of black self-respect and disciplined alienation salvaged crucial dimensions of the Black Church that were being severely challenged by my superb training in the Department of Religious Studies at the University of Tennessee at Knoxville.

As my professors at Tennessee introduced me to the ideas and history of modern European thought between 1600 and the 1960s, I resonated best with those thinkers—like Kierkegaard, Nietzsche, Barth, and Sartre—who grappled with the problem of the absurd. Thanks to my later exposure to the thought of Professor Charles Long of the University of California at Riverside, I now understand why. Professor Long, one of the seminal African-American religious scholars of this century, argues in his book *Signification: Signs, Symbols, and Images in the Interpretation of Religion* (1986), and elsewhere, that if the problem of meaninglessness, or the absurd, is the root metaphor of modernity, then the African-American experience of slavery and racism must be counted as a major embodiment of the modern problem of alienation. My own extensive research and writing in African-American religious history has confirmed the significance and veracity of this rich insight.

The absurdities of racism insinuate themselves in conscious and unconscious ways in the lives of black people. Religion has been a central way for us to maintain our sanity. But we live in a time when too many African Americans are being infected with the ensemble of societal viruses that Cornel West calls "nihilism." This undisciplined and callous anger grieves me deeply. And it offers a fundamental challenge to my own faith commitment in ways that my struggles with intellectual secularism have never succeeded in doing.

My experience in the pastorate taught me that spiritual malaise is the root cause of the social callousness that has befallen too many segments of African America. Given this belief, I have been asking myself several questions: Can I really prove that spiritual malaise is the cause and not the consequence of nihilism? And if I could succeed in proving this point, what difference would this make? How could I as a middle-aged black religious scholar address this crisis? Should I return to the pastorate and share in the valiant struggle to combat this evil that *Emerge* magazine has rightly called "the worst crisis since slavery"? Over the years several friends of mine, especially those who are pastors, have urged me to return to that most primary form of ministry. But when I recall the intellectual and social experiences that led me to leave the pastorate, my urge is tempered. I have been trying to recover the history of the spiritual disciplines that sustained my people through slavery, Jim and Jane Crowism, and the Civil Rights Movement. Some of those disciplines are still nurtured by institutional African-American religion. But many of them have been either deemed irrelevant or have been forgotten. Most have simply died with an older generation whose insights and practices were dismissed by well-meaning advocates of Black Power who saw such people as obstructions on their self-proclaimed "progressive" road to African-American nationalism.

As we have come to expect from him, Cornel West, in his brilliant manifesto *Prophesy Deliverance! An Afro-American Revolutionary Christianity* (1982), has telescoped the significance of the problem of both human and divine evil in the history of Christian thought. Indeed he examines the possibilities and contradictions of the major streams of progressive African-American religious history. Those who now regularly assess his work often fail to mention this book. They seem unaware of its emerging landmark status in the history of Christian thought in the United States precisely because he succeeds in making the connection between the crisis of modernity and religious responses to the terrors of African-American history.

When West and I began teaching at Union Theological Seminary in the late 1970s, we spent seven unforgettable years discussing problems and issues that still command the foci of our intellectual concerns. Among those issues were these questions he raised in his first book: "Why did large numbers of American black people become Christians? What features of Protestant Christianity persuaded them to become Christians?" He framed these questions in a way that demanded the largely philosophical and historical responses that he offers. But, as West would readily agree, far more historical and theological work is needed.

More than a decade later, I am still asking those kinds of questions. But I have also been asking the question of faith. That is, why do people who suffer continue to believe in a God who supposedly has the power to prevent and alleviate suffering? This question bedevils the history of Western monotheism. Indeed, some walk away from such questions because they no longer believe in the existence of God. I must confess that for the sake of my own peace of mind I sometimes wish that I could do the same. But I have been burdened with the assumptions and responsibilities of an intellectual monotheist who still believes in the God that I first came to acknowledge through the Hebrew and Christian scriptures.

The denial of the reality of God has become fashionable among the affluent. Such secularity often belittles folk thought as if learning how to read and write in the halls of academe is a guarantor of our supposedly greater wisdom. But one need only observe the stars on a clear evening to register the unimaginativeness of such cynicism. Indeed, stargazing, a favorite pastime of those, such as unmolested children, who still cherish wonder and curiosity, offers awesome, transporting access to the utter beauty and terrifying grandeur of the universe.[4] Such stargazing is pleasurable precisely because it defies the banal interests of our utilitarian age.

Prayer is an attempt to count the stars of our souls. Under its sacred canopy, an oratory of hope echoes the vast but immediate distances between who we are and who we want to be. This peculiar trek sentences its devotees to an arduous discipline. Prayer demands focus and obedience, as well as intimacy and faithful nurture. A certain civility is inherent in this transaction. Its requirements are both communal and individual. I accept Ludwig Wittgenstein's tightly reasoned convictions that language itself is social.[5] I guess that is why I believe that the oratory of prayer is deeply shaped by one's upbringing.

Those of us who cherish the fading art of counting the stars above, and the stars within, should not become despondent. Every minute of each fleeting day documents how human forgetfulness ends with someone's death, or is diminished by someone's birth. Children who have not been captured by the cynicisms of adulthood replenish the imagination of the human community. My personal experience and historical research have taught me that the children of God, when at their best, also inspire the best in us. My mother, Annie Beatrice Moore Washington, whose fifth-grade education could assist her in getting no further than a career as an honest domestic worker, has taught me more about prayer in the African-American community than anyone else I know. I wish I could remember the exact date, my age, the circumstance of what follows, but I cannot.

It was during the early morning hours, while the gladiatorial snores of my sleeping family rebuked silence, that two of us were actually awake. The window of the crowded children's bedroom framed the East Tennessee sky as I lay communing with the stars. A whisper from my parents' bedroom forced me to cease my transporting enterprise. I strained to hear what I would now call a divine soliloquy. It was Mama's voice. She was speaking in piteous hush. I yearn to recapture her exact words. I cannot. I do know that the drama of the moment demanded that I should stop counting stars. I could not resist the temptation to eavesdrop on a most unusual conversation. Mama said a few words about her burdens, anxieties, children. Then an awesome silence would punctuate her lamentation to . . . God? Who was her conversation partner? Daddy was working on the night shift. "Please, Jesus!" she cried. I felt she was hurt, maybe even dying. I ran to be with her. I rubbed her back while she sobbed.

In many ways I have been in spiritual solidarity with my mother since that moment. She taught me to pray. Her silence and her action taught me that I must pray. The distinction between necessity and instructions is paramount. There is a vast difference between giving directions and believing that those directions are either helpful or vital. As I watched her for most of my young life, I noticed that for her prayer is a way of life. At any moment, pray. I learned many things from that strange moment when my mother and I were on our knees in prayer. Indeed, more than any other, through precept and example, she taught me that prayer is a conversation with God. That was the reigning assumption of the African-American Christian community that nurtured me. God is a living, personal presence that is insinuated at all times and in all circumstances.

When I was eight years old, it was the custom in our small community to assign to youngsters responsibilities that would teach them "to respect their elders." There was a proud and severely crippled elderly black woman whose name was Mrs. Helen Grady. Because she was a good friend of both my mother and my grandmother, it gradually became my duty and privilege to perform errands for this strange woman. She had the dubious reputation among my playmates of being "an old grouch." But she had her reasons for being temperamental.

Her very physical presence would startle any "normal" person. A dark hue in a racist society was not an asset—even among her own people. Her face bore the imprimatur of deep pain, and I discovered later that she was indeed in constant agony. Polio, that dreaded disease, had dealt its greatest blow to her right side. Her shriveled right hand was permanently cupped. She often joked about this by saying it was always ready for work. It could only assist her left hand, however, since all its muscles were totally useless. She used a strong cane to help her left side drag her right side along. But Helen Grady's handicap did not define or fully describe the rich complexity of her personality.

I learned that her gruff manner was actually a protective facade developed to ward off busybodies. But she really loved children. I sensed this and learned to love her back. I eagerly looked forward to my daily visits to her home. She became a generous teacher, and I became an eager student. She taught me how to hoe a garden with only "one good arm," how to get eggs out of the chicken coop without getting pecked, how to light a fire in an old iron stove which burned coal and wood, and countless other practicalities of poor folk existence. But most important, she took time to introduce a small-town boy to black agrarian culture. She told me countless stories and interpreted the Bible to me after I read passages to her. Even though, I discovered later, she could read, she indulged my passion to display my ability.

She even became my confessor. She confronted the awful monsters of my childhood dreams with the tough realism of folk wisdom and Christian charity. She often ended our little dialogues by saying, "Now, honey, let's talk to the Lord." I cannot recall her exact words. But I can still relive, even now, the sense of God's presence her words invoked. I did not mistake her words for magical incantations. God was there. I could feel a third presence. When she finished what she had to say to God, she invited me to join the conversation. Sometimes we even prayed at the same time. After all, we believed that God is supralingual and omnipresent. As she appealed to "the Throne of Grace," she sobbed with tears of protest against the human condition; and, with tears of faith and thanksgiving, she told the Lord how grateful she was that the Lord God could care about "worms" like us. She asked the Lord to have mercy on my soul and lead me in "the paths of righteousness." These numinous moments captured my attention, affections, and faith. If God could make a crippled bulwark like Mrs. Grady break down in tears and shout with joy, how could I possibly escape this awesome power? I came to believe that such escape was both impossible and exceedingly unde-sirable.

Mrs. Grady taught me that I should not feel like a prisoner or a slave. She taught me that I am a free spiritual being. She taught me that true spirituality is the ability to see beyond my own prejudices and shortsightedness. Mrs. Grady introduced me to the reality of the spiritual world. She, along with numerous other saints, convinced me that there is a spiritual realm that is available to all who find its many entrances.

In the Mount Olive Baptist Church, where I belonged and was later ordained, I often watched oppressed black women, and some-times even men, offer shouts of joy embellished with fierce, holy gesticulations. The first enduring sounds of black worship I saw and heard included the strangely warm and often intense cadence of black preachers like Dearing E. King and Charles Dinkins. I also witnessed the prayers of Deacons C. L. Bell, Robert Minter, and George Thor-ton; the testimonies of Mothers Eliza Dunlap and Lizzie Bates, as well as the angelic singing of Sister Mary Usher and Brother Murphy Strong. Their praise still rings with delight within my memory.

Mrs. Grady revealed to me that these "friends of Jesus" actually slipped into a different time zone, a different realm of existence. I saw these glorious excursions most intensely in her local church. She was a member of the Mothers' Board of the Victory Baptist Church, a tiny congregation endeavoring to maintain the "Ole-Time Reli-gion." The residuals of African-American Slave Religion were quite evident here, where they moaned and groaned before God. Her pastor whooped, and her church relied on common meter hymn singing more than my home church.

Mrs. Grady, my beloved friend and spiritual counselor, is dead now. Perhaps the only recognizable living form of the religious culture she loved so dearly exists in black congregations like Mount Olive and Victory. When I attend black worship services of nu-merous denominations as either a guest preacher or fellow worshiper, I often see Mrs. Grady's face, and feel her presence among my sisters and brothers in the faith as they pray, sing, testify, and shout about what the Lord has done for them. But where I experience her companionship the most is in my own peculiar prayer life. For me prayer is not a ritual. It is a mode of being. I agree with John

Macquarrie in his *Paths to Spirituality* that prayer is "a way of thinking." I also like the way my colleagues Ann and Barry Ulanov define and describe prayer as "primary speech." These assessments of the meaning of prayer only ratified what I first learned in the African-American religious community. I was taught that we must know how to talk and think with God.

One need only look at the prayers in this book to see that African Americans have believed fervently that prayer is a necessity in time of crisis. Those who have been the victims of what Orlando Patterson has called "natal alienation" understand this. Prayer in the midst of the abortion of one's human, political, and social rights is an act of justice education insofar as it reminds the one who prays, and the one who overhears it, that the one praying is a child of God. The Reverend Horace J. Bailey, pastor of the Payne Avenue Baptist Church (Knoxville, Tennessee), reminded me of this in 1970.

That year I learned from him that prayer is more than ordering from the menu of divinity, as if God is some cosmic waiter who serves us at our convenience. I found myself undergoing the humiliations of the sacrament of imprisonment, in jail for a righteous cause. I carried a sign amidst a small group of antiwar demonstrators who were protesting the presence of the president of the United States, Richard M. Nixon, at a Billy Graham Crusade which was being held at the University of Tennessee at Knoxville's Neyland Stadium. The authorities issued John Doe warrants with the cooperation of the university administration and the local media.[6] For the first time in my life, I discovered that righteousness and "good" citizenship are often incompatible. This was a painful lesson in its own right. But an even more profound lesson awaited me when I visited the pastor's study of the very pious Reverend Bailey. I recounted the experience of being arrested in the middle of campus, carted in a paddy wagon, fingerprinted, photographed, and slammed behind bars for several hours until the Reverend Robert Parrott, director of the Wesley Foundation at the university, secured a bail bond. A sense of rejection, alienation, humiliation, and defeat impeded my spirit from rallying.

The good pastor interrupted my self-pitying litany of woes when he said, "Wait a minute, James." He was an old minister of the gospel. The arthritis that had taken residence in his body made his movements slow and agonized. He kneeled in front of his desk chair.

"Let's talk to God about this," he said. He prayed for my soul and my ministry, and against the demons of bitterness. He asked God to give me strength to look beyond the faults of others. "Keep James in your care, O Lord! He will be a mighty strong weapon in your warfare against evil!" My Black Power outlook disliked his tolerance for human evil. But I have come to see that he was more concerned about what human evil was doing to my soul than about what human evil was doing to my body. This might be a false dichotomy. But it is a real distinction in many African-American prayers.

A satisfactory comparative history and anthropology of prayer has yet to be written. But whenever such a study appears, surely Theodore Parker Ferris's apt description of the transaction called prayer will be uncontested. According to Ferris, "People who pray feel that they are in some communication with God." Millions believe in the power of this mysterious transaction. Yet few can translate the spiritual content of this peculiar form of communication. In fact many believe that it is impossible.

The prayers in this book were all uttered within the last 230 years under various circumstances, which will be described whenever possible in the Contributors section. A common mood of resistance to racial oppression informs the authors' petitioning for divine affirmation, yearning for divine presence, protesting the seeming absence thereof, and finally feelings and manifestations of divine grace. Sometimes these varied moods and purposes appear so rapidly that they are indistinguishable. This prayerful thought of David Walker illustrates this point:

> I aver, that when I look over these United States of America,
> and the world, and see the ignorant deceptions and consequent
> wretchedness of my brethren, I am brought ofttimes solemnly to
> stand, and in the midst of my reflections I exclaim to my God,
> "Lord didst thou make us to be slaves to our brethren, the
> whites?" But when I reflect that God is just, and that millions
> of my wretched brethren would meet death with glory—yea,
> more, would plunge into the very mouths of cannons and be
> torn into particles as minute as the atoms which compose the el-
> ements of the earth, in preference to a mean submission to the
> lash of tyrants, I am with streaming eyes, compelled to shrink
> back into nothingness before my Maker, and exclaim again, "thy
> will be done, O Lord Almighty."[7]

Without his saying it explicitly, Walker's moment of liberation came when he recalled that God had nurtured a community of resisters. Walker assumed that a community of what Karl Rahner called "anonymous Christians" constitute a corporation committed to the sanctity of freedom and the liberation of the oppressed.[8] Many African Americans believe that this sanctified corporation exists both within and beyond the Christian churches. For them prayer is not the possession either of white folk or of the churches. Prayer is something that all human beings have a right to do. But they believe that "the prayers of the righteous prevaileth much." If one has a right relationship with God, certain activities are inexcusable. They believe that the truly righteous do not pull black preachers like Richard Allen and Absalom Jones from their knees while they are praying. The truly righteous do not deny slaves the right to pray and worship.

Greenburg W. Offley, a black Methodist minister, expressed the social nature of this tradition in the following story. He was careful to assert that a theology of resistance was imbued in the relative privacy of the slave cabin.

> Our family theology teaches that God is no respecter of persons, but gave his Son to die for all, bond or free, black or white, rich or poor. If we keep his commandments, we will be happy after death. It also teaches that if God calls and sanctifies a person to do some great work, that person is immortal until his work is done; that God is able and will protect him from all danger or accident in life if he is faithful to his calling or charge committed by the Lord. This is a borrowed idea from circumstances too numerous to mention. Here is one man we present as a proof of the immortality of man, while in the flesh: Praying Jacob. This man was a slave in the State of Maryland. His master was very cruel to his slaves. Jacob's rule was to pray three times a day, at just such an hour of the day; no matter what his work was or where he might be, he would stop and go and pray. His master had been to him and pointed his gun at him, and told him if he did not cease praying he would blow out his brains. Jacob would finish his prayer and then tell his master to shoot in welcome— your loss will be my gain—I have two masters, one on earth and one in heaven—master Jesus in heaven, and master Saunders on earth. I have a soul and a body; the body belongs to you, master Saunders, and the soul to master Jesus. Jesus says men ought always to pray, but you will not pray, neither do you want to

have me pray. This man said in private conversation that several times he went home and drank an unusual quantity of brandy to harden his heart that he might kill him; but he never had power to strike or shoot him, and he would freely give the world, if he had it in his possession for what he believed his Jacob to possess. He also thought that Jacob was as assured of Heaven as the apostle Paul or Peter. Sometimes Mr. S. would be in the field about half drunk, raging like a madman, whipping the other slaves; and when Jacob's hour would come for prayer, he would stop his horses and plough and kneel down and pray; but he could not strike the man of God.

Hardly any slaves or slave masters are still living, thus we are dependent on their competing historical tracings. Each oftentimes made quite different claims about the nature of that social order. If an interpreter sides with the beneficiaries of the system, it is usually because he or she is in sympathy with that kind of social philosophy. I am not. Therefore, I find the reports of the slaves to have more moral cogency. We are living in a period when our social memories are constantly being dislocated by too much information and not enough insight. Russell Jacoby calls this phenomenon "social amnesia." I believe there are grave consequences when we cannot locate and integrate the memories of our forebears. Perhaps the most ominous consequence is what I call soul murder.[9]

I believe that somewhere in the infrastructure of the human soul there dwells a dormant anger poised to register its complaint about the unfairness of life. The public and collective expression of this rage oftentimes comes in the form of perverse and harmful civic arrangements that lead to what I call social murder. Every social murder is the consequence of public expressions of this perversion of the human soul. If we look only at the consequence and not at the genesis of social murder, however, we will never be in a position to develop an antidote.

Therefore, we need to understand how social homicides germinate. This requires an examination of the sequence of psychic events that precedes collective demonic deeds. I call my analytical procedure "historical demonology." This strategy assumes that demons are intelligible. And all intelligent beings have a history that yearns for exposure and analysis. Demons thrive best in the dark intervals of human history, and the parentage of real power lies in the sinister womb of negativity. Plato tried to express this in his *Republic* by characterizing humanity as cave dwellers who define reality as a reflection of a reflection of a beam of light forced through a shaft of light. Hegel defined this negativity as "the unhappy conscious." Freud called it "the psyche." Jean-Paul Sartre said in his *Being and Nothingness* that all of reality is like looking through a keyhole. Carl Jung called it "the shadow." But Jesus called it "sin." Whatever we call it, it does exist. All it requires is our cooperation. Unfortunately, the dynamics of demonology are propelled by our tendency to deny its existence. We repress it into the regions of our unconscious where it becomes powerful because it is in the dark, seamy recesses of our soul where it constantly vies for attention and control. We need a historical analysis of these mysterious intervals in order to develop a spiritual practice capable of fortifying our souls against the inevitable assaults of the wiles of the devil.

Let me illustrate what I mean by historical demonology by examining this struggle within the soul as it has manifested itself in an old African-American bread-and-water forgiveness festival. On Sunday, 4 January 1884, the first Sunday of the new year, Charles Edwardes attended a black worship service in Jacksonville, Florida. Edwardes described the elderly black pastor's homily that opened this special 11 A.M. service.

> It was the old lesson and story which clergymen have to teach
> and tell while they have breath for speech—the old lesson, new
> dressed. The first Sunday in the new year! He told them that
> they were, one and all, at a crisis in their lives; they might have
> been, as he hoped they had been, good men and women in the
> past; but now they were facing the future, they were beginning a
> new year. How could they best start afresh? he asked them.
> How? Why, by clearing all the naughty weeds out of the garden
> of their souls, to be sure; and the way to do that was by prayer
> and asking forgiveness of friends and neighbors for the injuries
> they had done them last year. Some might say they had done no
> wrong to nobody. But they made a mistake if they said that—
> for they *must* do no wrong, whether they mean it or not. It's hu-
> man nature to do it, and they can't help themselves. This, then,
> was what they were met for this first Sunday in the new year.
> There was bread and there was water by his side—a good quan-
> tity of both—and he hoped they would all be so hungry and

thirsty for the forgiveness of each other that they would use them both up very soon; for if they didn't he should have to finish them, and it was too cold to drink much cold water, in his opinion.

The pastor then invited his assistants to distribute bread from the table below the däis. This was not a communion service, nor was the table an altar. The bread was passed to members of the congregation who desired to forgive their neighbors for any offense. The aggrieved sister or brother in the faith would then use his or her right hand to pinch a morsel of bread that was held in the left hand of the one willing to forgive. Everyone who so desired sought those willing to forgive. Apparently the water was used to wash down the bread of those who required much forgiveness.

They then followed this practice with prayers and testimonies of faith. In the midst of this segment of the service, one of the most graphic illustrations of the pastoral problem faced by African-American spirituality can be found.

Then a yellow girl, shapely and well-dressed, with tears coursing down her cheeks, cried out and besought that she too might be prayed for. This said, she moved rapidly from her seat, and walked towards the clergyman, with a strange look in her eyes. The worthy man encountered her gaze with his old smile, though it froze somewhat when the girl stopped and continued staring at him—face to his face, with only a few inches between them—in the presence of the whole congregation. "Well!" he said, "what's the matter with you?" and by now his smile had lost all its cordiality; the spirit of it had, as it were, departed.

The question arosed the girl from her trance. Shaking her head from side to side madly, and stamping with her feet, she cried—

"Brothers and sisters, pity me. Oh, how I hates myself! I don't know why such a young girl as me was sent into this 'ere earth, 'cept to be made miserable, which don't seem as if it ought to be. I'm all bad, every part of me, and the devil, he's got a finger in everything I do. Yet I hates him, friends, as much as I hates myself. I hate him more than I can say—I'd like to tear his nasty black eyes out of his lying head, that I would! Nor I don't think it a wrong passion to go into! But, dear brothers and sisters, I don't know what to do to be made happy—I don't know what to do. Oh, pray for me, dear brothers and all, pray for me!"

And sobbing aloud, with her hands to her face, the poor girl retraced her steps, and sat down.

This young woman's experience of radical alienation, as well as her willingness to embrace hatred to cure her own self-hatred, illustrates the rampant plague of nihilism that infests parts of black America.

In his best-selling book, *Race Matters*, Cornel West offers a powerful analysis of the reasons for the moral collapse of large segments of the African-American communities in America's cities. Why all the murders, drug addiction, teen pregnancy, broken homes, and other various forms of violence? Here, West argues more explicitly than ever before that a pervasive nihilism is at fault. This sense that life is useless and worthless, and that values, beliefs, and tradition are for chumps, describes the psychic and spiritual impoverishment of a forgotten people, often odiously referred to as "the underclass." West rightly places these developments at the feet of the general deterioration of values and justice in a racist and classist society that has minimized its commitments to democracy. I agree with him. But I want to examine some of the religious dimensions of these developments.

I could focus on institutional religion's failure to respond adequately to the challenge of nihilism. I do not feel, however, that institutional religion can respond to this challenge. Its own infighting over theological and ethical issues since the 1890s has spent its energies, and driven away much-needed talent. Moreover, its often uncritical acceptance of the excesses of industrial capitalism, anticommunism, racism, and sexism has severely weakened its moral credibility. Whether Protestant, Catholic, Jewish, or African American, institutional religion has had its potentially sharp prophetic edge dulled by its overt or silent complicity in maintaining the status quo. If the powerful, affluent machineries of institutional religion have been so disabled, who then can respond? I believe that this is the wrong question. I believe we need to ask, what is there about the nature of the present cultural crisis that makes it almost impervious to religion? The answer is both simple and complex.

Nathan Hatch recently captivated devotees of American religious history with the obvious but powerful argument that the United States is responsible for the democratization of Christianity. Yet at this crucial moment, the role of religion with regard to racism is unclear. There are many possible explanations, but perhaps some psychological insights would be most helpful in conveying my viewpoint about this subject.

I begin with the hypothesis that the roots and rationale for systemic racism have become an unconscious social creed, with all the traits of a folk religion. I invoke the notion of "folk" here not as a trivializing gesture but as an attempt to suggest how thoroughly unconscious the processes of racism can be. Racism is the perversion of the primeval impulse to protect, advance, and enhance one's tribe. Although we need not pursue interesting questions about the degree to which biology determines this noble phenomenon, this set of impulses undoubtedly underwrites the self-justifying fears that fuel racist attitudes and practices.

Fears become a clinical issue when they can no longer be influenced by the legislative, judicial, or executive inquiries of communal forms of reason. Much hinges here on the breadth of our notions of community. But what is clear is that the narrower our conception of community, the narrower our conception of what is reasonable. Racists believe that the reasoning of their own particular tribe is exclusively correct. Erik Erikson has called this modern phenomenon "pseudospeciation" because racism makes the absurd assumption that one race is the quintessential embodiment of the entire species. Thus other racial groups are seen as expendable. If those who hold this assumption acquire the awesome destructive power that nuclear weapons provide, such racism is not a matter of merely mean social practices. Whole segments of the human race find their existence threatened.

Racism is therefore a more dangerous social practice than tribalism and nationalism. Its modern history crosses all these boundaries. It constitutes a conglomerate of cultural and social forces that sanction political and economic privileges as a natural or divine right. Such cultural enclaves become a set of religious practices and beliefs when they are placed beyond the critical borders of discussion. That was one of the central problems with racism in the South between 1865 and 1965. Everyone with a minimal amount of common sense knew that racism existed, but southern moderates did not want to speak about it lest they disrupt delicate local political coalitions. And religious leaders did not want to talk about it because many considered lynchings, and mean political tactics, such as gerrymandering and voting tests, to belong to the domain of "politics as usual."

Such popular political cynicism has become a degenerative tradition in this country. It is a form of hoodwinking, a set of unprincipled rituals that foster false appearances in the service of disguising where real power lies. This is why during the 1960s white thugs eagerly accepted the dubious "honor" of "eliminating" black civic "irritants" like Medgar Evers or northern white righteous "invaders" such as the Reverend James Reeb.[10] The state could not summon enough moral courage to be true to its own principles of justice because it had no desire to disclose or expose the white male power structure. Few in that power structure were as vociferous in their defense of this sinful arrangement as were right-wing ministers such as the Reverends Billy Hargis and Jerry Falwell.[11] They condemned Martin Luther King, Jr., and his cohorts for daring to challenge the racist privileges exercised by the white community with brazen impunity. And they insisted that politics and religion should have nothing to do with each other. Once political "problems" lie beyond the precincts of public discussion, however, they themselves become religious artifacts.

A religion without theological discussion is a religion that has no room for negotiation, no room for change. White people utter constant refrains such as "I am not a racist. I am not responsible for creating oppression. That's the way the world is!" Carl Jung once said that unconsciousness is the greatest sin that bedevils humanity. At the root of racist unconsciousness is a social anemia that prevents the oxygen of cultural knowledge from circulating throughout the body politic. Something akin to a religion of social fears sanctifies the tribalism that keeps us apart. This peculiar faith in genetic superiority, however, receives more unwarranted solace from the plagues of forgetfulness than from a sinister plot to bolster the privileges of the privileged.

I recall an important comment by Herbert Marcuse in his book *Eros and Civilization*. Marcuse argued that it is practically impossible to remember what you never knew. Several thoughtful analysts of the national soul, such as Frances FitzGerald, have been warning us for more than two decades that our country places itself at serious intellectual risk when it does not have public history textbooks that recount the rich diversity of this nation's history.

But what if the problem is not mere ignorance but forgetfulness understood in an immediate as well as a primeval sense? Is it possible, as Freud suggested in *The Psychopathology of Everyday Life,* that the phenomenon of forgetfulness represents incursions of a repressed unconscious into the realm of consciousness?

When my book *A Testament of Hope: The Essential Writings of Martin Luther King, Jr.* appeared in January 1986, my publisher arranged for me to be on several radio "talk shows" to promote it. I was astonished at how many white people literally hate Martin Luther King, Jr. Some of the calls were from individuals who identified themselves as religious who felt that King was more of an agitator than a reconciler. I have a nagging feeling that there is more to the hatred against King's ministry within white America than meets the eye. After much reflection, I have concluded that King's determination to insist that America be conscious about its history of mistreating black Americans is a rather perverse example of the classic transference syndrome.[12] As a therapeutic prophet, Dr. King insisted that his nation of patients (white and black) confront their repressed social history not with tribalistic bloodshed but with forgiving love baptized in the caldrons of racial justice.

My own experience of growing up in Knoxville, Tennessee, introduced me quite early to the absurdities of segregation. I attended totally black schools from kindergarten to high school, and was forbidden by law from using the magisterial Lawson McGhee Library. From a youngster's perspective, it was a huge, Romanesque building with big marble columns and a seemingly endless supply of books. I, however, had to use the old, dingy, poorly equipped and staffed Andrew Carnegie Library on Vine Avenue. Finally, though, after the local newspapers announced that the library had agreed to desegregate, I entered the portals of the white people's library, a white building that seemed to me bigger than a whale.

And like Captain Ahab I resolved immediately to pursue my white whale. I walked into its jaws, approached the frowning commander at its mouth, the person behind the circulation desk, and asked, "May I use the library?" She glared at me with an air of stark incredulity. "Listen, little nigger," she whispered with righteous indignation, "colored people are not allowed to use this library! I must ask you to leave immediately!" My bruised ego retorted, "But I read in the newspaper that—" She interrupted my pending recitation with a humiliating interjection delivered with whispered ferocity, "Out!" The acoustics of this temple of learning seized her malevolent whisper and transformed it into a jolting crescendo. The eyes of the white users quickly executed my already bruised ego with glares that sought to incinerate my soul. I wanted to join this anonymous fraternity of learners. Unfortunately, however, I became a victim of social fratricide.

I grew up in a family that could not afford to buy books for me. I worked at odd jobs to amass about twenty books by age fifteen. Books were my extended family, especially philosophical and historical ones. Why would anyone want to keep me from my family? I left not only dejected but with a deficit in my reservoir of unused tears. This self-pity quickly turned to anger, however. I felt like many black youngsters in the 1960s. I wanted to burn that "damn" building down. I reasoned, If I don't have the right to use the *public* library, then why should I obey a system that deceives, belittles, and degrades me for trying to cultivate my intellectual gifts? Should I torch the white library like some Black Power anarchists advised, or should I continue to emulate the model of gentle strength I cherished in my pastor, the Reverend Dr. William T. Crutcher, who was the leader of the Civil Rights Movement in Knoxville, Tennessee?[13]

I found myself caught between the powerful sway of the religions of tribalism and racism, and the prophetic interpretation of the Bible which I had learned at the Mount Olive Baptist Church under the guidance of Dr. Crutcher. As I reflected on what to do, I realized that I also needed to analyze what had happened at that circulation desk. I concluded that a righteous sense of racial and intellectual pride had emboldened me to go to the white library in the first place. Perhaps I was the one in the wrong. I recall wondering whether or not such a conclusion was an instance of what Black Power advocates called "Uncle Tomism." I thought, Am I blaming myself for offending white sacred space? Who designated this space, "For White People Only"? I wondered why white people needed to exclude people who looked like me from *public* space. From a practical standpoint, I decided not to either burn the building or "cast my pearls before swine." I decided to retreat to the safety of the black communal womb.

The black congregation, when at its best, is a cultural system that teaches self-respect as well as advocates and promotes initiative. My decision to do nothing, however, was an affirmation of my tribal religion's long-standing teaching that self-respect demands that you not go where you are not wanted. I decided to continue building my own personal library. But civil rights integrationism was challenging the separatist social doctrine prevalent in the Black Church as well as in the African-American community at large. The universalist assumptions of the Civil Rights Movement strongly objected to decisions not to confront systemic racial evil. Movement apologists, such as Professor George Kelsey in his *Racism and the Christian Understanding of Man,* argued that the spiritual and intellectual problems such compromises engender are an offense to our common humanity and to God because they make an idol of white claims for genetic superiority. In fact the more I retreated, the more I realized that the system invades the precincts of conscience most effectively at the primal level of culture and religion.

I began to ask questions that I later pursued more systematically in my undergraduate work in religious studies. I have learned much since I began in 1967, but one of the most enduring lessons is that religion does as much to divide humanity as it does to help us grasp meaning. For proof of this, we have only to recall that religious doctrines sanctioned white supremacy among the Mormons, many Southern Baptists, Methodists, and Presbyterians, as well as within the Dutch Reformed Church in South Africa.

The sin is to do nothing to resist and change the conditions that encourage us to remain either ignorant or forgetful. Resistance, however, requires the prophetic insight and guts to examine the infrastructure of our own souls in search of the contours of the social malignancy of racism. As Abraham Heschel reminds those who still read him, God is a God of "pathos." God feels and responds to the oppressed. Can we religious people possibly do any less? Past betrayals of the best in our religious cultures do not give us license to continue the same degenerative habits. We must respond to the sins of exploitation, injustice, violence, hatred, and war with something more than bureaucratic finesse.[14] We need to respond also as individuals who, to quote Howard Thurman, the great African-American Christian mystic, have yielded "the nerve center of our consent" to God, and consequently to the noblest impulses of the human spirit.[15]

The disease of social amnesia plagues the African-American community. Large segments of our community have lost the discipline of humanity bestowed upon us by our foreparents. As Ralph Ellison once said in response to a white critique of his work, "He seems never to have considered that American Negro life (and here he is encouraged by certain Negro 'spokesmen') is, for the Negro who must live it, not only a burden (and not always that) but also a *discipline*—just as any human life which has endured so long is a discipline teaching its own insights into the human condition, its own strategies of survival." This discipline is at risk because we have sacrificed the virginity of our cultural womb on the altar of integration.

The myth of integration—historically conceived—assumed that racism was caused by the difference of black people as evidenced in their physiognomy. The doctrine of integration argued that African-Americans needed to become as close to perfect copies of white people as possible. This required the emasculation of their culture and history. In order to do this, one had to infantilize African-American history by placing black people on a lower scale of historical development.

A close examination of the genealogy of this argument would reveal that some African-American leaders, such as Alexander Crummell, prepared the way for this historical condescension in their arguments for supporting home missions and African missions.[16] Both the liberated slaves and the colonialized Africans became examples of historical progress. Proponents of racial reform saw cultural homogeneity as the necessary condition for black "uplift." African culture in any form was viewed as animistic, deformed, indeed, pathological.

This concession to white supremacy oftentimes unwittingly or tacitly endorsed what James William Charles Pennington called that "stupid theory" that *"nature has done nothing but fit us for slaves, and that art cannot unfit us for slavery!"* This has led to what Carter G. Woodson has called "the miseducation of the Negro." Prayer becomes the *primal* way of conducting "justice education."

African-American prayers as a literary genre, and a religious social practice, assume that God is just and loving, and that the human dilemma is that we cannot always experience and see God's justice and love. We pray for faith to trust God's ultimate disclosure.

Thus prayer as act and utterance teaches the believer to exercise what Adrienne Rich calls "revolutionary patience." But the literary history of African-American prayers suggests that, besides anticipating God's ultimate self-disclosure in the history of the oppressed, we are the trustees of a spiritual legacy paid for with the blood, sweat, tears, and dreams of a noble, even if not triumphant, people. The culture, grammar, and promise of the African-American prayer tradition is in our hands. Only time will tell whether or not their faith in us was worth the price they paid.

Thus, in editing this book, my first urge was to protect the preciousness of the spiritual womb that birthed and now continuously nourishes my soul. Fortunately, the critical historian in me vetoed that paternalistic impulse. I felt a professional responsibility and personal urge to share my knowledge of the history of African-American spirituality in order to combat misunderstandings of its value and culture. Before I could do this, however, I had to ponder where I had seen prayers in the course of more than two decades of arduous research. The prayers in this book are the by-product. When I really put my mind to the task, I began to find prayers seemingly everywhere.

I have organized these prayers chronologically. In order to give a sense of the general circumstance that framed these prayers in particular periods, I have subdivided them into six parts: Part I. Slavery and the Eclipse of the African Gods, 1760–1860; Part II. The Crucible of the Anglo-African Conscience, 1861–1893; Part III. The Vale of Tears, 1894–1919; Part IV. The New Negro, 1920–1955; Part V. The Civil Rights Ethos, 1956–1980; Part VI. Postmodern African-American Worlds, 1981–1994. The names I have given for these periods reflect the central crisis out of which and to which these prayers come. It is a mistake to see these prayers *only* as the personal conversations that each of these African-Americans has had with God. They are certainly this. But from a cultural and social standpoint, as Benjamin Mays tried to argue in his *The Negro's God As Reflected in His Literature,* these prayers represent major moods in the complex spiritual history of a people who have obvious reasons to be angry with God.

Each division represents the invasions of a new form of the absurd: Part I, the experience of being chattel with the failure of the African gods to prevent enslavement, as well as the various forms of racism in the antebellum period; Part II, the struggle to define what kind of community could be created in the face of the nation's unwillingness to compensate ex-slaves justly; Part III, the moral dilemma of what to do in the face of the murders and lynching of black people especially in the period between 1889 and 1919; Part IV, the place of African-American Christianity in the face of a nascent agnosticism and atheism that was sometimes evident as a young generation emerged in the Harlem Renaissance; Part V, facing the flaws in the myth of the American Dream as evident in the successes and failures of the Civil Rights Movement; and Part VI, the increasing decline of the moral influence of African-American Christianity.

The prayers in this anthology are attempts to converse with God about the joys, burdens, and hopes of being African people in a racist society. All these prayers trusted that the Lord would make a way somehow.

NOTES

1. From the standpoint of late-twentieth-century American usage, Du Bois's use of "awful" is somewhat archaic. If he were writing today, he would probably use "awesome."

2. Studies of African-American humor have been written by William Schechter, Lawrence Levine, and Mel Watkins. Langston Hughes also edited a very useful anthology on the subject.

3. The complexity of the notion of the soul is reflected in recent religious scholarship on this subject contained in the nine articles on the concept of soul in primitive, Ancient Near Eastern, Greek and Hellenistic, Indian, Buddhist, Chinese, Jewish, Christian, and Islamic religions in Eliade's *The Encyclopedia of Religion*.

4. I use "stargazing" as a metaphor for the experience of the numinous conveyed through sight—with an acute awareness of the experiential limitations and intellectual difficulties of the use of ocular metaphors. Taking the metaphor at its face value, sightless people like John M. Hull remind us that listening and touching can have the same effect as seeing. On a deeper level, I use this metaphor despite my understanding of the intellectual hegemony of the assumptions and metaphors about sight in modern thought as reflected in recent discussions about "representation." This subject has been explored with much vigor and

brilliance by students of modern and postmodern culture. Martin Jay calls it the problem of ocularcentrism. Jay rightly identifies Jacques Ellul as having an important influence on his understanding of ocularcentrism's evolution. Major religious historians, theologians, and biblical scholars have explored ocularcentrism under the rubric of the idolatry of culture that is oftentimes called "henotheism." But even though H. Richard Niebuhr appealed to the transcendent regime of radical monotheism as an antidote to henotheism, he did not reduce the problem of idolatry to its ideational plenipotentiary, ideology, nor to the distortion of vision or language. A very helpful attempt to relate this problem to African-American cultural studies can be found in a recent study by W. T. J. Mitchell.

5. The primal role of nurture in what Wittgenstein calls "the language game" is accented in his pregnant exegesis of how a language is acquired by a child. According to Wittgenstein, especially in his *Brown Book,* "The child learns this language from grown-ups by being trained to its use." Language is acquired through *"demonstrative* teaching of words." I am suggesting that prayer is an acquired ontology often of a religious cultus that offers a grammar whose objective is to proffer a "cure of disease based on dogma set forth by its promulgator." The role of metaphors and assertions of contamination in religious language and practice has been explored by several scholars, including Mary Douglass and Paul Ricoeur, whose works have influenced me the most. I am acutely aware of the complexity of using metaphors to express religious ideas and describe religious practices despite my rather shameless deployments in this introduction. Nonetheless, I have been helped most recently by the quite engaging study work of Janet Martin Soskice.

6. Peace demonstrators at the Billy Graham Crusade were particularly offended that President Nixon's visit was his first to a college campus after the United States invaded Cambodia. For a somewhat fuller description of this event, see some of the contemporary local newspaper accounts in the *Knoxville News-Sentinel* (1–4 November 1971) and the *Knoxville Journal* (1–4, 11, and 17 November 1971), as well as books by Michael J. McDonald, Judith Isenhour, and Marshall Frady.

7. David Walker's *Appeal* is a jeremiad that has a secure place in American history. Like most jeremiads, *Walker's Appeal* uses righteous indignation both to lament and condemn American slavery and racism. The broader literary and ideological context of the jeremiad has been studied by Sacvan Bercovitch and David Howard-Pitney.

8. Karl Rahner, S.J. (1904–1984), a famous and distinguished Roman Catholic theologian, used this term to grapple with the proposition that there are those who are seemingly predisposed to be theists and Christians without formally being so. He included ethical agnostics and even atheists as possible members of this righteous conventicle. Several theologians have strongly objected to Rahner's imaginative idea. I invoke it even though Rahner believed that this is "first and foremost a controversy internal to Catholic theology," because I believe that the African-American community, agnostics and atheists included, have often seen themselves as morally superior to White America. Some even believed that the so-called "Invisible Institution" of free and enslaved Christians were the true church. Among Abolitionist Christians who practiced "comeouterism," true Christians had to break all ties with slaveholding Christians. The best study on comeouterism was written by John R. McKivigan. Other studies by Albert J. Raboteau and James M. Washington offer useful information about this subject as it relates to slave religion and African-American Baptists.

9. I am using the concept of soul murder to suggest that the defamation of the character and human worth of African Americans has historically been used to belittle the collective ego of African Americans. Scholarly studies and literary depictions of this phenomenon are vast. Of course this is not a new idea. The prevalence of racial stigmas and systematic discrimination were cited in the famous case *Brown v. Board of Education* (1954). Major studies on the effects of racism on African-American children informed the Supreme Court's decision, which mandated the desegregation of American public education. Perhaps the best-known psychological studies were those of Kenneth and Mamie Clark. Beyond the Clarks, the most helpful and critical influence upon my thinking about this was written by William E. Cross, Jr. I have also learned much from other general studies on the spirituality of children by Robert Coles and Dorothy W. Martyn.

10. The Reverend James Joseph Reeb (1927–1965), a white minister, was assassinated while participating in the famous Civil Rights demonstrations in Selma, Alabama. He was the Associate Minister of All Souls Unitarian Universalist Church in Washington, D.C.

11. John Redekop has written a very reliable analysis of the opposition of Billy James Hargis's Christian Crusade to the Civil Rights Movement, as well as other progressive movements. One of the sermons in which Falwell attacks Martin Luther King, Jr., can be found in the appendix to a recent book by Perry Deane Young.

12. I use the term *transference* to describe the human proclivity to predict and project one's own desires and interests, as well as the desires and interests of others. My views on this psychological and philosophical concept have been deeply influenced by the work of psychoanalysts Nelson Goodman and Paul Ricoeur. Indeed, Ricoeur's work has especially enabled me to see how it is possible to recast Freud's psychological theory of transference to mesh with various hermeneutical and phenomenological theories. Much work lies ahead for those like myself who believe that these ideas would greatly assist students of racism, race relations, cultural studies, and the history of spirituality. Some very important suggestions along these lines can be found in the work of Richard Wright, Ralph Ellison, Franz Fanon, James Baldwin, and Toni Morrison. Getting psychologists and historians to appreciate the importance of the history of African-American spirituality is a somewhat more difficult task.

13. Crutcher is one of the major subjects of a recently reprinted book by Merrill Proudfoot on the Civil Rights Movement in Knoxville, Tennessee.

14. Like many other scholars, my view that violence is an archetypal form of sin has been influenced by Rene Girard, the most well known and influential student of the relationship between violence and religion. His work is having a profound effect on the study of religion.

15. Thurman offered a deeply affective explication of his frequently used phrase, "the nerve center of consent," in the chapter titled "Commitment" in his *Disciplines of the Spirit*. He said, "The yielding of the deep inner nerve center of consent is not a solitary action, unrelated to the total structure or context of the life." Indeed, he continued to explain, "It is a saturation of the self with the mood and the integrity of assent."

16. Wilson Jeremiah Moses has written excellent studies of Crummell's life and thought that focus on this irony.

Part I

Slavery and the

Eclipse of the

African Gods

1760–1860

Penitential Cries to God (1760)

Jupiter Hammon

Salvation comes by Jesus Christ alone,
    The only Son of God;
Redemption now to every one,
    That love his holy Word.

Dear Jesus we would fly to Thee,
    And leave off every Sin,
Thy tender Mercy well agree;
    Salvation from our King.

Salvation comes now from the Lord,
    Our victorious King;
His holy Name be well ador'd,
    Salvation surely bring.

Dear Jesus give thy Spirit now,
    Thy Grace to every Nation,
That hasn't the Lord to whom we bow,
    The Author of Salvation.

Dear Jesus unto Thee we cry,
    Give us Thy Preparation;
Turn not away thy tender Eye;
    We seek thy true Salvation.

Salvation comes from God we know,
    The true and only One;
It's well agreed and certain true,
    He gave his only Son.

Lord hear our penitential Cry:
    Salvation from above;
It is the Lord that doth supply,
    With his Redeeming Love.

Dear Jesus by thy precious Blood,
  The World Redemption have:
Salvation comes now from the Lord,
  He being thy captive Slave.

Dear Jesus let the Nations cry,
  And all the People say,
Salvation comes from Christ on high,
  Haste on Tribunal Day.

We cry as Sinners to the Lord,
  Salvation to obtain;
It is firmly fixt his holy Word,
  Ye shall not cry in vain.

Dear Jesus unto Thee we cry,
  And make our Lamentation:
O Let our Prayers ascend on high;
  We felt thy Salvation.

Lord turn our dark benighted Souls;
  Give us a true Motion,
And let the Hearts of all the World,
  Make Christ their Salvation.

Ten thousand Angels cry to Thee,
  Yea louder than the Ocean.
Thou are the Lord, we plainly see;
  Thou art the true Salvation.

Now is the Day, excepted Time;
  The Day of Salvation;
Increase your Faith, do not repine:
  Awake ye every Nation.

Lord unto whom now shall we go,
  Or seek a safe Abode;
Thou hast the Word Salvation too
  The only Son of God.

Ho! every one that hunger hath,
    Or pineth after me,
Salvation be thy leading Staff,
    To set the Sinner free.

Dear Jesus unto Thee we fly;
    Depart, depart from Sin,
Salvation doth at length supply,
    The Glory of our King.

Come ye Blessed of the Lord,
    Salvation gently given;
O Turn your Hearts, accept the Word,
    Your Souls are fit for Heaven.

Dear Jesus we now turn to Thee,
    Salvation to obtain;
Our Hearts and Souls do meet again,
    To magnify thy Name.

Come holy Spirit, Heavenly Dove,
    The Object of our care;
Salvation doth increase our Love;
    Our Hearts hath felt thy fear.

Now Glory be to God on High,
    Salvation high and low;
And thus the Soul on Christ rely,
    To Heaven surely go.

Come blessed Jesus, Heavenly Dove,
    Accept Repentance here;
Salvation give, with tender Love;
    Let us with Angels share.

A Prayer for New Birth (1776)
Lemuel Haynes

Lastly. Let all those that are strangers to the new birth be exhorted no longer to live estranged from God, but labour after this holy temper of mind. Flee to Christ before it is too late. Consider that there is an aggravated condemnation that awaits all impenitent sinners. There is a day of death coming. There is a day of judgement coming. A few turns more upon the stage and we are gone. Oh how will you answer it at the bar of God, for your thus remaining enemies to him? It is sin that separates from God. But it is the *being* or *remaining* such that will eternally separate you from him. Never rest easy till you feel in you a change wrought by the Holy Spirit. And believe it,—until then you are exposed to the wrath of God; and without repentance you will in a few days be lifting up your eyes in torment.

The Lord grant that we may lay these things suitably to heart;— that we, having the kingdom of Christ set up in our hearts here, may grow up to the stature of perfect men in Christ Jesus. This will lay a foundation for union with all holy beings, and with this everlasting happiness in the kingdom of glory is inseparably connected, through Jesus Christ our Lord. Amen.

A Mother's Prayer for the Child in Her Womb (1779)

Phillis Wheatley

Oh my Gracious Preserver! hithertoo thou hast [brought] [me,] be pleased when thou bringest to the birth to give [me] strength to bring forth living and perfect a being who shall be greatly instrumental in promoting thy [glory]. Though conceived in Sin and [brought] forth in iniquity yet thy infinite wisdom can bring a clean thing out of an unclean, a vesse[l] of Honor filled for thy glory[.] Grant me to live a life of gratitude to thee for the innumerable benefits. O Lord my God! instruct my ignorance and enlighten my Darkness[.] Thou art my King, take [thou] the entire possession of [all] my powers and faculties and let me be no longer under the dominion of sin[.] Give me a sincere and hearty repentance for all my [many][1] offences and strengthen by thy grace my resolutions on amendment and circumspection for the time to come[.] Grant me [also] the spirit of Prayer and Suppli[cation] according to thy own most gracious Promises.

---

[1] There is a word missing at this point. The anonymous transcriber inserted the following handwritten note: "cannot decipher this word." I am suggesting this word for rhetorical consistency.

A Prayer for Faith (1787–1830)

Richard Allen

I BELIEVE, O God, that Thou are an eternal, incomprehensible spirit, infinite in all perfections; who didst make all things out of nothing, and dost govern them all by Thy wise providence.

Let me always adore Thee with profound humility, as my Sovereign Lord; and help me to love and praise Thee with godlike affections and suitable devotion.

I believe, that in the unity of the Godhead, there is a trinity of persons; that Thou art perfectly one and perfectly three; one essence and three persons. I believe, O blessed Jesus, that Thou art one substance with the Father, the very and eternal God; that Thou didst take upon Thee our frail nature; that Thou didst truly suffer, and wert crucified, dead and buried, to reconcile us to Thy Father and to be a sacrifice for sin.

I believe, that according to the types and prophecies, which went before, of Thee, and according to Thy infallible prediction, Thou didst by Thy own power rise from the dead the third day, that Thou didst ascend into Heaven, that there Thou sittest on Thy throne of glory adored by angels and interceding for sinners.

I believe, that Thou hast instituted and ordained holy mysteries, as pledges of Thy love, and for a continual commemoration of Thy death; that Thou hast not only given Thyself to die for me, but to be my spiritual food and sustenance in that holy sacrament to my great and endless comfort. O may I frequently approach Thy altar with humility and devotion, and work in me all those holy and heavenly affections, which become the remembrance of a crucified Saviour.

I believe, O Lord, that Thou hast not abandoned me to the dim light of my own reason to conduct me to happiness, but that Thou has revealed in the Holy Scriptures whatever is necessary for me to believe and practice, in order to my eternal salvation.

O, how noble and excellent are the precepts; how sublime and enlightening the truth; how persuasive and strong the motives; how powerful the assistance of Thy holy religion, in which Thou hast instructed me; my delight shall be in Thy statutes, and I will not forget Thy word.

I believe it is my greatest honor and happiness to be Thy disciple; how miserable and blind are those that live without God in the world, who despise the light of Thy holy faith. Make me to part with all the enjoyments of life; nay, even life itself, rather than forfeit this jewel of great price. Blessed are the sufferings which are endured, happy is the death which is undergone for heavenly and immortal truth! I believe that Thou hast prepared for those that love Thee, everlasting mansions of glory; if I believe Thee, O eternal happiness. Why does anything appear difficult that leads to Thee? Why should I not willingly resist unto blood to obtain Thee? Why do the vain and empty employments of life take such vast hold on us? O, perishing time! Why dost Thou thus bewitch and deceive me? O, blessed eternity! When shalt Thou be my portion for ever?

A Prayer for Hope (1787–1830)
Richard Allen

O, MY God! in all my dangers, temporal and spiritual, I will hope in thee who art Almighty power, and therefore able to relieve me; who are infinite goodness, and therefore ready and willing to assist me.

O, precious blood of my dear Redeemer! O, gaping wounds of my crucified Saviour! Who can contemplate the sufferings of God incarnate, and not raise his hope, and not put his trust in Him? What, though my body be crumbled into dust, and that dust blown over the face of the earth, yet I undoubtedly know my Redeemer lives, and shall raise me up at the last day; whether I am comforted or left desolate; whether I enjoy peace or am afflicted with temptations; whether I am healthful or sickly, succored or abandoned by the good things of this life, I will always hope in thee, O, my chiefest, infinite good.

Although the fig-tree shall not blossom, neither shall fruit be in the vines; although the labor of the olive shall fail, and the fields yield no meat; although the flock shall be cut off from the fold, and there shall be no herd in the stalls, yet I will rejoice in the Lord, I will joy in the God of my salvation.

What, though I mourn and am afflicted here, and sigh under the miseries of this world for a time, I am sure that my tears shall one day be turned into joy, and that joy none shall take from me. Whoever hopes for the great things in this world, takes pains to attain them; how can my hopes of everlasting life be well grounded, if I do not strive and labor for that eternal inheritance? I will never refuse the meanest labors, while I look to receive such glorious wages; I will never repine at any temporal loss, while I expect to gain such eternal rewards. Blessed hope! be thou my chief delight in life, and then I shall be steadfast and immovable, always abounding in the work of the Lord; be thou my comfort and support at the hour of death, and then I shall contentedly leave this world, as a captive that is released from his imprisonment.

A Prayer for Love (1787–1830)
Richard Allen

O, INFINITE amiableness! When shall I love Thee without bounds? without coldness or interruption, which, alas! so often seize me here below? Let me never suffer any creature to be Thy rival, or to share my heart with Thee; let me have no other God, no other love, but only Thee.

Whoever loves, desires to please the beloved object; and according to the degree of love is the greatness of desire; make me, O God! diligent and earnest in pleasing Thee; let me cheerfully discharge the most painful and costly duties; and forsake friends, riches, ease and life itself, rather than disobey Thee.

Whoever loves, desires the welfare and happiness of the beloved object; but Thou, O dear Jesus, can'st receive no addition from my imperfect services; what shall I do to express my affection towards Thee? I will relieve the necessities of my poor brethren, who are members of Thy body; for he that loveth not his brother whom he has seen, how can he love God whom he hath not seen?

O, crucified Jesus! in whom I live, and without whom I die; mortify in me all sensual desires; inflame my heart with Thy holy love, that I may no longer esteem the vanities of this world, but place my affections entirely on Thee.

Let my last breath, when my soul shall leave my body, breathe forth love to Thee, my God; I entered into life without acknowledging Thee, let me therefore finish it in loving Thee; O let the last act of life be love, remembering that God is love.

A Thanksgiving Prayer for the Abolition of the African Slave Trade (1808)

Absalom Jones

Oh thou God of all nations upon the earth! we thank thee, that thou art *no respecter of persons,* and that thou *hast made of one blood all nations of men.*[1] We thank thee, that thou hast appeared, in the fullness of time, in behalf of the nation from which most of the worshipping people, now before thee, are descended. We thank thee, that the sun of righteousness[2] has at last shed morning beams upon them. *Rend thy heavens,* O Lord, and *come down* upon the earth; and grant that *the mountains,* which now obstruct the perfect day of thy goodness and mercy towards them, may *flow down at thy presence.*[3] Send thy gospel, we beseech thee, among them. May the nations, which now *sit in darkness,* behold and rejoice in its *light.* May *Ethiopia soon stretch out her hands unto thee,* and lay hold of the gracious promise of thy everlasting covenant. Destroy, we beseech thee, all the false religions which now prevail among them; and grant, that they may soon *cast* their *idols, to the moles and the bats* of the wilderness. O, hasten that glorious time, when the knowledge of the gospel of Jesus Christ, shall cover the *earth, as the waters cover the sea,* when *"the wolf shall dwell with the lamb, and the leopard shall lie down with the kid, and the calf and the young lion and the fatling together, and a little child shall lead them"*;[4] and when, *"instead of the thorn, shall come up the fir tree, and, instead of the brier, shall come up the myrtle tree: and it shall be to the Lord for a name and for an everlasting sign that shall not be cut off."*[5] We pray, O God, for all our friends and benefactors in Great Britain, as well as in the United States: reward them, we beseech thee, with blessings upon earth, and

---

[1] See Acts 17:26 (KJV).

[2] See Malachi 4:2 (KJV).

[3] Beginning with *"Rend thy heavens"* and concluding with *"at thy presence"* Jones was paraphrasing Isaiah 64:1 (KJV).

[4] Isaiah 11:6 (KJV).

[5] Isaiah 55:13 (KJV).

prepare them to enjoy the fruits of their kindness to us, in thy everlasting kingdom in heaven; and dispose us, who are assembled in thy presence, to be always thankful for thy mercies, and to act as becomes a people who owe so much to thy goodness. We implore thy blessing, O God, upon the President, and all who are in authority in the United States. Direct them by thy wisdom, in all their deliberations, and O save thy people from the calamities of war. Give peace in our day, we beseech thee, O thou *God of peace!* and grant, that this highly favoured country may continue to afford a safe and peaceful retreat from the calamities of war and slavery, for ages yet to come. We implore all these blessings and mercies, only in the name of thy beloved Son, Jesus Christ, our Lord. And now, O Lord, we desire, with angels and arch-angels, and all the company of heaven, ever more to praise thee, saying, *"Holy, holy, holy, Lord God Almighty: the whole earth is full of thy glory."*[6]

---

[6] See Isaiah 6:3 (KJV) and Revelation 4:8 (KJV).

A Prayer for Sanctification (1808?)
Jarena Lee

. . . A Certain colored man, by name William Scott, came to pay me a religious visit. He had been for many years a faithful follower of the Lamb; and he had also taken much time in visiting the sick and distressed of our color, and understood well the great things belonging to a man of full stature in Christ Jesus.

In the course of our conversation, he inquired if the Lord had justified my soul. I answered yes. He then asked me if he had sanctified me. I answered no; and that I did not know what that was. He then undertook to instruct me further in the knowledge of the Lord respecting this blessing.

He told me the progress of the soul from a state of darkness, or of nature, was three-fold; or consisted in three degrees, as follows: First, conviction for sin. Second, justification from sins. Third, the entire sanctification of the soul to God. I thought this description was beautiful, and immediately believed in it. He then inquired if I would promise to pray for this in my secret devotions. I told him yes. Very soon I began to call upon the Lord to show me all that was in my heart, which was not according to his will. Now there appeared to be a new struggle commencing in my soul, not accompanied with fear, guilt, and bitter distress, as while under my first conviction of sin, but a laboring of the mind to know more of the right way of the Lord. I began now to feel that my heart was not clean in his sight; that there yet remained the roots of bitterness, which if not destroyed, would ere long sprout up from these roots, and overwhelm me in a new growth of the brambles and brushwood of sin.

By the increasing light of the Spirit, I had found there yet remained the root of pride, anger, self-will, with many evils, the result of fallen nature. I now became alarmed at this discovery, and began to fear that I had been deceived in my experience. I was now greatly alarmed, lest I should fall away from what I knew I had enjoyed; and to guard against this I prayed almost incessantly, without acting faith on the power and promises of God to keep me from falling. I had not yet learned how to war against temptation of this kind. Satan well knew that if he could succeed in making me disbelieve my conversion, that he would catch me either on the ground of complete despair, or on the ground of infidelity. For if all I had passed through was to go for nothing, and was but fiction, the mere ravings of a disordered mind, that I would naturally be led to believe that there is nothing in religion at all.

From this snare I was mercifully preserved, and led to believe that there was yet a greater work than that of pardon to be wrought in me. I retired to a secret place, (after having sought this blessing, as well as I could, for nearly three months, from the time brother Scott had instructed me respecting it,) for prayer, about four o'clock in the afternoon. I had struggled long and hard, but found not the desire of my heart. When I rose from my knees, there seemed a voice speaking to me, as I yet stood in a leaning posture—"Ask for sanctification." When to my surprise, I recollected that I had not even thought of it in my whole prayer. It would seem Satan had hidden the very object from my mind, for which I had purposely kneeled to pray. But when this voice whispered in my heart, saying, "Pray for sanctification," I again bowed in the same place, at the same time, and said, "Lord *sanctify* my soul for Christ's sake." That very instant, as if lightning had darted through me, I sprang to my feet, and cried, "The Lord has sanctified my soul!" There was none to hear this but the angels who stood around to witness my joy—and Satan, whose malice raged the more. That Satan was there, I knew; for no sooner had I cried out "The Lord has sanctified my soul," than there seemed another voice behind me, saying, "No it is too great a work to be done." But another spirit said, "Bow down for the witness—I received it—*thou art sanctified!*" The first I knew of myself after that, I was standing in the yard with my hands spread out, and looking with my face toward heaven.

I now ran into the house and told them what had happened to me, when, as it were, a new rush of the same ecstacy came upon me, and caused me to feel as if I were in an ocean of light and bliss.

During this, I stood perfectly still, the tears rolling in a flood from my eyes. So great was the joy, that it is past description. There is no language that can describe it, except that which was heard by St. Paul, when he was caught to third heaven, and heard words which it was not lawful to utter.[1]

---

[1] See II Corinthians 12:2.

A Prayer for Africa's Children (1808)
Peter Williams, Jr.

Oh, God! we thank thee, that thou didst condescend to listen to the cries of Africa's wretched sons; and that thou didst interfere in their behalf. At thy call humanity sprang forth, and espoused the cause of the oppressed: one hand she employed in drawing from their vitals the deadly arrows of injustice; and the other in holding a shield to defend them from fresh assaults: and at that illustrious moment, when the sons of '76 pronounced these United States free and independent; when the spirit of patriotism erected a temple sacred to liberty; when the inspired voice of Americans first uttered those noble sentiments, "we hold these truths to be self-evident, that all men are created equal; that they are endowed by their Creator with certain unalienable rights; among which are life, liberty, and the pursuit of happiness"; and when the bleeding African, lifting his fetters, exclaimed, "am I not a man and a brother"; then with redoubled efforts, the angel of humanity strove to restore to the African race the inherent rights of man.

A Prayer for Trust (1817)
Peter Williams, Jr.

O, Lord! we presume not to arraign thy counsels. Thou knowest what is best. Though clouds and darkness are around thee, justice and judgement are the habitation of thy seat. Teach us, O heavenly father, teach us resignation to thy will, and we shall find it all to be right in the end.

A Prayer for the Abolition of Slavery (1813)

George Lawrence

And, O! thou father of the universe and disposer of events, thou that called from a dark and formless mass this fair system of nature, and created thy sons and daughters to bask in the golden streams and rivulets contained therein; this day we have convened under thy divine auspices, it's not to celebrate a political festivity, or the achievement of arms by which the blood of thousands were spilt, contaminating thy pure fields with human gore! but to commemorate a period brought to light by thy wise counsel, who stayed the hand of merciless power; and with hearts expanded with gratitude for thy providences, inundated in the sea of thy mercies, we farther crave thy fostering care. O! wilt thou crush that power that still holds thousands of our brethren in bondage, and let the sea of thy wisdom wash its very dust from off the face of the earth; let Liberty unfurl her banners, Freedom and Justice reign triumphant in the world, universally.

A Slave Woman's Prayer (1816)
{Stephen Hays}

O Lord, bless my master. When he calls upon thee to damn his soul, do not hear him, do not hear him, but hear me—save him—make him know he is wicked, and he will pray to thee.

I am afraid, O Lord, I have wished him bad wishes in my heart—keep me from wishing him bad—though he whips me and beats me sore, tell me of my sins, and make me pray more to thee—make me more glad for what thou hast done for me, a poor [N]egro.

A Desire to Know Our Characters (1816)

John Jea

Lord, I desire for to know
How to serve my God below?
How to serve thee with my heart?
How to choose the better part?

Tis a point I long to know,
Oft it causes anxious thought—
Do I love the Lord or no?
Am I his, or am I not?

If I love, why am I thus?
Why this dull and lifeless frame?
Hardly, sure, can they be worse
Who have never heard his name.

Could my heart so hard remain;
Never to cry to God within;
Every trifle give me pain;
If I knew a Saviour's name?

When I turn my eyes within,
All is dark, and vain, and wild,
Fill'd with unbelief and sin;—
Can I deem myself a child?

O my God to thee I cry,
Save my soul from sin and hell!
Send thy Spirit in my heart,
Bid my unbelief depart.

For the Morning (1816)

John Jea

I hear thy voice, O God of grace,
    That loudly calls for me;
That I may rise and feel thy face,
    Before the dawning day.

While others still lie in their beds,
    And have no thought to pray,
Their sleep doth still keep them secure,
    Like death, upon the frame.

But, O my God, 'tis thou that hears
    My mourning feeble cries;
I cry for grace, thy Spirit's aid,
    Before the sun do rise.

That like the sun I may fulfil,
    My bus'ness of the day;
To give the life that Jesus did,
    To go and preach to-day.

O like the sun I would fulfil,
    My duties and obey;
Thy Spirit's voice that speaks within,
    And tells me keep the day.

Prayers from a Pilgrim's Journal (1820)
Daniel Coker

PRAYER AT SEA, SATURDAY, FEBRUARY 12, 1820

This morning, I awoke, and found that the wind had greatly abated; the vessel had got under sail. Mr. Bacon call unto me, (as I slept in the next berth) to know how my faith was, I told him it was not moved. He interrogated each of the agents to the same purpose, Mr. Bankson, spoke in language that shewed strong faith in the arrival of the vessel in Africa. Indeed, we all seemed to believe that so many were praying for us, that we should arrive in Africa. We had not been long under sail, before we espied a wreck, and the captain gave orders to steer for it. We found it to be the ship *Elizabeth,* of Boston, the chief mate and two of the sailors got into the long-boat, and ventured to go to the windows to see if any crew were on board; but found none. No doubt but they are all drowned. O God! why were we spared? Surely because this expedition is the care of God, as it is the object of sincere prayer of thousands in America. My soul travails that we may be faithful. And should God spare us to arrive in Africa that we may be useful.

PRAYER AT SEA, THURSDAY, FEBRUARY 24, 1820

This day it is fine and pleasant weather. We are at last in what is called the trade winds, latitude 25, north. Our minds and conversation much taken up with our expected arrival at the colony, and the reception that we shall meet with. Think some difficulty is anticipated at Sherbro, by our agents; still our confidence is unshaken, for the hearts of all men are in God's hands. O! that he may direct us in all our movements! May we be able at all times, and in every place, to say

> Only thou our leader be,
> And we still will follow thee!
> *Wesley*

All seem tolerably well on board; I have a violent pain in my head. To-morrow is set apart as a day of fasting and prayer, and humiliation; we believe that there are dangers and trials ahead. May He that was with Moses in the wilderness, be with us; then all will be well.— This is a great undertaking, and I feel its importance more and more, daily.

PRAYER AT SEA, FRIDAY, FEBRUARY 25, 1820

Oh God! help me to be true to my trust, and to act for the good of my African brethren in all things.

I feel a great responsibility to rest upon me; may nothing move me from the right way. I am more and more pleased with the agents; Mr. Bacon only wanting a sable skin to make him an African. Never could there have been a better choice, in my opinion, as a leader. I believe he loves America, Africa, and his God. This day was a fast day; it was a good day at public worship; it was a melting time among us. Oh my soul! praise thou the Lord. Surely, the Lord will bless the colonizing society's exertion. We are in latitude 22°2′, longitude 29°54′. Oh, how happy is my soul while I write these lines.

PRAYER AT SHERBRO ISLAND, SATURDAY, MARCH 18, 1820

We have anchored about twenty or thirty miles from Sherbro island. The sand has a handsome appearance, looks level. I have to labour between hope and fear as to our reception. At this moment the language of my heart is, while I write and look at the vast tracts of land in sight, —Oh, God! is there not for us a place whereon to rest the soals [soles] of our feet? Will not Africa open her bosom, and receive her weeping and bleeding children that may be taken from slave ships or come from America?

> When will Jehovah hear our cries?
> When will the sun of freedom rise?
> When will for us a Moses stand,
> And bring us out from Pharaoh's hand?

PRAYER AT SHERBRO ISLAND, WEDNESDAY, MARCH 29, 1820

This morning, about thirty of our people, Mr. Kezzel, and myself, started in a canoe to king Sherbro. About nine o'clock, we arrived at the king's town. We intended to pass on to prince Concuber, but we were hailed, and put in; found the people friendly, but had soon to start to the prince's, as it is he who must introduce us to the king. On our arrival, we found that the king's power is merely a nominal thing; for he has no power. All the power is in the prince Concuber. On our arriving at his town, all the people were introduced to him; after which, Mr. Kezzel took me by the arm and led me into his house, and introduced me to the old man. He received me cordially, and said he was glad to see me, &c. Had supper got for all our people. After supper, I felt it to be my duty to go to prayers in his house. So, after singing a hymn, we kneeled down, and I offered up a prayer to God for the conversion of Africa, &c. He, and a number of his people were present, and attentive. I felt strange feelings in prayer. Great God! what darkness reigns here. He gave me excellent lodging.

A Prophet's Plea to God (1829)
David Walker

O! save us, we pray thee, thou God of Heaven and of earth, from the
devouring hands of the white Christians!!!

Oh! thou Alpha and Omega!
The Beginning and the end,
Enthron'd thou art, in Heaven above,
Surrounded by Angels there.

From whence thou seest the miseries
To which we are subject;
The whites have murder'd us, O God!
And kept us ignorant of thee.

Not satisfied with this, my Lord!
They throw us in the seas:
Be pleas'd, we pray, for Jesus' sake,
To save us from their grasp.

We believe that, for thy glory's sake,
Thou wilt deliver us;
But that thou may'st effect these things,
Thy glory must be sought.

And Now What Wait We For? (1835)

Maria W. Stewart

Almighty God, it is the glorious hope of a blessed immortality beyond the grave, that supports thy children through this vale of tears. Forever blessed be thy name, that thou hast implanted this hope in my bosom. If thou hast indeed plucked my soul as a brand from the burning, it is not because thou hast seen any worth in me; but it is because of thy distinguishing mercy, for mercy is thy darling attribute, and thou delightest in mercy, and art not willing that any should perish, but that all should come to the knowledge of the truth as it is in Jesus. Clothe my soul with humility as with a garment. Grant that I may bring forth the fruits of a meek and quiet spirit. Enable me to adorn the doctrines of God my Saviour, by a well regulated life and conversation. May I become holy, even as thou art holy, and pure, even as thou art pure. Bless all my friends and benefactors: those who have given me a cup of cold water in thy name, the Lord reward them. Forgive all my enemies. May I love them that hate me, and pray for them that despitefully use and persecute me. Preserve me from slanderous tongues, O God, and let not my good be evil spoken of. Let not a repining thought enter my heart, nor a murmuring sigh heave from my bosom. But may I cheerfully bear with all the trials of life. Clothe me with the pure robes of Christ's righteousness, that when he shall come in flaming fire to judge the world, I may appear before him with joy and not with grief; and not only for myself do I ask these blessings, but for all the sons and daughters of Adam, as thou art no respecter of persons, and as all distinctions wither in the grave. Grant all prejudices and animosities cease from among men. May we all realize that promotion cometh not from the East nor from the West, but that it is God that putteth up one and setteth down another. May the rich be rich in faith and good works towards our Lord Jesus Christ, and may the poor have an inheritance among the saints in light, a crown incorruptible that fadeth not away, eternal in the heavens. And now what wait we for? Be pleased to grant that we may at last join with all the Israel of God, in celebrating thy praises.

A Prayer for Divine Companionship (1835)

Maria W. Stewart

O Lord God, as the heavens are high above the earth, so are thy ways above our ways, and thy thoughts above our thoughts. For wise and holy purposes best known to thyself, thou hast seen fit to deprive me of all earthly relatives; but when my father and mother forsook me, then thou did take me up. I desire to thank thee, that I am this day a living witness to testify that thou art a God, that will ever vindicate the cause of the poor and needy, and that thou hast always proved thyself to be a friend and father to me. O, continue thy loving kindness even unto the end; and when health and strength begin to decay, and I, as it were, draw nigh unto the grave, O then afford me thy heart-cheering presence, and enable me to rely entirely upon thee. Never leave me nor forsake me, but have mercy upon me for thy great name's sake. And not for myself alone do I ask these blessings, but for all the poor and needy, all widows and fatherless children, and for the stranger in distress; and may they call upon thee in such manner as to be convinced that thou art a prayer-hearing and prayer-answering God; and thine shall be the praise, forever. Amen.

A Prayer for Holy Zeal (1835)

Maria W. Stewart

O, thou sin-forgiving God, they that are whole need not a physician, but they that are sick. Lord, I am sick, and full of diseases. If thou wilt, thou canst make me clean. Though my sins have been as scarlet, thou canst make them as wool; and though they be red like crimson, thou canst make them whiter than snow. Were it not that there is a sufficiency in thy blood to atone for the vilest, the view of my past sins and transgressions would sink me in despair. But thou hast said, him that cometh to thee, thou wilt in no wise cast out. Lord, I come, pleading alone the merits of my Redeemer; not only for myself do I plead, but for the whole race of mankind; especially for the benighted sons and daughters of Africa. Do thou loose their bonds, and let the oppressed go free. Bless thy churches throughout the world. Clothe thy ministers with salvation, and cause thy saints to shout for joy. Grant that the time may soon come, that all may know thee from the rising of the sun unto the going down thereof. In an especial manner wilt thou look down upon the church to which I belong. Fire our souls with a holy zeal for thy cause, and let us not rest at ease in Zion, whilst souls are perishing for lack of knowledge. Wilt thou increase her number of such, and such only, as shall be saved. Bless our pastor with a double portion of thy Spirit. Encourage his heart, and strengthen him in the inward man, and may he see the work of the Lord prosper in his hands. And now, Lord, what wait I for? Dispel every gloomy fear that pervades my mind, and enable me to hope in thy mercy, and to thee will I ascribe praises everlasting.

A Prayer for the Children of Africa in America (1835)

Maria W. Stewart

O, Lord God, the watchmen of Zion have cried peace, peace, when there was no peace; they have been, as it were, blind leaders of the blind. Wherefore hast thou so long withheld from us the divine influences of thy Holy Spirit? Wherefore hast thou hardened our hearts and blinded our eyes? It is because we have honored thee with our lips, when our hearts were far from thee. We have polluted thy Sabbaths, and even our most holy things have been solemn mockery to thee. We have regarded iniquity in our hearts, therefore thou wilt not hear. Return again unto us, O Lord God, we beseech thee, and pardon this the iniquity of thy servants. Cause thy face to shine upon us, and we shall be saved. O visit us with thy salvation. Raise up sons and daughters unto Abraham, and grant that there might come a mighty shaking of dry bones among us, and a great ingathering of souls. Quicken thy professing children. Grant that the young may be constrained to believe that there is a reality in religion, and a beauty in the fear of the Lord. Have mercy on the benighted sons and daughters of Africa. Grant that we may soon become so distinguished for our moral and religious improvements, that the nations of the earth may take knowledge of us; and grant that our cries may come up before thy throne like holy incense. Grant that every daughter of Africa may consecrate her sons to thee from the birth. And do thou, Lord, bestow upon them wise and understanding hearts. Clothe us with humility of soul, and give us a becoming dignity of manners: may we imitate the character of the meek and lowly Jesus; and do thou grant that Ethiopia may soon stretch forth her hands unto thee. And now, Lord, be pleased to grant that Satan's kingdom may be destroyed; that the kingdom of our Lord Jesus Christ may be built up; that all nations, and kindreds, and tongues, and people might be brought to the knowledge of the truth, as it is in Jesus, and we at last meet around thy throne, and join in celebrating thy praises.

A Prayer for Purification (1835)

Maria W. Stewart

O thou King eternal, immortal, invisible, and only wise God, before whom angels bow and seraphs veil their faces, crying holy, holy, holy, is the Lord God Almighty. True and righteous are thy ways, thou King of saints. Help me, thy poor unworthy creature, humbly to prostrate myself before thee, and implore that mercy which my sins have justly forfeited. O God, I know that I am not worthy of a place at thy footstool; but to whom shall I go but unto thee? Thou alone hast the words of eternal life. Send me not away without a blessing, I beseech thee; but enable me to wrestle like Jacob, and to prevail like Israel. Be graciously pleased, O God, to pardon all that thou hast seen amiss in me this day, and enable me to live more to thine honor and glory for the time to come. Bless the church to which I belong, and grant that when thou makest up thy jewels, not one soul shall be found missing. Bless him in whom thou hast set over us as a watchman in Zion. Let not his soul be discouraged. May he not fail to declare the whole counsel of God, whether sinners will hear or forbear. And now, Lord, what wait I for? My hope is in thee. Do more for me than I can possibly ask or think, and finally receive me to thyself.

A Prayer for Vision (1835)

Maria W. Stewart

O Lord God, Paul may plant, and Apollos water, but thou alone givest the increase.[1] We are sensible that without thee we can do nothing. Vain are all our efforts without thy blessing. But, O Lord God, thou hast the hearts of all thy creatures in hand; and thou canst turn them withersoever thou wilt. Strip the hearts of this people from their idols, we humbly beseech thee. Take off their eyes from beholding vanity. Thou canst glorify thyself in making them the monuments of thy mercy; and thou canst glorify thyself in making them the monuments of thy wrath. Glorify thyself in making them the monuments of victorious grace. Open their eyes that they may see that their feet stand upon slippery places, and that fiery billows roll beneath them. And, O Lord God, wilt thou in an especial manner have mercy on our unconverted brethren. Soften their proud and rebellious hearts, and be not angry with them forever. O, Jesus of Nazareth, hast thou not died that they might live? Hast thou not become poor, that they might become rich? Is not thy blood sufficient to atone? Wherefore, O Lord God, hast thou hardened their hearts, and blinded their eyes? Wherefore hast thou so long withheld from them the divine influences of thy holy Spirit? Open their eyes that they may see that they are going down to hell, as fast as the wheels of time can carry them. O, stop them in their mad career! Grant that a grievous cry might be heard among thy professing children, in behalf of perishing souls; and may it be like the cry of the Egyptians in the night that thou didst slay their first-born. And not only for ourselves do we pray, but for all nations, kindreds, tongues and people. Grant that an innumerable host, which no man can number, may be gathered in from the four winds of heaven; and when the last trumpet shall sound, grant that we may be caught up into the clouds of the air, and our ear saluted with the joyful sound, "Well done, thou good and faithful servant; thou hast been faithful over a few things, I will make thee ruler over many things; enter thou into the joy of thy Lord."[2]

---

[1] See I Corinthians 3:6 (KJV).

[2] See Matthew 25:21–23 (KJV).

O God, This Great Work Is Thine (1835)

Maria W. Stewart

O, Lord God, when I consider thy heavens, the work of thy fingers, the sun, moon and stars, what is man that thou art mindful of him, or the son of man, that thou shouldst visit him? Thou didst at first create man after thine image, pure and upright; but man, by his disobedience, fell from that holy and happy state, and hath involved all posterity in guilt and ruin. Thine awful sentence was just: "Dust thou art, and unto dust thou shall return."[1] Help me to realize that thou art a consuming fire to those that obey thee not, and that thou art arrayed in terrible majesty. Thou chargest thine angels with folly, and the heavens are not clean in thy sight; how much more filthy and abominable must be man, who drinketh in iniquity like water? Thou canst not look upon the least sin but with abhorrence, and thou wilt by no means clear the guilty. But though thy name alone is so terrible, yet Mercy stands pleading at thy bar, saying, Father, I have died: behold my hands and my side! Spare them a little longer, and have mercy upon the souls that thou hast made. O God, help me to realize that "man that is born of a woman is of few days, and full of trouble: he cometh forth as a flower, and is cut down; yea, man giveth up the ghost, and where is he?" And help me to realize that it is with great tribulation that we enter through the gates into the holy city. Once more I beseech thee to hear the cry of thy children in behalf of the unconverted. O God, this great work is thine; thou alone canst perform it. My church and pastor I recommend to thee; it is all that I can do; and that thou wouldst supply them with all needful blessings is the prayer of thine unworthy handmaiden.

---

[1] Genesis 3:19 (KJV).

Purge Us from All Our Dross (1835)
Maria W. Stewart

"Our Father, which art in heaven, hallowed be thy name. Thy kingdom come. Thy will be done. . . ."[1] Enable me to say from my heart, "Thy will be done," O God. The heaven is thy throne, and the earth is thy footstool; neither may any say unto thee, what does thou? But thou art the high and lofty One that inhabiteth eternity, yet will thou condescend to look upon him that is of a humble, a broken, and a contrite heart. As such, enable me, O God, to bow before thee at this time, under a deep sense of my guilt and unworthiness. It was my sins that caused thee to arise in thy wrath against me. Be pleased, O God, to blot them from thy book, and remember them no more for ever. Bless the church to which I belong. Thine arm is not shortened that it cannot save, neither is thine ear heavy that it cannot hear; but it is our sins that have separated thee from us.[2] Purge us from all our dross;[3] hide thy face from our iniquities, and speak peace to our troubled souls. Bless thy servant, our pastor; let not his soul be discouraged, but may an angel appear unto him, strengthening him. Bless all the benighted sons and daughters of Africa, especially my unconverted friends. Send them not away from thy presence into that lake that burneth with fire and brimstone, but magnify the riches of thy grace in plucking their souls as brands from the burning; and though I may long sleep in death before thou wilt perform this work, yet grant that in the resurrection morn we may all awake in thy likeness, and our souls be bound in the sure bundle of eternal life.

---

[1] Matthew 6:9–10 (KJV).

[2] This sentence is a slight restatement of Isaiah 59:1–2 (KJV).

[3] See Isaiah 1:25 (KJV).

The Hour of Prayer (1837)

Daniel Alexander Payne

Haste thee, haste thee, hour divine,
Joys ecstatic[1]—bliss is thine.
And raptures from the throne above—
Sweeter those, than life to me,
When the world and cares do flee;
And Jesus speaks, in tones of love,
O, time of prayer! O, hour divine!—
Ecstatic joys and peace are thine!

Fairer thou than sunny rays—
Holiest time of all my days!
O, hour of love and joy, draw nigh—
Spread my faith, these eagle wings—
Speed thee where the angels sing:
Where Jesus pleads my cause on high.
O, time of prayer! O, hour divine!
Ecstatic joys and peace are thine!

Now is come the hour of prayer—
Lovely, precious Jesus, hear:
Stoop thou from thy throne above—
Bless me, bless me, Son of God!
Shed thou in my heart, abroad,
Thy saving grace, thy dying love.
O, time of prayer! O, hour divine!
Ecstatic joys and peace are thine!

O, Jesus, thou my portion art:—
Sun of my life—joy of my heart.
O, raptures! bliss—O, God of love!

---

[1] Bishop Payne consistently used *extatic,* now the obsolete spelling of the word *ecstatic.* See *The Compact Edition of the Oxford English Dictionary.* To avoid confusion, I have used the modern spelling.

Exalt my thoughts, my hopes, my soul,
Higher than where the planets roll—
Up to thy dazzling throne of love.
O, time of prayer! O, hour divine!
Ecstatic joys and peace are thine!

Prayer for Dedication of a Church Edifice

(1848)

Daniel Alexander Payne

And now, O, Lord God, Most High, whom the heaven, and heaven of heavens cannot contain, we dedicate this house to thy service, receive it, we humbly beseech thee, receive it unto thyself, and number it among thine earthly Sanctuaries; that thine own presence, the presence of thy Son, Jesus Christ, and the presence of thy Holy Spirit, may ever fill this house, which we have builded and called by thy name; so that whensoever the Gospel is preached in this house, it may descend with all its purity, power, and demonstration upon the hearts of the impenitent, turning them from darkness to light, and from power of sin and Satan unto God; that its sanctifying influences may be felt in the souls of all believers, lifting their desires, their hopes, and their affections, from earth to heaven, and leading back the wandering sheep of the house of Israel, into the fold of eternal life. Amen.

Hear us, O, merciful Father, and grant, that whosoever shall be dedicated to thee, in this house, by the holy ordinance of baptism, may also receive the fullness of thy grace; be made useful members of the Church militant, and finally obtain an abundant entrance into the Church triumphant through Jesus Christ, our Lord. Amen.

Hear us, O, merciful Father, and grant, that whosoever shall, in this house, partake of the symbols of the Saviour's broken body and shed blood, may also realize by faith, that he is indeed the lamb of God, that taketh away the sin of the world, and thus being regenerated and sanctified, stand spotless and life-crowned, at thy right hand, world without end. Amen.

Hear us, O, thou who art the spouse of the Church, and grant, that whosoever shall, in this house, be joined together in holy matrimony, may also live as did Isaac and Rebecca, in the purest enjoyment of connubial love, mutually assisting each other, in the way to heaven, and training their children for usefulness in this world, and for glory in that which is to come, through Jesus Christ, our Lord. Amen.

O, O thou high and Holy One of Israel, regard, we beseech thee, the prayers of thy servants, and grant, that whosoever shall, in this house, make confession of their sins, or lift their voices in praise and thanksgiving for mercies past or benefits received, may also rejoice in the light of thy countenance, with the peace that passeth all understanding, with the joy that is unspeakable and full of glory. Amen.

Great Head of the Church, we beseech thee hear us, and grant, that whosoever shall, in this house, be set apart and ordained to the holy offices of the ministry, may also receive the fullness of the blessings of the Gospel, to preach its unsearchable riches to a ruined world, then, having finished their course, fought the good fight, and kept the faith, receive the crown of life, and reign with thee, world without end. Amen.

Thou, God of Missions, hear us, and grant, that the sacred cause of missions, with every other institution of Christianity, may ever find, in this house, an able advocacy and an ample support, so as to be rendered instrumental in hastening on the day, when the kingdoms of this world shall become the kingdom of our Lord and his Christ. Amen.

Thus have we dedicated this house unto thee, O, thou that dwellest in heaven, receive it, O, receive it, among thine earthly sanctuaries, and grant, that all who may worship thee here, from Sabbath to Sabbath, and from generation to generation, even our children's children, may feel it to be indeed the house of God, and the gate of heaven! Amen.

A Teacher's Prayer (1841)

Ann Plato

Teach me, O! Lord, the secret errors of my way,
Teach me the paths wherein I go astray,
Learn me the way to teach the word of love,
For that's the pure intelligence above.
As well as learning, give me that truth forever—
Which a mere worldly tie can never sever,
For though our bodies die, our souls will live forever,
To cultivate in every youthful mind,
Habitual grace, and sentiments refined.
Thus while I strive to govern human heart,
May I the heavenly precepts still impart;
Oh! may each youthful bosom, catch the sacred fire,
And youthful mind to virtue's throne aspire.
Now fifteen years their destined course have run,
In fast succession round the central sun;
How did the follies of that period pass,
I ask myself—are they inscribed in brass!
Oh! Recollection, speed their fresh return,
And sure 'tis mine to be ashamed and mourn
"What shall I ask, or what refrain to say?
Where shall I point, or how conclude my lay?"
So much my weakness needs—so oft thy voice,
Assures that weakness, and confirms my choice.
Oh, grant me active days of peace and truth,
Strength to my heart, and wisdom to my youth,
A sphere of usefulness—a soul to fill
That sphere with duty, and perform thy will.

Instructions in the Midst of Prayer (1843)
Rebecca Cox Jackson

April the 1st, 1843. Sitting by a table, the wind blowing in a terrible
manner, I felt afraid, and thought it was not safe to be in the house.
Yet I felt not to do anything without knowing whether it was the
will of the Lord for me to go out, or to stay in the house. I felt
desirous to pray. I asked the Lord if I might, and what I might pray
for. He told me to pray to His Father to raise me up in the Resurrection of His Son. So down I kneeled in prayer, inwardly entreating the
Almighty to resurrect my soul into His dear Son.

[The more I prayed, the worse I felt.] And while I was weeping
and praying in the great agony of my soul, prostrated before God, the
Father spoke to me and said, "What is the matter? What ails thee?
What are you crying about? Have I not sent my Son to you? What
more do you want? [All you have to do is to obey Him in all things.]
What is the Resurrection but your rising out of your nature into the
nature of your Lord and Savior Jesus Christ, . . . [but being raised out
of your earthly thoughts into His heavenly thoughts?"]

"Pray to die to thy hearing. Then thou will rise in the hearing of
thy Savior and then thou will hear his voice, and know it from all
others. And you will be able to always obey. Pray to die to your
seeing and to rise in the seeing of thy Savior, and then thou will see
the difference between God's holy will, and thy carnal will. Pray to
die to thy smell, and then thou will rise in the smelling of thy blessed
Savior. And then thou will smell the odor of Holiness and the
sweetness of His kingdom. And then thou will desire to be fed at His
table in His kingdom, which is within thee, and not at thy table of
carnal desire. Pray to die to thy taste and to rise to the taste of thy
Savior, which is to do all His will in all things, which is the food of
thy soul, as it was the food of His soul to do His Father's will when
He was on earth. As He said, 'It is my meat and drink to do my
Father's will.' And in that He was always ready to suffer, for that was
His Father's will. He came into the world to suffer that we might be
saved. And that is what I have called thee for. And in thy taste, thou
never can do it. Thy taste is to do thy own will. His taste is to do my
will. Therefore thou must die that thou may live, because He lives.

A Pastor's Last Prayer for His People (1854)
London Ferrill

May the Great Father of Heaven and earth bless the citizens of Richmond, Virginia, for their kindness toward me in my youthful days,[1] but more particularly, O Lord, be merciful to the citizens of Lexington, Kentucky, and may it please Thee to bless, preserve, and keep them from sin. Guide them in all their walks; make them peaceable, happy and truly religious; and when they come to lie down on the bed of death, may Thy good Spirit hover around ready to waft their ransomed souls to Thy good presence. Lord, grant this for Christ's sake; and O God, bless the Church of which I am pastor, and govern it with Thy unerring wisdom, and keep it a church as long as time shall last.

And, O my Master! choose, when I am gone, choose some pastor for them who may be enabled to labor with more zeal than your most humble petitioner has ever done, and grant that it may continue to prosper and do good among the colored race. And, Merciful Father, bless the white people who have always treated me as though I were a white man; and bless, I pray Thee, all those who, through envy or malice, have mistreated me, and save them—is my prayer. Bless the Church of Christ everywhere—bless Christians in every land—bless, O Lord, my two adopted children, and keep them in Thy way— bring all sinners, in all countries, to feel their need of a Savior, and pardon all their sins; and when they come to die, take them unto Thyself, and the glory shall be to the Father, Son, and Holy Ghost, forever and ever. Amen.

---

[1] They raised money to buy him out of slavery in order to free him to preach the Gospel.

A Slave Mother's Doleful Prayer (1858?)
Fannie Woods

We stopped at this boarding house. This was our first night's stop after leaving Wilmington [, Delaware]. The keeper of the boarding house tried to buy Fannie Woods' baby, but there was a disagreement regarding the price. About five the next morning we started on. When we had gone about half a mile a colored boy came running down the road with a message from his master, and we were halted until his master came bringing a colored woman with him, and he bought the baby out of Fannie Woods' arms. As the colored woman was ordered to take it away I heard Fannie Woods cry, "Oh God, I would rather hear the clods fall on the coffin lid of my child than to hear its cries because it is taken away from me." She said, "good bye, child." We were ordered to move on, and could hear the crying of the child in the distance as it was borne away by the other woman, and I could hear the deep sobs of a broken hearted mother. We could hear the groans of many as they prayed for God to have mercy upon us, and give us grace to endure the hard trials through which we must pass.

A Piteous Prayer to a Hidden God (1861)

{Harriet A. Jacobs}

I well remember one occasion when I attended a Methodist class meeting. I went with a burdened spirit, and happened to sit next [to] a poor, bereaved mother, whose heart was still heavier than mine. The class leader was the town constable—a man who bought and sold slaves, who whipped his brethren and sisters of the church at the public whipping post, in jail or out of jail. He was ready to perform that Christian office any where for fifty cents. This white-faced, black-hearted brother came near us, and said to the stricken woman, "Sister, can't you tell us how the Lord deals with your soul? Do you love him as you did formerly?"

She rose to her feet, and said, in piteous tones, "My Lord and Master, help me! My load is more than I can bear. God has hid himself from me, and I am left in darkness and misery." Then, striking her breast, she continued, "I can't tell you what is in here! They've got all my children. Last week they took the last one. God only knows where they've sold her. They let me have her sixteen years, and then—O! O! Pray for her brothers and sisters! I've got nothing to live for now. God make my time short!"

She sat down, quivering in every limb.

A Poor Negro's Prayer (1864)
{Anonymous}

Masser Jesus, like de people ob de ole time, de Jews, we weep by the side ob de ribber, wid de strings ob de harp all broken. But we sing ob de broken heart, as dem people could not do.[1]

Hear us, King, in de present state ob our sorrows. You know, King Jesus, honey, we just got from de Red Sea, and wander in de dark wilderness, a poor feeble portion ob de children ob Adam, feeble in body, feeble in mind, and need de help ob de good Mighty God. Oh! help us, if you please, to homes; for we's got no homes, Masser Jesus, but de shelter ob de oak-tree in de day-time, and de shelter ob de cotton tent at night. Help us for our own good, and de good ob God's blessed Union people, dat want all people free, whatsomebedder de color.

Masser Jesus, you know de deep tribulation ob our hearts, dat sickness is among us, dat our children dying in de camp, and as we tote dem from one place to tudder, and bury dem in de cold ground, Jesus, to go in spirit, to de God ob de people whare de soul hab no spot nor color.

Great King ob Kings, and Doctor ob Doctors, and God ob Battles, help us to be well. Help us to be able to fight wid de Union sogers de battle for de Union—help us to fight for liberty—fight for de country—fight for our own homes, and our own free children, and our children's children. Fotch out, God ob battles, de big guns, wid de big bustin' shells, and give dem God-forsaken secesh,[2] dat would carry to shame our wives and daughters, O Mighty Jesus! if you please, a right smart charge ob grape[3] and canniser.[4]

---

[1] This is an allusion to Psalm 137:1–4 (KJV).

[2] This utterance, "and give dem God-forsaken secesh," was this slave's way of praying for the defeat of Confederate soldiers.

[3] A *grapeshot* was "a cluster of small iron balls used as a cannon charge." See *Webster's Seventh New Collegiate Dictionary*.

[4] *Canniser* is mistakenly used for *cannon*.

Make 'em glad to stop de war, and come back to shoes and de fatted calf, and de good things ob de Union, no more murdering brodder ob de North States, no more ragged, barefoot, no more slave-whippers, and slave-sellers, no more faders ob yellow skins, no more meaner as meanest niggers.[5]

---

[5] This is a reference to the fact that some black slave drivers (or foremen) were sometimes harsher than white slave drivers. For an introduction to this viewpoint, see John W. Blassingame, *The Slave Community: Plantation Life in the Antebellum South,* rev. and enl. ed. (New York and Oxford: Oxford University Press, 1979), 258–260.

A Sacred Ode: A Prayer for the Consecration of a Pulpit (1866)

Daniel Alexander Payne

Descend! descend! Thou gracious God of Heaven!
    And with Thy glory fill this beauteous fan;
Descend! and let Thy mercy here be giv'n;
    Descend! and let Thy statutes here obtain.
O, *here,* the mantle of Thy love outspread,
And let Thy richest blessings *here* be shed.

Here may the light of holy truth dispel
    The moral darkness of the human mind,
Defeat the combined power of earth and hell,
    And achieve all the heart of Christ design'd;
Here let the dews of Christian love distil.
And peace divine each faithful bosom fill.

Speak here, great Saviour, and the blind will see;
    The deaf will hear, the dumb will sing Thy praise;
Lepers be cleansed; the maimed will worship Thee;
    And from their graves the sleeping dead be raised;
The halt will leap and tread the heavenly way,
While flying devils shall Thy word obey!

Lord, when Thy people in this house shall raise
    Their voice melodious, to extol thy power,
Be they the morning or the evening lays,
    Or in a mournful or a joyous hour,
O, let their songs, sweet as the voice of love,
Borne up by angels, rise to Thee, above!

And when Thy children in this house shall pray,
    And lift to heaven their confidential eyes,
O, hear, benignant, every word they say,
    And hasten hither from the op'ning skies,
To press this altar with Thy viewless feet,
And round this shrine Thy willing people meet.

Here, let the thunders of Thy law resound,
  Its light'nings flash on omnipresent pain,
Its tyrant-hearts, till every slave unbound
  Shall shout for joy, and crush th' oppressor's chain;
O, here! let Holy Freedom speak aloud,
And Freemen plead the cause of Freedom's God!

Redeemer! may the cause of missions here,
  Receive a high, a most exalted place,
And many a herald go from hence to bear
  The joyful message of redeeming grace;
Bid home-born heathens and the Pagans far,
Receive the light of Zion's blazing Star!

Here may the blood-stained banners of the cross
  In pristine beauty now begin to wave,
To guide the bark on sin's dark billows tost,
  And show a ruined world that God can save;
Here may the heralds of salvation be
A spotless priesthood, and from error free.

Come! quickly come! Thou God of Israel, here,
  Eternal Spirit, let thy peace abound,
Make Bethel now a crown of honor wear,
  And like the sun, shed light and heat around;
Then shall the glory of this latter place,
Shine forth resplendent with superior grace.

Adoring angels! from clouds descend!
  And promenade this consecrated aisle;
Bright cherubim! your unheard voices blend
  T' inspire our worship with celestial style;
And Thou! blest Saviour—Thou, our hearts inspire
With holy zeal, and love's ethereal fire.

Bethel! awake! and educate thy sons,
  Who bear the message of the Lord of Hosts!
Let science elevate thy sacred ones,
  And God inspire them with the Holy Ghost,

A flood of light this pulpit then shall pour,
And *baptized infidels thy God adore.*

Here may repenting sinners be forgiven,
    Through faith in Jesus and His cleansing blood,
Then have their names recorded in high heaven,
    On tablets lasting as the throne of God;
0, Bethel! then how dreadful wilt thou be!
The Gate of Heaven—a house, O God, for Thee!

A Prayer for the Mourner's Bench (1867)

An Anonymous "Colored" Woman

O Father Almighty, O sweet Jesus, most glorified King, will you be so pleased to come dis way and put you eye on dese poor mourners? O sweet Jesus, ain't you the Daniel God? Didn't you deliber de tree [three] chillun from the fiery furnis? Didn't you heah [hear] Jonah cry in de belly ub de whale? O, if dere be one seekin' mourner here dis afternoon, if dere be one sinkin' Peter, if dere be one weepin' Mary, if dere be one doubtin' Thomas, won't you be pleased to come and deliber 'em? Won't you mount your Gospel hoss, an' ride roun' de souls of dese yere mourners, and say, "Go in peace and sin no moah?" Don't you be so pleased to come wid de love in one han' and de fan in de odder han', to fan away doubts? Won't you be so pleased to shake dese here souls over hell, an' not let 'em fall in! [Amen.]

Poetic Prayer for a New Day (1870)
Charles Henry Phillips

O Lord, to thee we raise
Our hearts in joy and praise
   This natal day.
Long may our Zion bright
Shine forth with divine light;
"Protect us by thy might"
   This happy May.

When life's journey is run
And all our work is done,
   Great God, our King:
O, may we live with thee
Through all eternity,
Thy face and glory see,
   While angels sing!

A Prayer At Westminster Abbey (1878)

James Theodore Holly

And now on the shores of old England, the cradle of that Anglo-Saxon Christianity by which I have been in part, at least, illuminated, standing beneath the vaulted roof of this monumental pile redolent with the piety of bygone generations during so many ages; in the presence of the "storied urn and animated bust" that hold the sacred ashes and commemorate the buried grandeur of so many illustrious personages, I catch a fresh inspiration and new impulse of the Divine Missionary spirit of our common Christianity. And, here, in the presence of God, of angels and of men, on this day sacred to the memory of an apostle whose blessed name was called over me at my baptism, and as I lift up my voice for the first time, and perhaps, the last time in any of England's sainted shrines, I dedicate myself anew to the work of God, of the Gospel of Christ, and the salvation of my fellow-men in the far distant isle of the Caribbean Sea[1] that has become the chosen field of my special labors.

O Thou Saviour Christ, Son of the Living God, who, when Thou wast spurned by the Jews, of the race of Shem; and who, when delivered up without a cause by Pontius Pilate and the Roman soldiers, of the race of Japheth, on the day of Thy ignominious crucifixion,[2] hadst Thy ponderous cross borne to Golgotha's summit on the stalwart shoulders of Simon, of Cyrene, of the race of Ham; I pray Thee, O precious Saviour, remember that forlorn, despised and rejected race whose son bore Thy cross, when Thou shalt come in the power and majesty of Thy eternal kingdom, to distribute Thy crowns of everlasting glory.

---

[1] Holly was elected the first black Anglican bishop of Haiti.

[2] Although Alonzo Potter Holly's version of his father's prayer uses *crucified*, I am opting for *crucifixion*, the term used in the version of this prayer printed in *The People's Advocate* (19 April 1879). The Alonzo Holly version, however, seems to be more complete, and much more akin to Bishop Holly's usually gracious writing style.

And, give to me, then, not a place at Thy right hand, nor at Thy left, but only the place of a gate-keeper at the entrance of the Holy City, the New Jerusalem, that I may behold my redeemed brethren [, the saved of the Lord, entering therein to be][3] partakers with Abraham, Isaac and Jacob, of all the joys of Thy glorious and everlasting kingdom.

O Jesus, son of the living God; who, when Thou wast spurned and rejected and delivered in the hands of sinful men, by the Jews, of the race of Shem; and, who, when Thou wast mocked and cruelly ill treated by Pontius Pilate and the Roman soldiers, of the race of Japheth; hadst Thy ponderous cross borne to the summit of Golgotha on the stalwart shoulders of Simon of Cyrene, of the race of Ham; remember this poor, forlorn, and despised race when Thou art come into Thy kingdom. And give me, not a place at Thy right, nor at Thy left, but as a door keeper, that I may see the redeemed of my race sweeping into the new Jerusalem, with the children of Abraham, Isaac, and Jacob.[4] Amen.

---

[3] The bracketed insertion is not included in the Alonzo Holly version of this prayer. See *The People's Advocate* (19 April 1879). I am grateful to Dr. Randall K. Burkett, associate director, W. E. B. DuBois Institute for Afro-American Research at Harvard University.

[4] This last paragraph is missing from *The People's Advocate* version of this prayer but is included in Alonzo Holly's version.

Always Pray (1878)
Sojourner Truth

She avers that, in her darkest hours, she had no fear of any worse hell than the one she then carried in her bosom; though it had ever been pictured to her in its deepest colors, and threatened her as a reward for all her misdemeanors. Her vileness and God's holiness and all-pervading presence, which filled immensity, and threatened her with instant annihilation, composed the burden of her vision of terror. Her faith in prayer is equal to her faith in the love of Jesus. Her language is, "Let others say what they will of the efficacy of Prayer, *I* believe in it, and *I* shall pray. Thank God! Yes, *I shall always pray,*" she exclaims, putting her hands together with the greatest enthusiasm.

For some time subsequent to the happy change we have spoken of, Isabella's[1] prayers partook largely of their former character; and while, in deep affliction, she labored for the recovery of her son, she prayed with constancy and fervor; and the following may be taken as a specimen:—"Oh, God, you know how much I am distressed, for I have told you again and again. Now, God, help me get my son. If you were in trouble, as I am, and I could help you, as you can me, think I wouldn't do it? Yes, God, you *know* I would do it. Oh, God, you know I have no money, but you can make the people do for me, and you must make the people do for me. I will never give you peace till you do, God. Oh, God, make the people hear me—don't let them turn me off, without hearing and helping me."

---

[1] Isabella was actually Sojourner Truth's first name.

We Bless God (1888)

Alexander Crummell

We bless God for all the favors and the mercies of the year! for health, comfort, prosperity, the means of grace and for the hope of glory. We bless Him for even the tribulations of our lot in this land, which is, without doubt, a schooling for future greatness. We bless Him for the promise, discovered to sight by signal providences, of usefulness and exalted service, for Him, in this nation, in coming times. And we beseech Him, for the Redeemer's sake to make us faithful men and women, in our families, with our children, in the church. In the entire Race: for the glory of His great name, for the succor and safety of the nation and for the good of man.

A Benediction for a Peaceful Soul (1889)
Anthony Binga, Jr.

May the Lord save you from any painful regrets when the reaping time shall come. But may you all have so lived, that no arrow from God's quiver of justice can pierce your soul, nor mountain of guilt sink you down.

But may you all find your portion, with the redeemed and sanctified out of every nation, tongue and people, around the burnished throne of God, with everlasting shouts of joy and praise upon your lips. Amen.

A Prayer for Power (1889)

Orrin Stone

O Lawd, gib dy sarvint, dis Sunday mawnin', de eye of an eagle dat he may see sin f'om afar. Put his han's to de gospel pulpit; glue his ears to the gospel telefoam an' conneck him wid de Glory in de skies. 'Luminate his brow wid a holy light dat will make de fiahs of hell look like a tallah candle. Bow his head down in humility, in dat lonesome valley wheah de pearl of truth is much needed to be said. Grease his lips wid possum 'ile to make it easy fo' love to slip outen his mouth. . . .

Turpentine his 'magination; 'lectrify his brain wid de powah of the Word. Put 'petual motion in his arms. Fill him full of de dynamite of Dy awful powah; 'noint him all ovah wid de kerosene of Dy salvation, an' den, O Lawd, sot him on fiah wid de sperrit of de Holy Ghos'.

Doxology (1890)

Josephine Delphine Henderson Heard

Great God accept our gratitude,
For the great gifts on us bestowed—
For Raiment, shelter and for food.

Great God, our gratitude we bring,
Accept our humble offering,
For all the gifts on us bestowed,
Thy name be evermore adored.

I Will Look Up (1890)

Josephine Delphine Henderson Heard

I will look up to Thee
    With faith's ne'er-failing sight,
My trust repose in Thee,
    Though dark and chill earth's night.

I will look up to Thee,
    Though rough and long the way,
Still sure Thou leadest me
    Unto the perfect day.

I will look up to Thee
    When lone and faint and weak.
"My grace sufficeth Thee";[1]
    I hear Thy soft voice speak.

I will look up to Thee,
    For if Thou, Lord, art near,
Temptations quickly flee,
    And clouds soon disappear.

I will look up to Thee
    With feeble voice I cry.
Lord, pity helpless me—
    Without Thy aid I die.

I will look up to Him
    Who died my soul to save;
Who [bore][2] my load of sin—
    His blood a ransom gave.

---

[1] See II Corinthians 12:9 (KJV).

[2] The word *boar,* apparently a typographical error, appears here in the original printed text.

I will look up to Thee,
    The all-anointed one,
Who opes the gate for me,
    To the eternal throne.

I will look up to Thee;
    I feel my sins forgiven—
Thy footprints Lord I see,
    They mark the way to heaven.

I will look up to Thee,
    When doubt and fear arise;
Though dangers compass me,
    Upward I lift mine eyes.

I will look up to Thee,
    Who knoweth all my needs;
Thy spirit Lord grant me,
    My soul in anguish leads.

I will look up to Thee!
    Though all I have below,
Thou takest Lord from me,
    Thou canst the more bestow.

I will look up to Thee,
    Thou bright and morning star;
With eyes of faith I see,
    Thy glory from afar.

I will look up to Thee,
    My hand shall rest in thine;
Where e'er thou wilt lead me,
    Thy will, O Lord, not mine!

I will look up to Thee,
    When death's relentless hand,

Has laid its weight on me,
   Save—Thou atoning Lamb!

I will look up to Thee,
   When crossing Jordan's wave;
Then Lord, I look to Thee—
   Whose power alone can save!

Matin Hymn (1890)

Josephine Delphine Henderson Heard

Is this the way my Father,
That Thou wouldest have me go—
Scaling the rugged mountain steep,
Or through the valley low?
Walking alone the path of life,
With timid, faltering feet;
Fighting with weak and failing heart,
Each conflict that I meet?

"Nay! nay! my child," the Father saith,
"Thou dost not walk alone—
Gird up the loins of thy weak faith,
And cease thy plaintive tone.
Look thou with unbeclouded eyes
To calvary's gory scene—
Canst thou forget the Saviour's cries?
Go thou, on His mercy, lean."

My Father, brighter grows the way,
Less toilsome is the road;
If Thou Thy countenance display,
O, lighter seems my load!
And trustingly I struggle on,
Not murmuring o'er my task;
The mists that gather soon are gone,
When in Thy smile I bask.

Turn not from me Thy smiling face,
Lest I shall surely stray,
But in Thy loving arms' embrace,
I cannot lose my way.
My Father when my faith is small,
And doubting fills my heart,
Thy tender mercy I recall.
O, let it ne'er depart!

Thou Lovest Me (1890)

Josephine Delphine Henderson Heard

Gracious Saviour let me make,
   Neither error or mistake—
Let me in Thy love abide,
   Ever near Thy riven side.

Let me, counting all things dross,
   Find my glory in the cross;
Let me daily with Thee talk,
   In Thy footsteps daily walk.

I would gladly follow Thee,
   For Thou gently leadest me,
Where the pastures green doth grow,
   Where the waters stillest flow.

For me is Thy table spread,
   And Thou doth anoint my head,
And my cup of joy o'erflows
   In the presence of my foes.

Unuttered Prayer (1890)

Josephine Delphine Henderson Heard

My God, sometimes I cannot pray,
    Nor can I tell why thus I weep;
The words my heart has framed I cannot say,
    Behold me prostrate at Thy feet.

Thou understandest all my woe;
    Thou knows't the craving of my soul—
Thine eye beholdest whereso'er I go;
    Thou can'st this wounded heart make whole.

And oh! while prostrate here I lie,
    And groan the words I fain would speak:
Unworthy though I be, pass not me by,
    But let Thy love in showers break.

And deluge all my thirsty soul,
    And lay my proud ambition low;
So while time's billows o'er me roll,
    I shall be washed as white as snow.

Thou wilt not quench the smoking flax,
    Nor wilt thou break the bruised reed;
Like potter's clay, or molten wax,
    Mould me to suit Thy will indeed.

A Slave Mother's Prayer (1890)
Sallie Smith

Madam, although I did not have religion when I used to live in the woods, yet it seemed I could not keep from praying. I'd think of my mother, how, just before she died, she told me to "come." And that word always followed me. I used to lie out in the woods on logs, with moss under my head, and pray many and many a night. I hardly knowed what to say or how to pray, but I remembered how I used to hear my mother praying, on her knees, in the morning before day, long before she died, and I just tried to say what she used to say in her prayers. I heard her say many a time, "O, Daniel's God, look down from heaven on me, a poor, needy soul!" I would say, "O, Daniel's God, look down from heaven on me in these woods!" Sometimes it seemed I could see my mother right by my side as I laid on the log asleep. One time I talked with her in my sleep. I asked her, "Mother, are you well?" And it seemed I could hear her saying, as she beckoned to me, "Come, O come; will you come?" And I did try to get up in my sleep and start to her, and I rolled off the log. By that time I woke up, and the sun was shining clear and bright and I was there to wander about in the woods?

Some Prayers of Slave Children (1890)
Sallie Smith

Aunt Sallie, what did you and your brother decide upon in the woods!

O, we wandered about in the woods, I don't know how long. We would pick berries to eat, and would get any thing we came upon. I told Warren about my dream of our mother, and that I saw her come up to me, and that I had been praying every night on my moss bed. I wanted to get him to pray too. I said to him, "Warren, you know how our poor mother used to pray way before day in the morning, and how we used to hear her cry and say, "O, Daniel's God, have mercy on me!" And it makes me feel glad every time I pray, Warren; and now let us pray every time before we go to sleep." Warren said, "Well, let us pray to Daniel's God just like our poor mother did." And we did every night before we went to sleep, after wandering all through the woods all day. Me and Warren would pray. We prayed low and easy; we just could hear each other. Warren used to pray, "O, Daniel's God, have mercy on me and Sallie. Mother said you will take care of us, but we suffer here; nobody to help us. Hear us way up in heaven and look down on us here." Madam, we did not know hardly what to say, but we had heard mother and other people praying, and we tried to do the best we could.

A Bishop's Benediction (1892)

Singleton Thomas Jones

God grant that we may stand before that throne with the consciousness of sins pardoned. May we look upon the bow around it as one of promise to us, and under its beauteous light may we be guided to "mansions in the skies." Amen and Amen.

O God, Save Me (1893)

Frederick Douglass

Sunday was my only leisure time, I spent this under some large tree, in a sort of beast-like stupor between sleeping and walking. At times I would rise up and a flash of energetic freedom would dart through my soul, accompanied with a faint beam of hope that flickered for a moment, and then vanished. I sank down again, mourning over my wretched condition. I was sometimes tempted to take my life and that of Covey, but was prevented by a combination of hope and fear. My sufferings, as I remember them now, seem like a dream rather than like a stern reality.

Our house stood within a few rods of the Chesapeake Bay, whose broad bosom was ever white with sails from every quarter of the habitable globe. Those beautiful vessels, robed in white, and so delightful to the eyes of freemen, were to me so many shrouded ghosts, to terrify and torment me with thoughts of my wretched condition. I have often, in the deep stillness of a summer's Sabbath, stood all alone upon the banks of that noble bay, and traced, with saddened heart and tearful eye, the countless number of sails moving off to the mighty ocean. The sight of these always affected me powerfully. My thoughts would compel utterance; and there, with no audience but the Almighty, I would pour out my soul's complaint in my rude way with an apostrophe to the multitude of ships.

"You are loosed from your moorings, and free. I am fast in my chains, and am a slave! You move merrily before the gentle gale, and I sadly before the bloody whip. You are freedom's swift-winged angels, that fly around the world; I am confined in bonds of iron. O, that I were free! O, that I were one of your gallant decks, and under your protecting wing. Alas! betwixt me and you the turbid waters roll. Go on, go on; O, that I could also go! Could I but swim! If I could fly! O, why was I born a man, of whom to make a brute! The glad ship is gone: she hides in the dim distance. I am left in the hell of unending slavery. O, God, save me! God, deliver me! Let me be free!—Is there any God? Why am I a slave? I will run away. I will not stand it. Get caught or get clear, I'll try it. I had as well die with ague as with fever. I have only one life to lose. I had as well be killed running as die standing. Only think of it: one hundred miles north, and I am free! Try it? Yes! God helping me, I will. It cannot be that I shall live and die a slave. I will take to the water. This very bay shall yet bear me into freedom.

A Conversation with the Lord (1893)

Amanda Smith

May God in mercy save us from the formalism of the day, and bring us back to the old time spirituality and power of the fathers and mothers. I often feel as I look over the past and compare it with the present, to say: "Lord, save, or we perish."

As the Lord led, I followed, and one day as I was praying and asking Him to teach me what to do I was impressed that I was to leave New York and go out. I did not know where, so it troubled me, and I asked the Lord for light, and He gave me these words: "Go, and I will go with you."[1] The very words he gave to Moses, so many years ago.

I said, "Lord, I am willing to go, but tell me where to go and I will obey Thee"; and clear and plain the word came, "Salem!" I said, "Salem! why, Lord, I don't know anybody in Salem. O, Lord, do help me, and if this is Thy voice speaking to me, make it plain where I shall go." And again it came, "Salem."

"O, Lord, Thou knowest I have never been to Salem, and only have heard there is such a place."

I remembered that five years before while in Philadelphia, I was at Bethel Church[2] one morning, and the minister gave out that their quarterly meeting was to be held in Salem the next Sunday. I could not go—I was at service—this was all that I had heard about Salem, or knew. I said: "O, Lord, don't let Satan deceive me, make it plain to me, and if this is Thy voice, speak again to me, do Lord, make it clear, so as to make me understand it, and I will obey Thee. Now, Lord, I wait to hear Thee speak to me, and tell me where to go," and I heard the word coming, I was afraid, it seemed as though the Lord would strike me down, and I drew down as though to hide, and the word came with power, "Salem," and I said, "Lord, that is enough, I will go."

---

[1] See Exodus 4:12 (KJV).

[2] Mother Bethel African Methodist Episcopal Church, the first congregation of the famous denomination the African Methodist Episcopal Church, whose official date of founding is 1787. Some scholars question the accuracy of this date. See Albert J. Raboteau, "Richard Allen and the African Church Movement," in Leon Litwack and August Meier, eds., *Black Leaders of the Nineteenth Century* (Urbana and London: University of Illinois Press, 1988), 1–18.

A few weeks passed. O, how I was tested to the very core in every way. My rent was five dollars a month, and I wanted to pay two months before I went. I prayed and asked the Lord to help me to do this. It was wonderful how He did. I needed a pair of shoes. I told the Lord I was willing to go with the shoes I had if He wanted me to, but they were broken in the sole, and I said: "Lord, Thou knowest if I get my feet wet I will be sick; now, if it is Thy will to get the shoes, either give me some work to do or put it in the heart of somebody to give me the money to get the shoes." And these words came from God to my heart: "If thou canst believe; all things are possible to him that believeth."[3] And I said, "Lord, the shoes are mine," and I put them on as really as ever I put on a pair of shoes in my life! O, how real it was. I claimed them by faith. When I got up I walked about and felt I really had the very shoes I had asked for on my feet. O, how very true that blessed promise—"What things so ever ye desire, when ye pray, believe that ye receive them and ye shall have them."[4] I know that truth. Hallelujah! [Amen.]

---

[3] Mark 9:23 (KJV).

[4] Mark 11:24 (KJV).

Part III

The Vale of Tears

1894–1919

A Prayer for Spiritual Assurance (1894)
Charles Price Jones

One day as I staggered under the weight of this obligation, under the necessity of this ministry, I felt that I must be alone and especially talk with God about it. I went to the home of Sister Rachel Williams, a God-fearing woman, the widow of Deacon Ben Williams, and asked if I might lock myself in her parlor and remain unmolested till I had reached the Lord with this matter. Oh the relief and help possible through prayer. It is good when burdened to pray it out; some phrase it "pray through." I prayed from about 9 a.m. to about 3 p.m. This was the burden of my prayer: "Lord, give me power to convince my people and my generation of the beauty of holiness and the advantages of righteousness."[1] My people loved beauty, but the beauty of the flesh is vain and deceiving and soon passes. They wanted to advance in the world; but worldly advantages proved only a snare; for wealth promotes robbery, engenders pride and breeds strife; which to my people was fatal. I saw that in God was our salvation temporal and eternal. I desired that they should see it. I saw how we could hasten the coming of the Lord and universal happiness and welfare. I wanted them to see it. And so I prayed. Between 3 and 4 o'clock in the afternoon I became exhausted. I lay down on the sofa on which I knelt and said, "Lord, I'm exhausted. I can pray no more." Then the Lord flooded me with blessing until laughing and crying and verily kicking like an infant for holy delight, I at last begged the Lord to desist. It seemed I could stand no more, my vision was clarified, my eyes were opened. I could see apparently the golden walls and pearly gates of the "city made without hand." Surely the heavens were opened. The Spirit spoke within from the holy of holies of my redeemed spirit, and said, "You shall write the hymns for your people." This He said six or seven times till it was fixed in my mind. I got up and went to the organ in the corner of the room, wrote a song titled "Praise the Lord," ruled off a tablet, set it to music, and sang it before I left the room.

---

[1] Deuteronomy 28.

As I Am Running (1906)

Charles Price Jones

As I am running this race of life,
Lord, I am looking to Thee;
Rugged the pathway and fierce tho' the strife,
Lord, I am looking to Thee.

Refrain:
Thou art my Saviour,
Thou art my friend.
My guardian angel to lead and defend;
Thou art at all times all things to me,
And I am looking to Thee,
Looking to Thee,
Looking to Thee,
Looking to Thee,
Looking to Thee,
Looking to Thee,
Yes, I am looking to Thee.

From ev'ry pitfall save me I pray,
Lord, I am looking to Thee;
From ev'ry danger that's found on the way,
Save me, I'm looking to Thee.

Tho' friends forsake me and all I lose,
Lord, I am looking to Thee;
Thee for my portion I gladly shall choose,
Save me, I'm looking to Thee.

Life is perplexing, make my way plain,
Lord, I am looking to Thee;
Give me the power that I need each day,
Lord, I am looking to Thee.

Teach me to follow, make strong my heart,
Lord, I am looking to Thee;
All that I need, O Lord, surely, Thou art,
Lord, I am looking to Thee.

Lord, Rebuke Thy Servant Not (1906)

Charles Price Jones

Lord, rebuke Thy servant not
In Thine anger fierce and hot,
For Thy wrath I cannot bear,
Pity me and hear my pray'r.
Leave me not in deep distress,
Look upon my helplessness;
Abba Father, oh, I pray,
Turn Thy heavy wrath away.

My shortcomings I confess,
But Thou art my righteousness,
Without Thee I would not dare
E'en attempt to make a pray'r.
Lord, if sin lies at the door,
Give me grace to sin no more,
But, O Lord, in pity heed
My heart-groanings as I plead.

Lord, Thy favor now restore,
Bind my wound and heal my sore,
Loose my body from this pain,
Give me health and peace again.
But, O Lord, deep in my soul
Let the floods of glory roll!
Hallelujah! I am free,
Lord, by faith, by faith in Thee.

Prayer for Consecration (1906)

Charles Price Jones

Jesus, Jesus, I would be
Consecrated all to Thee;
In Thee wholly sanctified,
Free from selfishness and pride.

Jesus, I am very sure
Thou canst ev'ry weakness cure;
If my feeble heart believe
All Thy fullness Thou wilt give.

Jesus, I am satisfied
If in Thee I may abide;
Cause all thoughts of earth to flee,
Set my mind alone on Thee.

Jesus, fix me just as Thou
Wouldst delight to have me now;
Nothing would I have but Thee,
Be Thou all in all to me.

Our Plea (1894)

Benjamin Tucker Tanner

To Thee, oh Lord, we make our plea
That human sorrows Thou wouldst see,
And human grief; and human tears
That flow throughout the life-long years.

Awake, O Lord, and speak the word,
Awake, assert Thyself as Lord,
And let the pain of head and heart
At thy dear coming, Lord, depart.

Awake and let thy people know
That from them Thou wilt never go;
And let the world be put to shame—
If, Lord, it rev'rence not thy name.

Hidden Grief[1] (1895)

Benjamin Tucker Tanner

Oh, the untold, secret grief,
That draws back from all relief,
Will not deign to have a cure—
Grieves and says: I must endure.

Ah, the tear—soon wiped away—
Wipes in haste with no delay
Lest some sympathizing eye
Might the weeping sad espy.

Ah, the heart's great heaving groan
Quickly silenced lest the moan
Might attack some friendly heart
And to save, at once to start.

God of mercy, known alone
To Thee is the saddening groan
To Thee is the falling tear,
God of mercy, hear, oh hear.

---

[1] After "seeing a young woman weeping on the street," presumably in Philadelphia, where he resided, on 1 November 1895 Bishop Tanner wrote this "impromptu" poem and concluded it with prayer.

Who? (1895)

Benjamin Tucker Tanner

QUIS EST QUI CONDEMNET *(Romans 8:28)*[1]

If Jesu, Lord, I come to thee,
And freely thou receivedst me,
   Who shall say, nay?
Who shall bring up the days of sin,
When earthly passions raged within?

If Jesu, Lord, I should profess
Thy name—Thy boundless love confess,
   Who shall deny?
That thou thyself hast made me bold
To claim the blessings long foretold?

If Jesu, in the throng I raise
My voice in notes of praise,
   Who say, be still?
Who chide me for the words I speak
And tell me I should be more meek?

Dear Jesu, 'tis thy precious Name
That doth alone my heart inflame—
   My heart inspire.
And makes me fearless of the world—
Thy children—of the arrows hurled.

---

[1] Bishop Tanner could read and write Latin. The inspiration for this poetic prayer was Romans 8, especially verse 28. Yet Bishop Tanner used the Latin translation of verse 34 as an epigram: *Quis est qui condemnet* [i.e., "Who is he that condemneth?"]. The King James Version of the Bible offers this translation of Roman 8:28: "And we know that all things work together for good to them that love God, to them who are called according to his purpose." The translation of verse 34 reads, "Who is he that condemneth? It is Christ that died, yea rather, that is risen again, who is even at the right hand of God, who also maketh intercession for us." This prayer embraces the doctrine of salvation as understood in the theology of the Apostle Paul.

Ah, Tender Soul[1] (1899)

Benjamin Tucker Tanner

Ah, tender Soul:
Already burdened with the woe
That doth from human ills outflow—
Already burdened with grief
That, save in Thee, finds no relief.
Ah, tender, loving Soul.

Ah, tender Soul:
And can it be that I will add
Unto the weight, make Thee more sad?
Add to the grief of Thy poor heart
More pain, have it more keenly smart?
Ah, tender, loving Soul.

Ah, tender Soul:
Ignoble is the part I play
Despite my groan, despite my say.
From out Thy sorrow, help me, Lord
And save, according to Thy word.
Ah, tender, loving Soul.

---

[1] Tanner's first-rate classical education is reflected in his epigram for this prayer. He cited these lines from Thomas à Kempis's *Imitatio Christi,* chapter 18: "My son, I descended from heaven for thy salvation; I took upon me thy sorrows, not necessity, but love drawing thereto; that thou thyself mightest learn patience, and bear temporal sufferings without repining."

Again and One More Time (1895)

{Anonymous}

O! Lord here it is again and again and one time more that we thine weak an' unprofitable servants has permitted to bow, and I ask you while I make this feeble attempt to bow that you would bow my head below my knees, and my knees away down in some lonesome valley of humility where you have promised to hear and answer prayer at every time of need and every stressful hour for Jesus sake. (*Moan*)

I ask you while I have bowed down upon my buckle and boquets to come this way. (*Moan*)

In thy mighty coming please don't come in wrath nor in strick judgement, but come sin-killing, soul-reviving, healing up all our backsliding ways and loving our little souls freely, I pray thee. (*Moan*)

We will ask you to mount your swift steed in Zion called Victoria and ride around and see what your people stand need of. (*Moan*)

Come riding over many hill, gill and poblication, tearing down the mighty works of Satan and building up the great walls in Zion, I pray thee. (*Moan*)

Thou has said in thy fore-written and divine words where there was one, two, three or ever so many of thy royal blood-bought purchase whom from hell their blood has ransom and their name truly cut on the chief corner stone that lies way in the courts of mount Sinai that thou would be a prayer hearing God, and the chiefest among their number. (*Moan*)

We believe that thou art a rock in the weary land, and a shelter in the mighty storm, a strong hold in the day of trouble and a cove in thy temple. (*Moan*)

We would ask you to lift high your dauman window in heaven this evening and take a gentle peep over Joshua's high white wall way down here in these low grounds of sorrow and sin and see what sin and flesh is doing with your people down here in this unfriendly world. (*Moan*)

We believe that love is growing old and sin is growing bold and Zion wheel is clogged and can't roll, neither can she put on her beautiful garments, but we ask you to come this way, seal her with love, type her with blood and send her around the hill sides clucking to her broods and bringing live sons and daughters to the marvelous light of thy glorious gospel as the bees to the honey comb and the little doves to the window of Noah's ark, I pray thee. (*Moan*)

We will ask you to ride out on the wings of the winds and on the chief pools of thy glorious gospel. (*Moan*)

Did you say if your servant would ben the bow that you would correct the arrow, so I ask you correct it to some dying sinner's heart. We ask you to hammer hard with Jeremiah's hammer and break their hearts in ten thousand pieces for Jesus sake. (*Moan*)

O, Lord you said it was not hear for the many words, or the words being many, but it was for the insincerity of heart that your darling Son crave and require, so when I come down to death please raise our blood-bought spirits high and happy and our bodies be lowed to our mother dust for Christ sake, A-men. (*Long moans*)

The Sun Done Rose (1895)
{Anonymous}

Who rules blue sky fellom city, whar no mortal eye can either come, nor except it come in and through menighted son Jesus the matchless land, the hope of eternal glory this evening. (*Moan*)

The sun done rose in yonders east and done take healin' in her wings and set back the hilly clouds in darkness. (*Moan*)

We believe since she rose in de east and stemmed her coast across the blue meridian, that many of our fellow traveller have been cut off and gone. (*Moan*)

Where they are gone we dars not say, but we believe some have fallen on the right hand and some on the left hand. (*Groans*)

Those that have fallen on the left hand have fallen in hell among the rich man Dives[1] and all the forgetters of God, crying pity and pardon written on the gates of hell to free no mortal soul. (*Groans*)

Those that have fallen on the right hand are in heaven feasting off milk and honey, and have golden slippers on their feet and silver trumpets in their mouth blowing a new song which was never known before. (*Shouts*)

---

[1] This is an allusion to Luke 16:19–31.

An Offering (1895)

Eloise Alberta Veronica Bibb

Lord, all I am and hope to be,
I humbly offer, King, to thee!
When clouds arise, thy guidance send,
Accept my life, and bless it, Friend.

O Father! let me rest in thee,
Resigned to what *thou* will'st for me;
Content, though all my fond hopes fade,
And visions bright in gloom are laid.

When I was but a tiny child,
Thou shielded me from tempests wild;
And gave me strength to do the right
Within temptation's treacherous sight.

And now in girlhood's solemn time,
Oh, make my life one perfect rhyme,
Sung to the air of sweet content,
With blended sounds of a life well spent.

Lead Gently, Lord (1895)

Paul Laurence Dunbar

Lead gently, Lord, and slow,
    For oh, my steps are weak,
And ever as I go,
    Some soothing silence speak;

That I may turn my face
    Through doubt's obscurity
Toward thine abiding-place,
    E'en tho' I cannot see.

For lo, the way is dark;
    Through mist and cloud I grope,
Save for that fitful spark,
    The little flame of hope.

Lead gently, Lord, and slow,
    For fear that I may fall;
I know not where to go
    Unless I hear thy call.

My fainting soul doth yearn
    For thy green hills afar;
So let thy mercy burn—
    My greater, guiding star!

The Warrior's Prayer (1895)

Paul Laurence Dunbar

Long since, in sore distress, I heard one pray,
  "Lord, who prevailest with resistless might,
Ever from war and strife keep me away,
  My battles fight!"

I know not if I play the Pharisee,
  And if my brother after all be right;
But mine shall be the warrior's plea to thee—
  Strength for the fight.

I do not ask that thou shalt front the fray,
  And drive the warring foeman from my sight;
I only ask, O Lord, by night, by day,
  Strength for the fight!

When foes upon me press, let me not quail
  Nor think to turn me into coward flight.
I only ask, to make mine arms prevail,
  Strength for the fight!

Still let mine eyes look ever on the foe,
  Still let mine armor case me strong and bright;
And grant me, as I deal each righteous blow,
  Strength for the fight!

And when, at eventide, the fray is done,
  My soul to Death's bedchamber do thou light,
And give me, be the field or lost or won,
  Rest from the fight!

When Storms Arise (1895)

Paul Laurence Dunbar

When storms arise
And dark'ning skies
    About me threat'ning lower,
To Thee, O Lord, I raise mine eyes,
To Thee my tortured spirit flies
    For solace in that hour.

The mighty arm
Will let no harm
    Come near me nor befall me;
Thy voice shall quiet my alarm,
When life's great battle waxeth warm—
    No foeman shall appall me.

Upon thy breast
Secure I rest,
    From sorrow and vexation;
No more by sinful cares oppressed,
But in thy presence ever blest,
    O God of my salvation.

The Soul's Thirst (1895)

Lewis Ruffin Nichols

My God I come to Thee,
  Thee only would I know,
Thy blood O Let me feel,
  And this will comfort me.

I still trust in Thy word,
  Oh gracious lamb of God;
Increase my faith in Thee
  And wash me in thy blood.

Thy word I know is truth
  And it can never fail,
All who in Thee confide
  Forever will prevail.

Accept me blessed Lord,
  Make me thy humble child,
Spirit, take thy abode,
  And with me e'er abide.

Give me the "shield of faith,"
  Baptize with righteousness;
The spirit's sword vouchsafe,
  My feet, shod Thou with grace.

Walk with me, blessed Lord,
  Till life's long journey ends,
Sin and temptation foil
  Till Thou the summons send.

And then beyond the flood
  On Canaan's blissful shore,
Where saints and angels dwell,
  Save me forever more.

A Psalm of the Soul (1896)

Katherine Davis Chapman Tillman

Oh, Father, my heart is heavy laden,
    And grief has settled o'er me like pall;
And behold in earth or Heaven,
    My anguished soul on none but thee can call.

No one but thee a word of cheer can give,
    In this the deepened gloom of a sad day;
Oh, come to my heart dear Father,
    And bid my bitter sorrow steal away.

Teach me to see how blessed good shall come
    From everything that seemeth to me ill;
If I but wait, but trust my all to thee
    And ever seek to do thy loving will.

And while I cannot see a ray of light,
    Yet lend me faith to love thee well;
And conquering grace for every trial,
    Till I beyond the pearly gates shall dwell.

Tonight I need thy rod and staff
    To comfort me, for I am travel-worn;
My hands are weary with much toil,
    My feet are badly bruised and torn.

Reach down and hide me in thy cleft,
    Where I may rest awhile my weary feet;
And there I pray that thine own voice
    In soothing tones my longing heart shall greet.

So shall I then be comforted,
    My soul shall then rejoice in thee;
The oil of joy thy presence sheds
    Shall fill my soul with ecstacy.

A Hymn of Praise (1902)
Katherine Davis Chapman Tillman

Oh, God, when days were dark indeed,
    When we were fast in Slavery's chain,
Thou then our parents' prayers did heed
    And helped us freedom to obtain.

And when adrift upon the world
    A child race 'mid the great and strong,
Thy banner o'er was unfurled
    And gently were we led along.

Help us to e'er remember Thee
    And e'er to endless homage pay
For all the great prosperity
    Enjoyed by our race to-day.

Elijah's Stay (1898)

John B. Smalls

God of gods, Elijah's stay, O hear and pity my condition. I would be thine, gracious Redeemer, cleanse and purify my heart. Light of light, eternal life, Thou alone can give grace to help in time of need; I need Thee, Saviour of all mankind, I need Thee, gracious Spirit, to build up the broken places of my weakened will; to bind up the wounds which sin has made and to mollify the raging of all sinful desires. Have pity upon me, Jesus of Nazareth, the sinner's friend— the world's Redeemer. Grant me perfect peace, and henceforth enable me to resist all temptations; to resist evil thought or action of every kind. Set up Thy throne in this unworthy heart of mine and never from it more depart, but lead me unto everlasting life; I will bless and praise Thy name forever.—Amen.

A Prayer for the Human Heart (1898)

John B. Smalls

Redeemer of mankind, lend a listening ear and turn a pitying glance; a glance of heavenly day to lighten the darkness of this benighted Heart of mine. God of unbounded mercy, send the Divine Spirit in Jesus' name through the tender compassion manifested in His five bleeding wounds. Look favorably and mercifully upon this Heart, this forlorn Heart, in its state of worse than midnight darkness; let the light of the uplifted cross shed its halo of reconciliation, and break the grasp of the power of darkness and set my spirit free to act in obedience to the moving of the Holy Spirit. Break the power of my ghostly enemy, and the force of his combined influences.

Remove from my Heart Pride, Lewdness, Gluttony and Intemperance, Stupidity and Avarice, Anger, Sloth, and Enmity of every kind, and renew in me grace, through Thy Spirit, in Jesus' name and for His sake. Amen.

A Slave Father's Prayer (1898)

Jacob Stroyer

When the time came for us to go to bed we all knelt down in family prayer, as was our custom; father's prayer seemed more real to me that night than ever before, especially in the words, "Lord, hasten the time when these children shall be their own free men and women."

My faith in my father's prayer made me think that the Lord would answer him at the fartherest in two or three weeks, but it was fully six years before it came, and father had been dead two years before the war.

Lord God, To Whom Our Fathers Pray'd

(1899)

Benjamin Griffith Brawley

Lord God, to whom our fathers pray'd,
    To whom they did not pray in vain,
And who for them assurance made,
    Though oft repeated their refrain,
Hope of our race, again we cry,
Draw near and help us, lest we die.

The battle rages fierce and long,
    The wicked seem to triumph still;
Yet all things to the Lord belong,
    And all must bow beneath His will.
Lord God of old, again we cry,
Draw near and help us, lest we die.

If brooding o'er the wrongs we grieve,
    Our hearts forget to turn to Thee;
Or if they e'er do not believe
    That Thou in time wilt hear our plea,
Hope of our race, stand by us then,
And help us "quit ourselves like men."

As now we bend before thy throne,
    Upon us send Thy truth and light;
From us all other hopes are flown—
    We pray Thee, help us in the right.
Father of lights, Thy mercy send
Upon us, as we lowly bend.

Lord God, we pray Thee help us all
    To live in harmony and peace;
Help us to listen to Thy call,
    And from all evil-doing cease.
Hope of our people, hear our cry;
Draw near and help us, lest we die.

A Hymn (1900)

Priscilla Jane Thompson

Lord, within thy fold I be,
    And I'm content;
Naught can be amiss to me,
For thy helping hand I see,
Light'ning loads that heavy be;
    And I'm content.

Lord I've put my trust in thee,
    And I'm content;
Whatsoe'er my lot may be,
'Though my way I may not see;
    And I'm content.

Lord I feel thy Presence near,
    And I'm content;
In thy care, I know not fear,
'Though the Tempter's voice I hear;
I'm secure when Thou art near;
    And I'm content.

A Prayer (1907)

Priscilla Jane Thompson

Oh, Lord! I lift my heart,
　　In gratitude, to Thee,
For blessings, manifold,
　　Thou hast bestowed on me.

When conflicts raged within,
　　Too blinding to express,
Thou pitied my still tongue,
　　And soothed my heart to rest.

Keep me within thy care;
　　Compel me, to the right;
'Tis sweet to walk with Thee,
　　In darkness or in light.

The Century Prayer (1901)
James Ephraim McGirt

Lord God of Hosts incline thine ear
To this, thy humble servant's prayer:
May war and strife and discord cease;
This century, Lord God, give us peace!
Henceforth, dear Lord, may we abhor
The thought of strife, the curse of war.
One blessing more, our store increase,
This is our prayer, Lord, give us peace!

May those who rule us rule with love,
As thou dost rule the courts above;
May man to man as brothers feel,
Lay down their arms and quit the field;
Change from our brows the angry looks,
Turn swords and spears to pruning-hooks.
One blessing more, our store increase,
This is our prayer, Lord, give us peace!

May flags of war fore'er be furled,
The milk white flag wave o'er the world;
Let not a slave be heard to cry,
Lion and lamb together lie;
May nations meet in one accord
Around one peaceful festive board.
One blessing more, our store increase,
This is our prayer, Lord, give us peace!

Stand By Me (1905)

Charles Albert Tindley

When the storms of life are raging,
Stand by me;
When the storms of life are raging,
Stand by me.
When the world is tossing me,
Like a ship upon the sea;
Thou who rulest wind and water,
Stand by me.

In the midst of tribulation,
Stand by me;
In the midst of tribulation,
Stand by me.
When the hosts of hell assail,
And my strength begins to fail,
Thou who never lost a battle,
Stand by me.

In the midst of faults and failures,
Stand by me;
In the midst of faults and failures,
Stand by me.
When I do the best I can,
And my friends misunderstand,
Thou who knowest all about me,
Stand by me.

In the midst of persecution,
Stand by me;
In the midst of persecution,
Stand by me.
When my foes in battle array
Undertake to stop my way,

Thou who saved Paul and Silas,[1]
Stand by me.

When I'm growing old and feeble,
Stand by me;
When I'm growing old and feeble,
Stand by me.
When my life becomes a burden,
And I'm nearing chilly Jordan,
O Thou "Lily of the Valley,"[2]
Stand by me.

---

[1] This is an allusion to Acts 16:16–40.

[2] See Song of Solomon 2:1.

A Litany of Atlanta (1906)
William Edward Burghardt Du Bois

O Silent God, Thou whose voice afar in mist and mystery hath left our ears an-hungered in these fearful days—

Hear us, good Lord!

Listen to us, Thy children: our faces dark with doubt are made a mockery in Thy Sanctuary. With uplifted hands we front Thy Heavens, O God, crying:

We beseech Thee to hear us, good Lord!

We are not better than our fellows, Lord; we are but weak and human men. When our devils do deviltry, curse Thou the doer and the deed,—curse them as we curse them, do to them all and more than ever they have done to innocence and weakness, to womanhood and home.

Have mercy upon us, miserable sinners!

And yet, whose is the deeper guilt? Who made these devils? Who nursed them in crime and fed them on injustice? Who ravished and debauched their mothers and their grandmothers? Who bought and sold their crime and waxed fat and rich on public iniquity?

Thou knowest, good God!

Is this Thy Justice, O Father? that guile be easier than innocence and the innocent be crucified for the guilt of the untouched guilty?

Justice, O Judge of men!

Wherefore do we pray? Is not the God of the Fathers dead? Have not seers seen in Heaven's halls Thine hearsed and lifeless form stark amidst the black and rolling smoke of sin, where all along bow bitter forms of endless dead?

Awake, Thou that sleepest!

Thou art not dead, but flown afar, up hills of endless light, through blazing corridors of suns, where worlds do swing of good and gentle men, of women strong and free—far from the cozenage, black hypocrisy, and chaste prostitution of this shameful speck of dust!

Turn again, O Lord; leave us not to perish in our sin!

From lust of body and lust of blood,—

Great God, deliver us!

From lust of power and lust of gold,—
Great God, deliver us!
From the leagued lying of despot and of brute,—
Great God, deliver us!

A city lay in travail, God our Lord, and from her loins sprang twin Murder and Black Hate. Red was the midnight; clang, crack, and cry of death and fury filled the air and trembled underneath the stars where church spires pointed silently to Thee. And all this was to sate the greed of greedy men who hide behind the veil of vengeance!

Bend us Thine ear, O Lord!

In the pale, still morning we looked upon the deed. We stopped our ears and held our leaping hands, but they—did they not wag their heads and leer and cry with bloody jaws: *Cease from Crime!* The word was mockery, for thus they train a hundred crimes while we do cure one.

Turn again our captivity, O Lord!

Behold this maimed and broken thing, dear God; it was an humble black man, who toiled and sweat to save a bit from the pittance paid him. They told him: *Work and Rise!* He worked. Did this man sin? Nay, but someone told how someone said another did—one whom he had never seen nor known. Yet for that man's crime this man lieth maimed and murdered, his wife naked to shame, his children to poverty and evil.

Hear us, O heavenly Father!

Doth not this justice of hell stink in Thy nostrils, O God? How long shall the mounting flood of innocent blood roar in Thine ears and pound in our hearts for vengeance? Pile the pale frenzy of blood-crazed brutes, who do such deeds, high on Thine altar, Jehovah Jireh, and burn it in hell forever and forever!

Forgive us, good Lord; we know not what to say!

Bewildered we are and passion-tossed, mad with the madness of a mobbed and mocked and murdered people; straining at the armposts of Thy throne, we raise our shackled hands and charge Thee, God, by the bones of our stolen fathers, by the tears of our dead mothers, by the very blood of Thy crucified Christ: What meaneth this? Tell us the plan; give us the sign!

Keep not Thou silent, O God!

Sit not longer blind, Lord God, deaf to our prayers and dumb to our dumb suffering. Surely Thou, too, art not white, O Lord, a pale, bloodless, heartless thin!

Ah! Christ of all the Pities!

Forgive the thought! Forgive these wild, blasphemous words! Thou art still the God of our black fathers and in Thy Soul's Soul sit some soft darkenings of the evening, some shadowings of velvet night.

But whisper—speak—call, great God, for Thy silence is white terror to our hearts! The way, O God, show us the way and point us the path!

Whither? North is greed and South is blood; within, the coward, and without, the liar. Whither? To death?

Amen! Welcome, dark sleep!

Whither? To life? But not this life, dear God, not this. Let the cup pass from us, tempt us not beyond our strength, for there is that clamoring and clawing within, to whose voice we would not listen, yet shudder lest we must,—and it is red. Ah! God! It is a red and awful shape.

Selah!

In yonder East trembles a star.

Vengeance is Mine; I will repay, saith the Lord!

Thy Will, O Lord, be done!

Kyrie Eleison!

Lord, we have done these pleading, wavering words.

We beseech Thee to hear us, good Lord!

We bow our heads and hearken soft to the sobbing of women and little children.

We beseech Thee to hear us, good Lord!

Our voices sink in silence and in night.

Hear us, good Lord!

In night, O God of a godless land!

Amen!

In silence, O Silent God.

Selah!

Give Us Grace (1909–1910)
William Edward Burghardt Du Bois

Give us grace, O God, to dare to do the deed which we well know cries to be done. Let us not hesitate because of ease, or the words of men's mouths, or our own lives. Mighty causes are calling us—the freeing of women, the training of children, the putting down of hate and murder and poverty—all these and more. But they call with voices that mean work and sacrifice and death. Mercifully grant us, O God, the spirit of Esther,[1] that we say: I will go unto the King and if I perish, I perish—Amen.

---

[1] See Esther 4:16.

A Prayer for Endurance (1909–1910)
William Edward Burghardt Du Bois

In the midst of life and deeds it is easy to have endurance and strength and determination,[1] but Thy Word, O Lord, teaches us, that this is not enough to bring good to the world—to bring happiness and the worthier success. For *this* we must endure to the end—learn to finish things—to bring them to accomplishment and full fruition. We must not be content with plans, ambitions and resolves; with part of a message or part of an education, but be set and determined to fulfill the promise and complete the task and secure the full training. Such men and women alone does God save by lifting them above and raising them to higher worlds and wider prospects. Give us then, O God, to resist today the temptation of shirking, and the grit to endure to the end. Amen.

---

[1] Du Bois's prayers were often inspired by biblical passages, in this case Matthew 24:6–13.

A Prayer for Vision and Thought (1909–1910)
William Edward Burghardt Du Bois

May God deliver us from the curse of carelessness, from thoughtless ill-considered deed. The deliberate evil of the world, we know is great, but how much fortitude and strength and faith could we have to cure this and put it down, if only we were rid of the sickening discouraging mass of thoughtless careless acts in men who know and mean better. How willingly in all these years and now, have thousands of mothers and fathers toiled and sweat and watched from dawn till midnight over these children here, only to be rewarded— not indeed by crime, but by persistent carelessness almost worse than crime. The rules here are the simple rules of work and growth. We do not make them—the very circumstances of our life make them. And when we break them, it is *not* because we reason *out* their *un*reasonableness but usually because we do not think—because back of Law and Order we are too lazy to see the weary pain-scarred heart of the mother who sent us here. God give us vision and thought. Amen.

The Prayers of God (1914)

William Edward Burghardt Du Bois

Name of God's Name!
Red murder reigns;
All Hell is loose;
On gold autumnal air
Walk grinning devils barbed and hoofed,
While high on hills of hate,
Black-blossomed, crimson sky'd,
Thou sittest, dumb.

Father Almighty!
This earth is mad!
Palsied, our cunning hands;
Rotten, our gold;
Our argosies reel and stagger
Over empty seas;
All the long aisles
Of Thy great temples, God,
Stink with the entrails
of our souls.
And Thou art dumb.

Above the thunder of Thy thunders, Lord,
Lightening Thy lightnings,
Rings and roars
The dark damnation
Of this Hell of war.
Red piles the pulp of hearts and heads,
And little children's hands.

Allah!
Elohim!
Death is here!
Dead are the living, deep dead the dead.
Dying are earth's unborn—
The babes' wide eyes of genius and of joy;

Poems and prayers, sun-glows and earth-songs;
Great pictured dreams,
En-marbled phantasies,
Hymns of high Heaven,
All fade, in this dread night,
This long ghost night—
While Thou art dumb.

Have mercy!
Have mercy upon us, miserable sinners!
Stand forth, unveil[1] Thy face,
Pour down the light
That sees above Thy throne,
And blaze this devil's dance to darkness!
Hear!
Speak!
In Christ's great name—
    *   *   *   *   *
I hear.
Forgive me, God.
Above the thunder I hearkened;
Beneath the silence, now,
I hear.
    *   *   *   *   *
(Wait, God, a little space.
It is so strange to talk with Thee—
Alone!)
    *   *   *   *   *
This gold?
I took it.
Is it Thine?
Forgive; I did not know.
Blood? Is it wet with blood?
'Tis from my brother's hands.
(I know; his hands are mine.)
It flowed for Thee, O Lord.

---

[1] The metaphor of the veil is a crucial theme in DuBois's thought.

War? Not so, not war:
Dominion, Lord, and over black, not white.
Black, brown and fawn,
And not Thy chosen brood, O God,
We murdered.

To build Thy kingdom,
To drape our wives and little ones,
And set their souls a'glitter—
For this we killed these lesser breeds
And civilized their dead,
Raping red rubber, diamonds, cocoa, gold.

For this, too, once, and in Thy name
I lynched a Nigger—

> (He raved and writhed,
> I heard him cry,
> I felt the life light leap and lie,
> I watched him crackle there, on high,
> I saw him wither!)
> * * * * *

Thou?
Thee?
I lynched Thee?
 * * * * *

Awake me, God, I sleep!
What was that awful word Thou saidst?
That black and riven Thing—was it Thee?
That gasp—was it Thine?
This pain—is it Thine?
Are Then these bullets piercing Thee?
Have all the wars of all the world,
Down all dim time, drawn blood from Thee?
Have all the lies, and thefts, and hates—
Is this Thy crucifixion, God,
And not that funny little cross,
With vinegar and thorns?
 * * * * *

Help!
I sense that low and awful cry—

Who cries?
Who weeps
With silent sob that rends and tears—
Can God sob?

Who prays?
I hear strong prayers throng by,
Like mighty winds on dusky moors—
Can God pray?

*   *   *   *   *

Prayest Thou, Lord, and to me?
Thou needest me?
Thou *needest* me?
Thou needest *me?*
Poor wounded Soul!
Of this I never dreamed. I thought—
Courage, God,
I come!

A Vision at the Great Azusa
Prayer Meetings (1907)

Charles Harrison Mason

The first day in the meeting I sat to myself, away from those that went with me. I began to thank God in my heart for all things, for when I heard some speak in tongues, I knew it was right though I did not understand it. Nevertheless, it was sweet to me. I also thanked God for Elder [William] Seymour who came and preached a wonderful sermon. His words were sweet and powerful and it seems that I hear them now while writing. When he closed his sermon, he said, "All of those that want to be sanctified or baptized with the Holy Ghost, go to the upper room; and all those that want to be justified, come to the altar." I said that is the place for me, for it may be that I am not converted and if not, God knows it and can convert me . . ." Glory! The second night of prayer I saw a vision. I saw myself standing alone and had a dry roll of paper in my mouth trying to swallow it. Looking up towards the heavens, there appeared a man at my side. I turned my eyes at once, then I awoke and the interpretation came. God had me swallowing the whole book and if I did not turn my eyes to anyone but God and Him only, He would baptize me. I said yes to Him, and at once in the morning when I arose, I could hear a voice in me saying, "I see . . ."

I got a place at the altar and began to thank God. After that, I said Lord if I could only baptize myself, I would do so; for I wanted the baptism so bad that I did not know what to do. I said, Lord, you will have to do the work for me; so I turned it over into His hands. . . . Then, I began to seek for the baptism of the Holy Ghost according to Acts 2:44 which readeth thus: "Then they that gladly received His word were baptized." Then I saw that I had a right to be glad and not sad.

The enemy said to me, there may be something wrong with you. Then a voice spoke to me saying, if there is anything wrong with you, Christ will find it and take it away and will marry you. . . . Some said, "Let us sing." I arose and the first song that came to me was "He brought me out of the Miry Clay." The Spirit came upon the saints and upon me. . . . Then I gave up for the Lord to have His way within me. So there came a wave of Glory into me and all of my being was filled with the Glory of the Lord. So when He had gotten me straight on my feet, there came a light which enveloped my entire being above the brightness of the sun. When I opened my mouth to say Glory, a flame touched my tongue which ran down to me. My language changed and no word could I speak in my own tongue. Oh! I was filled with the Glory of the Lord. My soul was then satisfied.

An Exhortative Invocation[1] (1919)

Charles Harrison Mason

Father, thou openeth the gates of wonders, making us enjoy the gift of the Christ, his word standing. When the wicked comes against us the power of thy word is for us.

Open the gates of thy wisdom for us and rebuke the power of the wicked against us. In the glory of Thy council we stand. The Christ of thy word has made us stand.

We see the door of thy mystery. Let the poor confess their sins and see the glory of thy resurrection. Thy goodness and greatness is among the daughters. Fill these with the fullness of Christ. Bless us with light and prudence in the power of the Holy Ghost. The presence of God is with us and the blood prevails. Anoint us so we will in Thy pity come to thee.

Bless those who have died to sin finding in the spirit.

We enjoy saying the Lord gives us the living bread.

Look to God, be faithful to God, and say no more. I can't, God comes in you to do. Humble yourselves that Christ may be your portion.

Speaking from a sign of God, a cleaver. The day of the Lord never comes till the signs of the Lord appear. Man in God's hand is a sign. Thou art my battle axe, my weapon of war.[2] God's wonders coming, doing a strange work. Ministers of God preaching the word out of season and in season. Not using swords imposing God's little lambs.

God standing a wonder in man. Who can hinder God; His wonders are telling. We delight to see Jesus in signs. Confirming us out from snares, Jesus, great God at hand. His word telling about his ways bring us out from the mystery of evil. Watching for his wonders; telling God, I believe.

Scriptures are signs of the only Christ, the glory of God. From the

---

[1] This is a transcription of Mason's unusual form of extemporaneous, exhortative, and prophetic public prayers. In order to preserve the intentionally mystical quality of his style, I chose to conserve this transcription with its obvious lapses in grammar and syntax.

[2] Jeremiah 51:20 (KJV).

Scriptures Jesus spoke to the minds of the people, and they looked at Him and marveled. Jesus showing forth the wisdom of God. Jesus the sign spoken against.[3] Jesus, a sign overturning the evil time; gathers the nation with His understanding and binds His children together as one. Jesus, the wonder among nations, having done the work He came to do. Earth owned Him. When His soul was offered, His glory was upon Him. He was a Prince and a Son to rule. He obtained favor of the Father, but evil hearts abused Him. Through unbelief He cried out mercy for them who knew not what they did. The world looked on Him in a wonder. The sign of God's long-suffering. The sun, in obedience, acknowledged the Son of God's love and veiled His face. Darkness formed over the mountains, the earth trembled and said it is the Son of God. The veil in the temple parted itself from top to bottom. The mystery of God's greatness. Saints of God on earth. God's signs and wonders, witnesses of His glory and return. Jesus Christ, persecuted, led to the cross, crucified and said not a word; even so shall the children who are baptized in the glory of His death, be persecuted, tarred and feathered, imprisoned, lied on, and killed. Signs that their redemption draweth nigh.[4] Hated of all men for my namesake. The children of God hated because they enjoy wisdom from on high. Hating them because they love their enemies and pray for them that despitefully use them.

These signs follow believers.[5] The people receiving the Holy Ghost have something which the world cannot understand. The comforter proceeding from the Father going on in us, and through us. Earth testify to the shortage of the Church, knowing nothing of the greatness of God. All praise to God. Having found the faith, baptized in Him, I'm telling the story of Him. He is God for you. He is God to do. He is your thrilling life, the only help now we show. Pouring upon us the help of His power and love. Accept Him in might, saying God is right. Ask the Lord for help the more. Looking for God to guide the soul.

---

[3] Luke 2:34 (KJV).

[4] Luke 21:28.

[5] Mark 16:17–18.

I'll Follow Thee (1908)

Clara Ann Thompson

My Savior, let me hear Thy voice tonight,
    I'll follow Thee, I'll follow Thee;
The clouds that overhanging my way, obscure the light,
    And all is dark to me.

I'd hear Thy voice above the tempest's shriek;
    I'll follow Thee, I'll follow Thee;
And though my sight be dim, my spirit weak,
    I'll trust, though naught I see.

I'd feel Thy arm, supporting in the dark;
    I'll follow Thee, I'll follow Thee;
For Thou canst fan to flame, faith's sinking spark,
    And seal my loyalty.

I shall not sink, dear Lord, when Thou'rt my guide,
    I'll follow Thee, I'll follow Thee;
Though lashed by heavy waves, on ev'ry side,
    I'm safe, when Thou'rt with me.

Out of the Deep: A Prayer (1908)

Clara Ann Thompson

Out of the deep, I cry to Thee, oh Lord!
   Out of the deep of darkness, and distress;
I cannot, will not doubt Thy blessed word,
   Oh, God of righteousness!

I cry, and oh, my God, I know Thou'lt heed,
   For Thou hast promised Thou wouldst heed my cry;
I have no words to tell my deepest need,
   Thou knowest oh, Most High!

Thou knowest all the pain,—the agony,
   The grief I strive so vainly to express;
Oh let Thy shelt'ring wings spread over me,
   Great God of tenderness!

I cannot cease to cry to Thee,
   For oh, my God, this heart is not my own,
And as the streams press ever to the sea,
   My heart turns to Thy throne.

And when too weak to lift my voice, I lie
   In utter silence at Thy blessed feet,
Thou'lt know, that silence is my deepest cry,
   Thy throne, my last retreat.

And shouldst Thou hide Thy face for aye, from me,
   My heart, though shattered, evermore would grope
Out through the darkness, still in search of Thee,
   Oh God, my only hope!

Storm-Beaten (1908)

Clara Ann Thompson

Weary, worn, and sorrow-laden
 Jesus, I have come to Thee;
Shield me from the darts of Satan;
 Set my fettered spirit free.

Hearken to my plea for guidance,
 As I kneel before Thy throne;
Cheer me with Thy Holy Presence,
 When I feel I'm all alone.

Struggling with the cares that press me,
 Falling, when I fain would stand,
Thou alone, canst guide and keep me,
 Take, oh take my trembling hand!

Pity Thou my many failings!
 Strengthen Thou my falt'ring trust;
Keep me, 'mid the wind's loud wailing,
 Thou, the Pitiful and Just!

Appeal to Heaven (1914)

Maurice N. Corbett

The nation sleeps, Jehovah, Jove,
Thou Archive of incarnate love,
Our first, Beginning, Middle, End,
Thou man's Creator, Father, Friend,
Alpha, Omega, Source of Light,
Great God, Immortal, Infinite,
Exhaustless Fountain, Highest, Best,
Eternal Rock of Righteousness.

Thou Uncreated, Thou the Just,
Thou ruler, Whom Thy servants trust,
Preserver, Maker, Counsellor,
Omniscient Spirit, Governor,
Our Life, our Hope, our Guide, our Reed,
Our Refuge in the time of need,
Thou Dazzling Sun, incline Thine ear
Unto Thy servant's humble prayer.

Eternal God, Thy grace impart,
Look down in pity, Thou who art
The Ruler of the universe,
We pray Thee, Lord, remove the curse
Of hate and prejudice that stand
With ill design and fiery brand
Men's hearts to torture; on a race
Of helpless creatures, turn Thy face.

O God, this sleeping nation wake,
Ere men in desperation, take
To vengeance, as their moral guide,
And those now dwelling side by side,
Will ruthlessly be thrust apart,
While murder stalks in every heart,
And desolation's barren arms
Invade our factories and our farms.

Great God! Before me smells a flood
Of revolution's crimson blood;
Blood of the youthful and the old,
Blood of the timid and the bold,
Blood of the babe on mother's knee,
Blood of that mother, ruthlessly
Butchered to slake the raging thirst
For human blood, by men accurst.

O Lord, these visions chase away,
Bid Thou Thy tender love allay
The storm approaching, Mighty God,
With Thou in mercy stretch Thy rod
O'er this tempestuous hemisphere;
Let Thou the sun of peace appear
In glory from this murky sky,
Proclaiming death to enmity.

O Let Thy voice this nation hear,
And may its rulers live in fear
Of Thy just wrath, and may we see
Religion in its purity
Throughout this favored land prevail;
Let not the Savior's teachings fail
The purpose they to men were sent,
That men of wickedness repent.

Jehovah, let not patience cease
To be a virtue. Let men's knees
In prayer before Thy throne be bent;
Let man Thee worship 'neath his tent
Or in the forest's cooling shade
And none shall dare make him afraid.
Let wicked men no longer rule
That they may tarnish Thy footstool.

In nature, all things stay in bound;
The planets in their place are found;
The angry waves break on the shore;

The mountains check the deafening roar
Of raging storm; the gentle spring
Disarms grim winter of its sting;
Must not beyond a certain height
Ascend the eagle in its flight.

Vile man alone exceeds his bound,
Not where Thou placed him is he found,
For covetous has grown his heart
And conquest has become an art;
His brother's birthright doth he take,
Thy ten commandments doth he break,
Against Thy law doth he rebel,
And, knowingly sinks down to Hell.

Thou Righteous Lord, Thy spirit send
America, Do Thou defend
The helpless, yea, the poor and weak,
The destitute, the just, the meek,
From persecution's cruel lash;
The unjust Judge do Thou abash,
Confound, debase, expose, ungown,
And from his honored seat bring down.

O God of mercy, wilt Thou stay
The sword of vengeance; drive away
The fiery clouds of deadly wrath,
Let strangled conscience block the path
Of creatures on destruction bent,
Let love's entreaties eloquent
The rising tide of hate becalm
And men, of murder's thoughts disarm.

Avenging God, bid Thou be still
The winds of lawlessness which kill
The nation's conscience; let the light
Of Truth's bright garments chase the night
Of false pretensions far away;
Let visions of a brighter day,

In rainbow hue illume the sky
To warn men of Thy watchful eye.

Father, Thou hast all nations made
Of kindred blood, and Thou hast laid
The base for earth's foundation stone.
When Thou commandest there is none
Who dare oppose Thy sovereign will,
Thou canst create and Thou canst kill,
The worlds are holden in Thy hand,
By Thy decree, the heavens stand.

My God, Thy loving spirit give
To sinful man, that he may live
After the fashion of Thy son,
That when the monster death doth come
For him, with summons in his hand,
To join that silent caravan
For unknown regions swiftly bound,
That he with Thy mark may be found.

And now my Maker, to Thy trust
Do I consign the living dust.
A right to urge Thee do I claim
Through Thy dear son, the Savior's name,
That I these weak petitions make,
Which Thou wilt grant for his dear sake
And Thy name's praise shall never end,
Both now and ever more, Amen.

Amen! all Negro hearts reply,
Amen, is echoed from the sky,
Amen, all upright men repeat,
Amen, cries Virtue, from her seat,
Amen, says Justice, bruised and sad,
Amen, joins Mercy, looking glad,
Amen, Religion shouts with glee
To Him who died on Calvary.

Lord, Your Weak Servants Bow (1914)

Maurice N. Corbett

When nature reveleth in sleep,
Except those prowling beasts that creep
With muffled tread, in search of prey,
Or watch-dog holding thieves at bay,
In lonely spot, with face to ground,
Souls bowed in fervent prayer are found,
With trembling voices soft and low,
They thus tell Jesus of their woe.

"Lord, dis your weak servants bow,
In humbleness, to tell dee how
I longs ter die an' be wid dee
Fur eber, in eternity.
My Lord, you knows jes why I moans,
You knows de meanin' ob my groans;
If on my head, your jestice fell,
My naked soul would be in hell."

"Lord, you has hearn my prayers befo'
When I was layin' at hell's dark do',
You promised dat you'd not fersake
Your chilluns, who your cross would take,
But what we axed yer fer in faith,
You would be sure ter grant in grace;
Dat you cant stan' ter hear us pray,
An' from us turn your ears erway."

"Dear Lord, you heared ol' Daniel pray,
When in de lion's den he lay;
Shadrach, Meshach, an' Bednego,
From out de fire you heared, you know;
Jonah you heared from belly o' whale,
An' now my marster, please dont fail
Ter hear my prayer, if I prays right,
An' turn my darkness into Light."

"Lord, I am but a feeble worm;
Hide me I pray, from howling storm
Of cruel men who daily mock,
Anchor my soul wifin de Rock;
Make hase an' help, O Lord, come quick,
Fer now my weary soul is sick.
O tender lam' come here I pray,
An' break dese slavery chains erway."

"Lord, you said 'Seek an' you shall fin','
Come now an' ease my troubled min'.
You bid us ax an' You would give;
Please make us free so we kin live
Nearer each day, my God ter dee
In faith, hope, love, an' charity.
You said, if we'd obey your laws
You'd fight our battles, plead our cause."

"As you led Israel froo de sea,
Come now dear Lord, deliver me;
As Pharaoh in de sea you drowned,
So do my enemies confound,
Please throw dissensions inder gang,
Den dem, as high as Haman hang,[1]
Lord, I believes dat you is just
Den dese cole chains, remove you mus'."

"You said dat dem you jined in heart
No one should dare assunder part,
But my ol' marster, (cuss his hide),
Sol' my companion from my side;
An' while in agony I lay,

---

[1] This is a reference to the story of Haman, Esther 3:1–8:8. Indeed, Esther 8:8
(KJV) reads, "Then the king Ahasuerus said unto Esther the queen and
to Mordecai the Jew, Behold I have given Esther the house of Haman, and
him they have hanged upon the gallows, because he laid his hand upon
the Jews."

Dey come an' sol' my chile erway;
Dey lef me nuffin here ter luv,
Cep' you Dear Jesus, You, erbuv."

"You knows Lord, why dese tears I shed;
Deep waters overcomes my head,
My feet am stuck in miry clay,
Come now an' move it all erway;
You said ten Christians prayin' right,
Could er thousan' devils put ter flight;
You said you in our midst would be,
If too or three would jes ergree."[2]

"O Lord, my way is very dark;
Sometimes I thinks I hears de bark
Of hell-hounds howlin' on my track;
Come my good Lord, an' drive 'em back.
You will not let er sparrow fall,
Come ter my rescue when I call;
You clothed de lillies of de fiel'
O let dy bosom be my shiel'."[3]

"Lord, other refuge I have none,
So you mus' save an' you erlone,[4]
Marster, de trufe I mus' declar'
My load is more dan I kin bar';
Come lay dese slavery chains hard by,
An' I will serve you till I die,

_____

[2] See Matthew 18:18–20 (KJV).

[3] See Luke 12:22–28 (KJV).

[4] This is a paraphrase of a line from "Jesus, Lover of My Soul," the famous evangelical hymn by Charles Wesley (1707–1788), brother of John Wesley, who was founder of the Methodist Church in Great Britain and the United States. The second stanza reads, "Other refuge have I none—Hangs my helpless soul on Thee; Leave, ah, leave me not alone, Still support and comfort me! All my trust on Thee is stayed—All my help from Thee I bring; Cover my defenseless head With the shadow of Thy wing."

Free me from cruel marsters here,
An' I'll raise chilluns in dy fear."

"Sometimes when I kneels down ter pray,
I feels dat you fur erway;
Sometimes I feels so fur I stray
Dat you can't hear me when I pray.
Sometimes my faith grows very slack,
But den your spirit drawns me back;
You pormised jestice wid Your lip,
An' I won't let your mem'ry slip."

"O Lord, in dee I'll put my trus'
Tho You should turn me back to dus',
Jes how kin ennybody pray
When kep' in bondage night and day?
How could I still believe in Dee
Ef you should turn yer back on me?
An' now my marster, come dis way,
Don't let yer chariot wheels delay."

Thou Hast Supplied My Every Need (1916–1918)

Theodore Henry Shackelford

O God, to Thee I come today,
And with true repentance kneeling.
The while I bend my knee to pray,
The tears from mine eyes are stealing.
But for Thy grace lost would I be,
Or ship-wrecked on life's hidden shoals,
Or left to drift upon the sea
    Where dwelleth all earth's derelict souls.
But Thou didst free from all alarms
    And shield me from the tempter's power;
Thou broke the shackles from my arms
    And thou didst cheer my darkest hour.
Thou hast supplied my every need,
And made me free, and free indeed.

A Prayer for the Nations (1918)

Walter Henderson Brooks

As of old Jehovah's working
Out of his will, in every land,
And it runs through all the ages,
Like a weaver's hidden strand.

Centuries with God are moments,
And a thousand years a day;
Kingdoms rise and wane and perish,
Others come and pass away.

'Tis not wealth alone, nor numbers.
Justice makes a people strong,
Righteousness exalts a nation,
Victories to God belong.

Give us then, O God, thy blessing!
We rely upon thy might,
Gird our men, and make them heroes,
Glorify the *Cause of Right*.

Part IV

The New Negro

1920–1955

Cleave Us a Way, O Lord (1920)

Raymond Garfield Dandridge

Dear Lord we come to Thee,
In quest of Liberty
Thy mercy lend.
We know no better way
Than serve, obey and pray,
Almighty Friend.

Unsheathe Thy vengeful sword
Cleave us a way, O Lord,
As naught else can.
Let no base foe oppress,
Let no vain thought repress
Our future usefulness
To God and man.

We have no ancient creed,
We have no glutton's greed
To satisfy.
We seek the lofty height,
Where Justice, Truth and Right,
Condemn oppressor's might,
Like God on high.

May World Democracy
Include equality
For every one,
Father, all-wise and just,
Do as Thou wilt with us,
In Thee, alone, we trust
Thy will be done.

God of Our Weary Years (1921)

James Weldon Johnson

God of our weary years,
God of our silent tears,
Thou who hast brought us thus far on the way.

Thou who hast by Thy might
Led us into the light,
Keep us forever in the path, we pray;

Lest our feet stray from the places, our God, where we met Thee,
Lest, our hearts drunk with the wine of the world, we forget Thee.

Shadowed beneath Thy hand,
May we forever stand
True to our God, true to our native land!

A Prayer for Good Friday (1923)

George Alexander McGuire

Almighty Saviour, whose heavy Cross was laid upon the stalwart shoulders of Simon the Cyrenian, a son of Ham, in that sad hour of thine agony and mortal weakness, when the sons of Shem delivered thee into the hands of the sons of Japheth to be crucified, regard with thy favor this race still struggling beneath the cross of injustice, oppression, and wrong laid upon us by our persecutors. Strengthen us in our determination to free ourselves from the hands of our enemy; put down the mighty from their seat, and exalt thou the humble and meek; through thy mercies and merits who livest and reignest with the Father and the Holy Ghost, world without end. Amen.

A Prayer for the Synod of the African Orthodox Church (1924)

George Alexander McGuire

Bless, we beseech thee, O Lord Jesus Christ, thy Church throughout the world, and especially that portion thereof which thou hast graciously planted among our Race. Send, we pray thee, thy Holy Spirit to preside in the Synod (about to be) here assembled in thy Name and Presence. Direct us in all we undertake for the advancement of thy kingdom and the welfare of the Holy African Orthodox Church. Pour upon our Primate Alexander, our Bishop William and all our Clergy, and the Congregations committed to their charge, thy continual blessing. Regard with thy favor our struggling people who seek peace, justice and equality in things spiritual and temporal, and grant that our humble efforts to maintain ecclesiastical freedom may, by thy divine assistance, stimulate the vast millions of our blood-kin to stretch out their hands to the God of our forefathers, the God of Ham, of Simon the Cyrenian[1] and Endich the eunuch of Ethiopia. Then shalt thou be pleased with this thy people, and princes, priests and prophets shall come forth from among them, to truly preach and truly promote peace and goodwill among all mankind, looking to thy glorious appearing, who livest and reignest with the Father and the Holy Ghost, one God, world without end. Amen.

---

[1] According to Matthew 27:32, Mark 15:21, and Luke 23:26, Simon of Cyrene, whom tradition remembers as a black man, carried the cross of Jesus.

We Are Fully in Thy Sight (1924)
Charles Albert Tindley

Our Heavenly Father, we need not tell Thee that we are here. We are fully in Thy sight and are all known to Thee. And so we come in this opening session of the Conference to gather at Thy feet, to look in Thy face and to submit and commit ourselves and the program for the entire months to be and so we ask Thee to come not in the mornings only but through every hour of the day of the entire Conference sessions to be with every delegate and with everybody here, so that the work of this Conference may be done through us by Thee, so that when we have closed the Conference, the people may be able to say, "The Lord has been here: The Lord has done great things." We come to consecrate ourselves anew to Thee. We come to bind ourselves to the great and small tasks that lie before us. Thou art attempting still to redeem this world and to bring it to Christ. Much has been done and much remains to be done. Help us not to be fainthearted in the task. We are not machines. We are workers and we come asking Thee to use the best that is in us as Thou wilt that we may do our part in saving the world. Problems are confronting us that were not here the other day and that we were not asked to confront: but we are asked today to confront them. Help us to answer. Help us to witness, a witness for Thee and be instruments in Thy hands so that people may know that Thou art through us still redeeming the world. May folks, through us, find out Thou art still in the business of saving men. May folks find out that we have a relationship with Christ and that we have a vicarious atonement, that can cleanse from all sin. And help us to work with Thee that through us Thou shall do a mighty work. Clean up the world. Clear out all the saloons everywhere. Wipe our flag clean from all signs of war and may it be a signal of peace and a new paradise everywhere that men may walk and not be afraid.

Speak loudly to us Lord, and bless us in all things for Christ's sake. "Our Father who art in Heaven." Amen.

Pagan Prayer (1925)

Countée Porter Cullen

Not for myself I make this prayer,
    But for this race of mine
That stretches forth from shadowed places
    Dark hands for bread and wine.

For me, my heart is pagan mad,
    My feet are never still,
But give them hearths to keep them warm
    In homes high on a hill.

For me, my faith lies fallowing,
    I bow not till I see,
But these are humble and believe;
    Bless their credulity.

For me, I pay my debts in kind,
    And see no better way,
Bless these who turn the other cheek
    For love of you, and pray.

Our Father, God; our Brother, Christ—
    So are we taught to pray;
Their kinship seems a little thing
    Who sorrow all the day.

Our Father, God; our Brother, Christ,
    Or are we bastard kin,
That to our plaints your ears are closed,
    Your doors barred from within?

Our Father, God; our Brother, Christ,
    Retrieve my race again;
So shall you compass this black sheep,
    This pagan heart. Amen.

The Shroud of Color (1925)

Countée Porter Cullen

"Lord, being dark," I said, "I cannot bear
The further touch of earth, the scented air;
Lord, being dark, forewilled to that despair
My color shrouds me in, I am as dirt
Beneath my brother's heel; there is a hurt
In all the simple joys which to a child
Are sweet; they are contaminate, defiled
By truths of wrongs the childish vision fails
To see; too great a cost this birth entails.
I strangle in this yoke drawn tighter than
The worth of bearing it, just to be man.
I am not brave enough to pay the price
In full; I lack the strength to sacrifice.
I who have burned my hands upon a star,
And climbed high hills at dawn to view the far
Illimitable wonderments of earth,
For whom all cups have dripped the wine of mirth,
For whom the sea has strained her honeyed throat

Till all the world was sea, and I a boat
Unmoored, on what strange quest I willed to float;
Who wore a many-colored coat of dreams,
Thy gift, O Lord-I whom sun-dabbled streams
Have washed, whose bare brown thighs have held the sun
Incarcerate until his course was run,
I who considered man a high-perfected
Glass where loveliness could lie reflected,
Now that I sway athwart Truth's deep abyss,
Denuding man for what he was and is,
Shall breath and being so inveigle me
That I can damn my dreams to hell, and be
Content, each new-born day, anew to see
The steaming crimson vintage of my youth
Incarnadine the altar-slab of Truth?

Or hast Thou, Lord, somewhere I cannot see,
A lamb imprisoned in a bush for me?

Not so? Then let me render one by one
Thy gifts, while still they shine; some little sun
Yet gilds these thighs; my coat, albeit worn,
Still holds its colors fast; albeit torn,
My heart will laugh a little yet, if I
May win of Thee this grace, Lord: on this high
And sacrificial hill 'twixt earth and sky,
To dream still pure all that I love, and die.
There is no other way to keep secure
My will chimeras; grave-locked against the lure
Of Truth, the small hard teeth of worms, yet less
Envenomed than the mouth of Truth, will bless
Them into dust and happy nothingness.
Lord, Thou art God; and I, Lord, what am I
But dust? With dust my place. Lord, let me die."

Across the earth's warm, palpitating crust
I flung my body in embrace; I thrust
My mouth into the grass and sucked the dew,
Then gave it back in tears my anguish drew;
So hard I pressed against the ground, I felt
The smallest sandgrain like a knife, and smelt
The next year's flowering; all this to speed
My body's dissolution, fain to feed
The worms. And so I groaned, and spent my strength
Until, all passion spent, I lay full length
And quivered like a flayed and bleeding thing.

So lay till lifted on a great black wing
That had no mate nor flesh-apparent trunk
To hamper it; with me all time had sunk
Into oblivion; when I awoke
The wing hung poised above two cliffs that broke
The bowels of the earth in twain, and cleft
The seas apart. Below, above, to left,
To right, I saw what no man saw before:

Earth, hell, and heaven; sinew, vein, and core.
All things that swim or walk or creep or fly,
All things that live and hunger, faint and die,
Were made majestic then and magnified
By sight so clearly purged and deified.
The smallest bug that crawls was taller than
A tree, the mustard seed loomed like a man.
The earth that writhes eternally with pain
Of birth, and woe of taking back her slain,
Laid bare her teeming bosom to my sight,
And all was struggle, gasping breath, and fight.
A blind worm here dug tunnels to the light,
And there a seed, racked with heroic pain,
Thrust eager tentacles to sun and rain;
It climbed; it died; the old love conquered me
To weep the blossom it would never be.
But here a bud won light; it burst and flowered
Into a rose whose beauty challenged, "Coward!"
There was no thing alive save only I
That held life in contempt and longed to die.
And still I writhed and moaned, "The curse, the curse,
Than animated death, can death be worse?"

*"Dark child of sorrow, mine no less, what art
Of mine can make thee see and play thy part?
The key to all strange things is in thy heart."*

What voice was this that coursed like liquid fire
Along my flesh, and turned my hair to wire?

I raise my burning eyes, beheld a field
All multitudinous with carnal yield,
A grim ensanguined mead whereon I saw
Evolve the ancient fundamental law
Of tooth and talon, fist and nail and claw.
There with the force of living, hostile hills
Whose clash the hemmed-in vale with clamor fills,
With greater din contended fierce majestic wills
Of beast with beast, of man with man, in strife

For love of what my heart despised, for life
That unto me at dawn was now a prayer
For night, at night a bloody heart-wrung tear
For day again; for *this,* these groans
From tangled flesh and interlocked bones.
And no thing died that did not give
A testimony that it longed to live.
Man, strange composite blend of brute and god,
Pushed on, nor backward glanced where last he trod.
He seemed to mount a misty ladder flung
Pendant from a cloud, yet never gained a rung
But at his feet another tugged and clung.
My heart was still a pool of bitterness,
Would yield nought else, nought else confess.
I spoke (although no form was there
To see, I knew an ear was there to hear),
"Well, let them fight; they can whose flesh is fair."
Crisp lightning flashed; a wave of thunder shook
My wing; a pause, and then a speaking, "look."

I scarce dared trust my ears or eyes for awe
Of what they heard, and dread of what they saw;
For, privileged beyond degree, this flesh
Beheld God and His heaven in the mesh
Of Lucifer's revolt, saw Lucifer
Glow like the sun, and like dulcimer
I heard his sin-sweet voice break on the yell
Of God's great warriors: Gabriel,
Saint Clair and Michael, Israfel and Raphael.
And strange it was to see God with His back
Against a wall, to see Christ hew and hack
Till Lucifer, pressed by the mighty pair,
And losing inch by inch, clawed at the air
With fevered wings; then, lost beyond repair,
He tricked a mass of stars into his hair;
He filled his hands with stars, crying as he fell,
"A star's a star although it burns in hell."
So God was left to His divinity,
Omnipotent at that most costly fee.

There was a lesson here, but still the clod
In me was sycophant unto the rod,
And cried, "Why mock me thus? Am I a god?"

"One trial more: this failing, then I give
You leave to die; no further need to live."

Now suddenly a strange wild music smote
A chord long impotent in me; a note
Of jungles, primitive and subtle, throbbed
Against my echoing breast, and tom-toms sobbed
In every pulse-beat of my frame. The din
A hollow log bound with a python's skin
Can make wrought every nerve to ecstasy,
And I was wind and sky again, and sea,
And all sweet things that flourish, being free.
Till all at once the music changed its key.

And now it was of bitterness and death,
The cry the lash extorts, the broken breath
Of liberty enchained; and yet there ran
Through all a harmony of faith in man,
A knowledge all would end as it began.
All sights and sounds and aspects of my race
Accompanied this melody, kept pace
With it; with music all their hopes and hates
Were charged, not to be downed by all the fates.
And somehow it was borne upon my brain
How being dark, and living through the pain
Of it, is courage more than angels have. I knew
What storms and tumults lashed the tree that grew
This body that I was, this cringing I
That feared to contemplate a changing sky,
This I that grovelled, whining, "Let me die,"
While others struggled in Life's abattoir.
The cries of all dark people near or far
Were billowed over me, a mighty surge
Of suffering in which my puny grief must merge
And lose itself; I had no further claim to urge

For death; in shame I raised my dust-grimed head,
And though my lips moved not, God knew I said,
"Lord, not for what I saw in flesh or bone
Of fairer men; not raised on faith alone;
Lord, I will live persuaded by mine own.
I cannot play the recreant to these;
My spirit has come home, that sailed the doubtful seas."
With the whiz of a sword that severs space,
The wing dropped down at a dizzy pace,
And flung me on my hill flat on my face;
Flat on my face I lay defying pain,
Glad of the blood in my smallest vein,
And in my hands I clutched a loyal dream,
Still spitting fire, bright twist and coil and gleam,
And chiselled like a hound's white tooth.
"Oh, I will match you yet," I cried, "to truth."
Right glad I was to stoop to what I once had spurned,
Glad even unto tears; I laughed aloud; I turned
Upon my back, and though the tears for joy would run,
My sight was clear; I looked and saw the rising sun.

Prayer for Freedom from Race Prejudice (1925)
Robert C. Lawson

O God, who has made man in thine own likeness, and who doth love all whom Thou has made, suffer us not because of difference of race, color, or condition to separate ourselves from others and thereby from Thee; but teach us the unity of Thy family and universality of Thy Love. As Thou Saviour, as a Son, was born of an Hebrew mother, who had the blood of many nations in her veins; and ministered first to Thy brethren of the Israelites, but rejoiced in the faith of a Syro-Phoenician woman and of a Roman soldier, and suffered your cross to be carried by an Ethiopian; teach us, also, while loving and serving our own, to enter into the communion of the whole family; and forbid that from pride of birth, color, achievement and hardness of heart, we should despise any for whom Christ died, or injure or grieve any in whom He lives. We pray in Jesus' precious name. AMEN.

Keep Me from Sinkin' Down (1927)
{Robert Nathaniel Dett}

Oh Lord,
Oh, my Lord,
Oh, my good Lord,
Keep me from sinking down.

I tell you what I mean to do,
Keep me from sinking down,
I mean to go to heaven too;
Keep me from sinking down.

A Deacon's Campmeeting Prayer (1928)
{Anonymous}

Almighty! and all wise God our heavenly Father! 'tis once more and
again that a few of your beloved children are gathered together to call
upon your holy name. We bow at your foot-stool, Master, to thank
you for our spared lives. We thank you that we were able to get up
this morning clothed in our right mind. For Master, since we met
here, many have been snatched out of the land of living and hurled
into eternity. But through your goodness and mercy we have been
spared to assemble ourselves here once more to call upon a Captain
who has never lost a battle. Oh, throw round us your strong arms of
protection. Bind us together in love and union. Build us up where we
are torn down and strengthen us where we are weak. Oh, Lord! Oh,
Lord! take the lead of our minds, place them on heaven and heavenly
divine things. Oh, God, our Captain and King! search our hearts and
if you find anything there contrary to your divine will just move it
from us Master, as far as the east is from the west. Now Lord, you
know our hearts, you know our up-rising. Lord you know all about us
because you made us. Lord! Lord! One more kind favor I ask of you.
Remember the man that is to stand in the gateway and proclaim your
Holy Word. Oh, stand by him. Strengthen him where he is weak and
build him up where he is torn down. Oh, let him down into the deep
treasures of your word.

And now, oh, Lord; when this your humble servant is done down
here in this low land of sorrow: done sitting down and getting up:
done being called everything but a child of God; oh; when I am done,
done, done, and this old world can afford me a home no longer, right
soon in the morning, Lord, right soon in the morning, meet me down
at the River of Jordan, bid the waters to be still, tuck my little soul
away in that snow-white chariot, and bear it away over yonder in the
third heaven where every day will be Sunday and my sorrows of this
old world will have an end, is my prayer for Christ my Redeemer's
sake and amen and thank God.

De Same God (1928?)

{Anonymous}

You are de same God, Ah
Dat heard de sinner man cry.
Same God dat sent de zigzag lightning tuh
Join de mutterin'[1] thunder.
Same God dat holds de elements
In uh unbroken chain of controllment.[2]
Same God dat hung on Cavalry and died,
Dat we might have a right tuh de tree of life—
We thank Thee that our sleeping couch
Was not our cooling board,
Our cover was not our winding sheet . . .
Please tuh give us uh restin' place
Where we can praise Thy name forever, Amen.

---

[1] Given the tenor of this prayer, *mutterin'* might best be understood as *grumbling*. Anthropomorphic ascriptions to inorganic forces or objects are common practice in African-American folk culture.

[2] Substitute the word *control*. The prayer, in an effort to embrace sophistication, invents a word.

Draw Me, Dear Jesus (1928)

Garfield Thomas Haywood

Draw me, dear Jesus, draw me Nearer unto Thee;
Perils are lurking near me—Keep me close to Thee.
Thou are my soul's salvation, Thee would I adore;
Draw me, dear Jesus, draw me And I'll run after Thee.

Refrain:
I will follow Thee,
Yes, I will follow Thee,
I will follow Thee;
Yes, I will follow;
Draw me, dear Jesus,
And I will follow Thee.

Hear me, dear Jesus While I pray to Thee;
Bow down Thine ear in mercy—Grant my fervent plea;
Fill with Thy grace and power Every passing hour;
Draw me, dear Jesus, draw me And I'll run after Thee.

Guide me, dear Jesus, guide me All along my way;
Thou art my strong Deliverer—Help me, Lord, I pray;
Make me to ever follow, Hard after Thee;
Draw me, dear Jesus, draw me And I'll run after Thee.

A Marriage Prayer (1929)

Lewis Garnett Jordan

Our Father, who art in Heaven, who hast, in thy wise and tender care for mankind, ordained and blessed the institution of matrimony, we pray Thee, graciously to regard Thy servant and handmaiden, who have thus solemnly pledged themselves to each other, and sworn unto Thee; that, through Thy good care and guidance, they may evermore remember and keep these their vows; be kept themselves in unbroken concord and sympathy all the days of their earthly life; and be at the last, with all those most near and most dear unto them, gathered an unbroken household to Thy right hand on the day of judgement. And may all of us, here assembled, be of that blessed company who shall be called to go into the Marriage Supper of the Lamb.[1] And this we ask, only in the name and through the merits of Him, Thine own Son and our Redeemer, the Lord Jesus Christ. Amen.

---

[1] This is an allusion to Revelation 19:7–9.

O Lord, Have Mercy! (1930)

{James Cameron}

Cars, trucks, and policemen in blue uniforms—more than I had seen ever at one time—surrounded our house, and they were approaching with drawn revolvers. First one spotlight, then two, and finally, a dozen or more it seemed, began raking the house from every angle. I crouched below the window, cringing, wishing again that I could disappear and start my life over again.

"Who is it?" I heard my mother ask.

"The police," a gruff voice answered. "Open up!"

I summoned what little courage I had left to sneak to the top of the stairs just as my mother opened the door. Light coming from the searchlights outside the house flooded the bottom of the steps. "What do you want?" Mother asked them, nervously.

"Does James Cameron live here?" the officer wanted to know. It was the same gruff voice that answered with a demand. His question sounded more like an accusation.

"Yes," my mother told him. And then, sensing real trouble, she broke into uncontrollable tears that sounded almost hysterical. Words began tumbling out of her mouth, rushing between sobs. "What's he done? What do you want him for? He's a good boy. He's my only son. There must be some mistake . . . !"

The police cut her off. "Where is he?"

Mother told them I was upstairs asleep in bed. Then she begged them again to tell her why I was wanted.

"Oh, Lord, have mercy!" I heard my mother cry out. "Give me strength, dear Jesus. Help me!" Her voice trailed off and her words were lost in a fresh torrent of tears.

"Let's go," Officer Burden said to me. "The Chief wants to talk with you."

Two of the officers grabbed me by the arms and half dragged and half carried me down the narrow and steep stairway. I remember feeling a great sense of gratitude that Marie and Della [his sisters] on the other side of the partitions had not awakened.

Downstairs, my mother had collapsed on her bed, crying and praying all at once. "Lord, Jesus Christ, have mercy," she moaned over and over and over. "Give me strength."

The Inward Conflict (1932)

Walter Henderson Brooks

'Tis not for fame, nor fortune,
　　Nor length of days, I pray;
'Tis not for leadership of men:
　　God's will I would obey.

'Tis not for fleeting pleasures,
　　Therein may lie my fault,
I wish God's approbation:
　　His name I would exalt.

'Tis not to please the people
　　I serve, both young and old:
'Tis fellowship with God I crave;
　　I'd share his love untold.

And yet I'm prone to wander.
　　I do what I would not.
My strength is unavailing:
　　How wretched is my lot!

This one petition, therefore,
　　With earnest heart I plead,
That I, through God, may triumph:
　　His help alone I need.

I'm sure, this wished-for blessing
　　My Lord will give to me:
He knows my griefs and longings,
　　He knows what I would be.

Holy Spirit, Come! (1940)
Walter Henderson Brooks

Holy Spirit, come, possess me;
My whole being elevate,
As I search the Holy Scriptures,
Or in rapture meditate.

Make my thinking wise and reverent;
Let me see with vision clear;
Touch my lips, that I proclaim
Truth inspired, void of fear.

Fit me for my holy calling;
Make me harmless as a dove;
In the likeness of the Master,
Let me serve, with heart of love.

Give me grace, when wronged, to suffer,
Treading in the Savior's steaps;
Fill my soul with God-like pity,
In its fulness and its depths.

Crown with blessings all my labors,
Every day and every where,
As I serve in home or temple,
Giving counsel, or in prayer.

In This Hour (1941)
Walter Henderson Brooks

In this hour of darkness guide us,
Thou alone our sure defense.
All the world's at war around us:
Why these evils, and from whence?

Thou controllest every nation,
Shall the earth be drenched in fire?
Is this day a day of judgement,
Nations crazed with greed, and ire;

Nations hating one another,
In their pride and haughtiness;
All and each bent on destruction,
In their blood-thirst naughtiness?

Calm this raging sea of madness;
In their senses hold men fast,
Lest these Babylons shortly perish,
Fighting, struggling, to the last.

Usher in the reign of reason;
Turn the hearts of men to thee;
New-create the sense of justice;
Let mankind be one with thee.

Be thyself creation's ruler;
Peace and plenty grant to all,
Righteousness each nation's glory,
Blest of thee, the great and small.

One Thing I Crave (1945)

Walter Henderson Brooks

One thing, my Lord, I crave,
    Blest fellowship with thee;
Thy Spirit in me reigning,
    Thy likeness wrought in me.

In it lies sweetest peace,
    The highest, noblest worth,
The blessedness of heaven,
    The joy of second-birth.

I ask not fame, not riches,
    Grant oneness, Lord with thee:
Here, in this evil world,
    Enthroned, reign thou in me.

Then, in the realm eternal,
    I'll sing aloud thy praise,
With Saints, Apostles, Angels,
    The heavens shall ring with lays.

Precious Lord, Take My Hand (1932)

Thomas Andrew Dorsey

Precious Lord, take my hand,
Lead me on, let me stand,
I am tired, I am weak, I am worn;
Thru the storm, thru the night,
Lead me on to the light,
Take my hand, precious Lord,
Lead me home.

When my way grows drear, precious Lord, linger near,
When my life is almost gone,
Hear my cry, hear my call,
Hold my hand lest I fall;
Take my hand, precious Lord,
Lead me home.

When the darkness appears and the night draws near,
And the day is past and gone,
At the river I stand,
Guide my feet, hold my hand;
Take my hand, precious Lord,
Lead me home.

Sunday School Prayers (1933)

{Benjamin Elijah Mays and Joseph William Nicholson}

WE THANK THEE

We thank thee, Heavenly Father, for this great and grand opportunity; that You have spared us to turn out to the House of worship and hear Thy word once more. Have mercy upon us; bless the Sabbath school this morning; bless the teachers who are trying to instruct the little ones in Thy way as You have said; "Suffer the little children to come unto me, and forbid them not, for such is the Kingdom of Heaven."[1] Have mercy upon us. We are thankful that we are able to stand together and testify that we have seen another bright morning, while thousands have gone upward and onward. Bless all, Our Heavenly Father, that we are duty bound to pray for. Then, our Heavenly Father, when we have finished our work on earth; when there is no more space between the living and the dead, raise us up to Thy Kingdom. In Jesus' name. Amen.

THANKFUL PLEADING

Gracious Father, the father of us all and of our Lord and Savior, Jesus Christ, our elder brother. We thank Thee from the depths of our hearts that we are allowed to be present this morning within these consecrated walls. We thank Thee that this opportunity to worship Thee is denied no man but that every man and woman and child who believes can fall down and worship Thee. Lord, we come to Thee pleading no merits of our own. At best we are but poor feeble worms of dust, asking mercy that Thou abide with us. Sanctify our whole being. We know that we are short, Lord, but we are coming up to the throne of mercy pleading that Thou will make us the kind of servants that Thou would have us to be. Banish from our minds everything that destroys our faith in thee.

THY HOLY PRESENCE

We have come today, Father, into Thy Holy presence. We pray, Father, that as we gather here, we shall be conscious of Thy abiding

---

[1] Mark 10:14 (KJV).

presence, and that there shall be great rejoicing because Thou art with us. Abide with us. We thank Thee for this privilege.

A SUNDAY MORNING PRAYER

Lord, our Heavenly Father, we meet with you this morning to give Thee thanks for past blessings Thou hast bestowed upon us. We pray Thee sincerely for help; get into our wondering minds and faltering steps. We earnestly pray your blessings upon this great congregation. We pray Thy blessings upon the choir, preaching the gospel through song. Help them wake up to the understanding of their duty. We ask Thy blessings upon the personnel of this church.

WE BEG THEE

Lord, Thou knowest we can do nothing tangible without Thy assistance. We beg Thee, O Gracious God, give of Thy supernatural strength and power from on high, that we may do better. We ask Thy blessing for the speaker this morning; that his message will thrill our humble souls; strengthen him; help his family that they will be able to accomplish in every way their undertakings. We pray a prayer for the poor and needy, the sick and afflicted; we ask Thee to help all of us that we may do better for Thy glory.

WE ASK THEE

But we ask Thee for Thy holy privilege. We know we can do nothing without Thy aid or assistance. Make us conscious of the fact that we are all Thy children in that vineyard, striving to work out our souls' salvations. We ask Thee, give us the spirit of Christ and determination to press onward and upward. We ask Thee to give us, Father, grace, hope, patience, and keep our feet in the straight and narrow path and ever to be willing to do the task Thou hast assigned to us.

WE SURRENDER TO THEE

Help us, O Blessed Savior, that we may surrender ourselves to Thee, that we may come with humbler hearts. We come to Thee because we feel that we need Thee, we feel that we have need of Thee as never before. In these times when there is so much mistrust, in these times when sons and daughters are turning against their parents, and when there is so much suffering in this world, will Thou bless this pastor and give him courage this morning. Help us that we may give courage to some discouraged heart, help them so that they may not give up all hopes.

THY WONDERFUL BLESSINGS

We thank Thee that because of Thy wonderful blessings men no longer have to lay at the pool and wait for the troubling of the waters,[2] but that men and women may come and be reclaimed and fall out of their sinful ways.

FOREVER AND EVER

And when we are called from time to eternity, we will not go before the justice bar wanting, but having done the things commendable in Thy presence forever and ever. Amen.

THE SWEET VOICE

Bless Thy children, and when we come to press a dying pillow may we hear the sweet voice of Him, who taught us to say, [chanted] "Our Father which art in heaven, Hallowed be thy name. Thy kingdom come. Thy will be done in earth, as it is in heaven. Give us this day our daily bread. And forgive us our debts, as we forgive our debtors. And lead us not into temptation, but deliver us from evil: For thine is the kingdom, and the power, and the glory, for ever. Amen.[3]

DUTY BOUND TO PRAY

Bless all for whom we are duty bound to pray. Bless the unemployed, bless the suffering everywhere. Then, dear Father, when we have finished our work, when all our work is over here and when we can do no more for Thy Kingdom among the children of men, bring us into Thy presence where all the redeemed of God are blessed. Amen.

BLESS THE LOW IN SPIRIT

We pray for the sick. Bless the low in spirit. Bless this city of ours, O Lord. Bless this country and the world over. Bless the conditions of this country, we ask Thee. Give us peace and love and charity towards all mankind. Give us power. Give us a greater desire to serve Thee. We ask in Thy name.

---

[2] See John 5:2–9 (KJV).

[3] Matthew 6:9–13 (KJV).

Grant Me Strength (1934)

Esther Popel

Give me the strength
Of verdant hills
Washed clean by summer rain;
Of purple hills
At peace when weary Day
Sinks quietly to rest
In Night's cool arms;
Of rugged, wind-whipped hills
That lift their heads
Above the petty, lowland, valley things,
And shake their shoulders free
Of bonds that hold
Them close to earth;
Of snow-capped hills
Sun-kissed by day, by night
Companioned by the stars;
Of grim volcanoes
Pregnant with the fires
Of molten fury!

Grant me strength,
Great God,
Like that of hills!

A Thanksgiving Prayer (1935)

William Massie

Lord, keep me from all bitterness, I pray.
    In these perplexing days of doubt and strain.
When courage fails and faith and hope grow dim
    Oh, let me not complain.

Oh, save me from the ever haunting fear
    That clutches at my heart with wild demands,
That chills my love, that paralyzes faith,
    That blinds my eyes to all God's plans.

Lord, let me not feel pity for myself
    But go my way with laughter and good cheer;
With head held high and eye and heart aglow,
    With strength to scorn each tear.

Let me not feel that I alone do suffer,
    I would not doubt the wisdom of God's plan;
The world has ever groaned and sought release
    From pain, since time began.

So let me face the future unafraid.
    To-day is good: to-morrow taunts with fear.
To-morrow I shall find but God's to-day
    To prove anew His presence near.

A Prayer of Contrition (1935)

John Nathaniel Samuels-Belboder

Lord, God of Heaven, of Earth, of Hell!
Omnipotent of all that dwell
    In them, and in them is;
With penitent and painful sigh,
In deep contrition, Lord I cry
To Thee, great God! O Thou, most High
    Heal my infirmities.

Evening and morning, noon and night
My burdened soul a sorrowing sight
    Bleeds 'neath a chastening rod:
No pleasure, mirth, nor happiness
Lights up my heart; blind heaviness
Of what, I know not! wretchedness
    Obscures me from my God!

What have I in rude rashness done
To blear and blot my morning sun
    And darken all my life?
What have I, in my youthful rant,
Once sown, that now is grown a plant
Of bitter fruits, while devils chant
    Hell-hymns to cheer the strife.

Wrought in my soul?—the inward war—
Darkness impenetrable, far,
    Unpierced,—unsightly, cold!
No glimmer of some kindly ray;
No power to clear the hellish way;
No light; no path; nought but dismay
    Threat'ning my heart once bold.

Thou are the Only who can hear,
Answer and grant the contrite's pray'r

And richest blessings give!
Then, Lord, illumine my dark soul;
From off my heart this burden roll;
And let me reach the happy goal
Of life! and reaching, live!

A Mother's Desperate Plea (1939)
{Richard Wright}

They stood in the middle of the floor, crying, with their arms locked about Bigger. Bigger held his face stiff, hating them and himself, feeling the white people along the wall watching. His mother mumbled a prayer, to which the preacher chanted.

"Lord, here we is, maybe for the last time. You gave me these children, Lord, and told me to raise 'em. If I failed, Lord, I did the best I could. (*Ahmen!*) These poor children's been with me a long time and they's all I got. Lord, please let me see 'em again after the sorrow and suffering of this world! (*Hear her, Lawd!*) Lord, please let me see 'em where I can love 'em in peace. Let me see 'em again beyond the grave! (*Have mercy, Jesus!*) You said You'd heed prayer, Lord, and I'm asking this in the name of Your son."

"Ahmen 'n' Gawd bless yuh, Sistah Thomas," the preacher said.

They took their arms from round Bigger, silently, slowly; then turned their faces away, as though their weakness made them ashamed in the presence of powers greater than themselves.

"We leaving you now with God, Bigger," his mother said. "Be sure and pray, son."

They kissed him.

A Familiar Prayer (1940)

{J. G. St. Clair Drake}

Oh Lord, we come this morning *knee bowed and body bent before thy throne of grace.* We come this morning Lord, *like empty pitchers before a full fountain, realizing that many who are better by nature than we are by practice, have passed into the great beyond and yet you have allowed us your humble servants to plod along just a few days longer here in this howling wilderness.* We thank thee Lord that when we arose this morning, *our bed was not a cooling board, and our sheet was not a winding shroud.* We are not gathered here for *form or fashion,* but we come in our humble way to serve thee. We thank thee Lord that we are *clothed in our right mind*—Bless the sick and afflicted—those who are absent through no fault of their own. *And when I have done prayed my last prayer and sung my last song, and when I'm done climbing the rough side of the mountain, when I come down to tread the steep and prickly banks of Jordan,* meet me with thy rod and staff and bear me safely over. All these things I ask in Jesus' name, *world without end,* Amen.

Touch Me, Lord Jesus (1941)

Lucie Mae Campbell

Touch me, Lord Jesus,
With Thy hand of mercy,
Make each throbbing heartbeat
Feel Thy pow'r divine.
Take my will forever,
I will doubt you never,
Cleanse me, dear Savior,
Make me wholly Thine.

Mold me, dear Master;
As I bow before Thee,
Prostrate and helpless,
Make my heart Thy throne.
Purge my dross with hissop;[1]
Burn me with Thy fire;
Lord, make and use me;
Ever all Thine own.

Feed me, dear Jesus,
From Thy holy table,
Rain bread from heaven,
Let my cup o'erflow.
Naked, sick and hungry;
Poor and weak and lonely,
Feed me, Lord Jesus
Till I want no more.

Guide me, Jehovah,
Thro' this vale of sorrow,

---

[1] "Purge my *dross* with *hissop*" is an allusion to Psalm 51:7 and Isaiah 1:25 (KJV). The use of *hissop* rather than the correct spelling, *hyssop,* is apparently to facilitate pronunciation.

I am safe forever,
Trusting in Thy love.
Bear me thro' the current;
O'er the chilly Jordan,
Lead me, dear Master
To my home above.

God Speed the Day (1941)
Ralph Mark Gilbert

We wondered for a long while, how long it would be before our nation would be brought into this world conflict. By now we know that the days of peace are for a time, at least, ended. And while we know that we are engaged in a righteous cause, yet we feel the unrest that war inevitably stirs in our hearts. How much we do need an inner purging now! How close must all of us feel God around us! Let us keep the fire of true religion burning in our breasts and let us, as we bow tonight, and as we bow in the future, say, "Thy will, O God, be done!" Let us pray.

O Thou eternal God, Thou alone knowest what is in store for us. The distant unknown is dismal and dark; but we feel that the God who watches over His own, slumbers not nor sleeps; and the Captain who has never lost a battle will see His children through. God speed the day when righteousness, and justice, and freedom, shall spread over all mankind, and when bigotry, hatred, prejudice, pride, injustice, greed, and sin, shall perish from the earth. Forgive us all our sins. Bless, we pray Thee, those who mourn for the loss of loved ones, and all who are confined upon their sick beds or in prison cells. Bless the President of these United States in this, his crucial hour, and— GOD BLESS AMERICA. In Jesus' name we ask all this,—Amen.

Look Thou with Compassion upon Every Heart (1941)

Ralph Mark Gilbert

We come again to the mercy seat, and we come freely and boldly, because we have been bidden to approach our Father in that manner. Wherever you may be, we bid you to walk with us in that beautiful garden of prayer, and lay open your soul, and breathe out your burden, knowing as you do it, that by telling it to Jesus, you dissolve your doubts and solve your problems. Let us pray:

Almighty God, look Thou with compassion upon every heart that is now bowed in prayer. Bless every home that is tuned in to this service; continue them as houses of prayer, and bless them in storehouse and basket. Bless, we pray Thee, the sick, and give them a good night's rest this evening, and let Thy seamless robe pass through their bedchambers, that the virtue of Thy garment might bring quick relief and healing to them. Visit Thou the prisons and the jails, O God, and stir the hearts of men who are bound in a cell. And whoever approaches Thee tonight with a burdened heart, or an unsolved problem, or with a severe temptation,—whatever may be the burden of their petition, we know that Thou doest have the key, the remedy, the answer. And if, thru our ignorance, we ask the wrong thing, then, O Father, forgive us our foolish prayer, and give us that thing that in Thy wisdom, Thou seest we stand in need of. Forgive us our sins, we pray, and help us, by Thy spirit, to be the sort of Christians Thou wouldst have us to be. In the name of Jesus, our Master, we ask it all,—Amen.

O Shepard Divine (1941)
Ralph Mark Gilbert

At this Yuletide season, our whole thought for each and every one of you is that you might have a Merry, Merry Christmas. May this season take your minds back to the manger of Bethlehem, and as you gaze upon the Christ-child there, may you contemplate His goodness and meekness, and strive, in these materialistic days of warfare and strife, to find the peace of soul which He came into the world to show us how to achieve. Let us pray tonight for those less favored by circumstance than we are; for the homeless of Europe, and Asia, and Africa, made destitute by this World War; for the gallant men of our Army and Navy who are not seated around their own home firesides tonight, and will not be there on Christmas Day, but who are either defending our country, or preparing themselves for this nation's defense. Let us bow in prayer for all of these, and for all others who stand in special need of prayer.

Almighty God, Thou art always at hand to lend a listening ear to our petitions. When we consider all that Jesus Christ, Thy Son, meant to the world, and what His advent didst secure for humanity, we admit that this old world presents a sorry picture indeed. We cannot fathom Thy purposes, but somehow, as we feel out after Thee, we know that Thou hast not left us, and that in the midst of all our confused strife, still Thou art near us, and Thou shalt lead us thru. Bless Thou our great President in his personal and official crises, and as he must bear the travail of his soul thru these long, dreary days, don't allow him to falter or lose courage, and never let him for one moment feel that God is anywhere else but close to his side. Be Thou with all our boys who are fighting for our defense, and though they may be miles away from home and loved ones, give them during this season, the true spirit of Christmas. Bring cheer and healing to the sick, and comfort to those who are bereaved, and the light of Thy salvation to those who are in sin. Forgive each of us where we have sinned, and may Thy Holy Spirit guide us all our lives; and in the hour of death, be Thou there, O Shepard Divine, to pilot us safely across Jordan's stream of death. This we ask in Jesus's name,— Amen.

Our Need for Thee (1941)

Ralph Mark Gilbert

Without God, this world indeed would be a desert place without an oasis; but thank God, every once in awhile, in this waste howling wilderness, we come to a spot that we call, "The Sweet Hour of Prayer," and there this little caravan may stop for awhile, and be refreshed with a little talk with Jesus. Let us unload now at that spot, and bow our hands and hearts in earnest prayer.

Rising above every other need, O heavenly Father, is our great need for Thee. More than our bodies need food, and drink, and clothing, and shelter, do our souls need to feast and find refreshment upon Thee, and to feel Thy righteousness wrapped around us as our garment, and to find shelter and peace for our souls in the refuge of eternity, Thou great Rock of Ages. Make us know that Thou art here, O God, and let us realize Thy presence in the affairs of our lives. Forgive us where we have sinned. Touch Thou the sick who are listening in, and heal them. Visit the prison-bound, and bless every burdened soul, and liberate every bound spirit, we ask in Jesus' name,—Amen.

We Need Thy Hand (1941)

Ralph Mark Gilbert

Who of us has not experienced frustrated hopes? Who of us do not meet with experiences that baffle us? There are hindrances all along the pathway of our lives. At best, we cannot see far ahead. Every day impresses the fact upon us that we stand in need of God's grace. May we ask that we approach His throne tonight with this fact uppermost in our minds, and at the footstool of mercy, let us bow our heads in prayer for the divine guidance that we so sorely need.

Heavenly Father, we know from all of the experiences that have been ours, that we cannot make the journey by ourselves. All of life teaches us that we need Thy hand; we must be led by Thy counsel. We would walk daily with Thee, because of Thy help; but we also would walk with Thee for the joy that we obtain from Thy fellowship. Withdraw not Thy presence from us, for we are lost without Thee, and find ourselves stumbling blindly in the surrounding darkness. Bless the aged who can no longer come to the services in Thy house; bless those who are in prison, and consecrate the bitterness of their experience to their good; look with compassion, and healing, and strength, upon those who are upon their beds of affliction; be thou with every condition of mankind, and bless all our unseen congregation tonight in the way that they most need Thee. Forgive us all our sins, and give us strength day by day to do Thy will. This we ask in Jesus's name,—Amen.

Return, O Lord (1944)

Charles Eric Lincoln

Dear Lord, I am bewildered by the angry world.
I do not know the meaning of the flags unfurled.
The noisy skies, the tortured seas:
What sayest Thou, O Lord, to These?

I hear the strident call to arms; above the scenes
Of men in desperate debate, their war machines
Defile the skies, pollute the earth.
How much, O Lord, can peace be worth?

Hast Thou in merited disgust turned back from man
Who recklessly has broken trust and sinned again?
Forgive our selfish lust for power
And save us in this dreadful hour.

Return, O Lord, return and save this wretched race,
Save us, not by Thy justice Lord, but by Thy grace,
Forgive our foolish, pompous way,
And save us from ourselves, we pray.

They Would Pray (1945)
{Benjamin Albert Botkin}

My master used to ask us children, "Do your folks pray at night?"
We said, "No," 'cause our folks had told us what to say. But the Lord
have mercy, there was plenty of that going on. They'd pray, "Lord,
deliver us from under bondage."

Dear God, Thank You for the Morning Light (1945)

Elizabeth J. Dabney

Dear God, thank you for the morning light
This day I have lived to see.
Guide my speech, order my steps aright,
As I leave this place, to meet Thee.
I praise you for your training school,
The teaching you do impart,
Make me one of your praying tools:
Abide within my heart.
As I leave this home you gave;
Dear God, protect it for me.
Let the blood of Jesus save.
My prayers ascend to Thee.
If it pleases you to call me home
Before my covenant ends today,
Let me rest in Thine arms;
Accept this prayer I pray.
Bless all the leaders of the land;
Bless everybody everywhere.
The time has come. I must be on my way.
Look for me I shall meet you there. Amen.

O My God, Please Close This War (1945)

Elizabeth J. Dabney

Send the former and the latter rain, O my God.
Send the refreshing showers again.
Send help to those at home and abroad.
Give us godly patience to stand.
Our mothers and fathers are crying for meat.
The youth are deep in despair.
The nations can scarcely find enough to eat.
Forgive, dear God, and answer my prayer.
This generation ignored your great command.
Sometimes it's so cold we can not stand.
It has brought darkness, famine, and death.
Then it's so warm we can hardly draw our breath.
Please close this war which is very mean
Teach us how to live together again.
You are the greatest general, you are the greatest dean.
Forgive and blot out our sins.
Smile on the soil, touch it with your blood.
In Jesus' name I pray.
Rebuke the storms, and turn away the floods,
That will carry our products away.
Our God when you send rain upon the earth,
Give it healing balm to cure.
Unstop the blood streams, add forgiving myrrh.
Deliver your own once more.
Turn away your anger Lord, and smile.
Let nations repent, love, sow and reap.
The greater day shall come with trials.
I pray Thee our souls do keep.
Amen.

Please Send Our Boys Back Home (1945)

Elizabeth J. Dabney

Our Father, bless this distressed land,
Forgive our sins I pray.
Let us be delivered by Thy hand,
Turn death's destruction away;
Mothers and wives with broken hearts,
Are praying for peace to come.
Rebuke Satan and his fiery darts,
Please send our boys back home.
Oh, Father, stir your ministers to pray!
You gave to them the keys;
Lead them to that old way,
Humble repentance on their knees.
Bless the fields with harvest green,
The fowl, the birds and the flock,
Turn away the devourer that would destroy these,
Time our praying clock.
Bless the rulers of the law;
The children in the land.
Break the bands, lock the lion's jaw;
We will obey your commands. Amen.

What It Means to Pray Through (1945)
Elizabeth J. Dabney

I lifted my eyes heavenward and said: "Lord, if You will bless my husband in the place You sent him to establish Your Name, if You will break the bonds and destroy the middle wall of partition; if You will give him a church and congregation—a credit unto Your people and all Christendom, I will walk with You for three years in prayer; both day and night. I will meet You every morning at nine o'clock sharp; You will never have to wait for me; I will be there to greet You. I will stay there all day; I will devote all of my time unto You." I walked forward about five or six steps, and stood on the little stone which was at the edge of the water. I said unto Him, "Furthermore, if You will hearken unto the voice of my supplication and break through in that wicked neighborhood, and bless my husband, I will fast seventy-two hours each week for two years. While I am going through the fast, I will not go home to sleep in my bed. I will stay in church; if I become sleepy I will rest on newspapers and carpet."

As soon as I had made this covenant unto the Lord, the heavens opened on that river bank; and the glory of the Lord fell from heaven all around me. It fell in the water like large drops of hail and rain. I knew he had prepared me to enter into this Prayer Ministry Suffering. He let me know very definitely that it had to be real, wholehearted prayer business to keep this covenant.

I am unable to tell you how I felt, or to describe what it means to enter into such a covenant with the Lord.

Taking a memorandum book from my hand-bag, I tore out three pieces of paper, and wrote the covenant.

I ascended the hill, and found Elder Dabney waiting, with his eyes open to the utmost extent. I do not know what he thought about introducing me into this new field, but I am confident he was alarmed.

I told him the covenant I had made. I asked him if he would permit me the privilege and opportunity to fulfill this obligation; but he flatly refused. He tried to make me go home. I told him I would never return home again until he agreed to let me pray. I pleaded and, finally, I told him the Lord would kill me if I broke this covenant. He looked at me amazed. He told me it was not six months; it was not just a year: three years was too long for anybody to obligate herself to pray night and day, especially going to church daily at that early hour, and undergoing the suffering this would demand.

I made it very clear to him my life was doomed if he rejected. I wept, and the Lord touched his heart; he gave me his consent. He asked when would I enter into this Prayer Life. "Tomorrow morning," I replied. My heart leaped for joy; this was the happiest moment I ever experienced to do something for God.

The next morning at nine o'clock I met the Lord on time. I became so accustomed to meeting Him at that hour, I never had to look at my clock to find out the correct time; however I did.

At nine o'clock each morning the door knob of the church would turn. I knew it was the Lord; therefore I greeted Him with a hearty, "Good morning, Jesus."

His glory filled the room all day long. He was my guest. I would sit down and pray: I kneeled until I wore all the skin off of my knees on those hard floors. They were so sensitive, many times I was in great pain; however, I had to use them without murmuring or complaining. At times I was so worn in my body, I placed three chairs together and stretched out on them. At times I crocheted and prayed. I never permitted anything to interfere with my conversation with God. I suffered. The flesh on my bones was numb; I fasted, not eating or drinking natural food; but I had a direct supply from heaven. The days were dark, and I did not see my way; but of one thing I was confident, the Lord guided my footsteps; I enjoyed his company and he enjoyed mine.

I Ask You, Jesus, to Take Care of Me (1949)
Diana Brown

Our Father, who art in heaven, hallowed be thy name, thy kingdom come, thy will be done on earth as it done in heaven. Give us this day our daily bread, and forgive those trespass against us. Lead us not into temptation, but deliver us from all thing like evil. Thine the kingdom, power, and thy glory.

Oh, God, I have a chance for another July meet me here. [I] stagger up and down hills and mountains; but I ask you, Jesus, to take care of me and want you, Master, to be to the head and one be to the foot for the last morning. Oh! stand to the bedside, oh, God! this morning. And Lord, when you see Diana done knock from side to side on Edisto—no mother, no father, no brother, no sister—I ask you, Jesus, to be me mother and be me father for the last morning. Oh, God! stand to me as my hair to my head, because you is the only one I can look upon if I call you. And you is me mother; you is me father; you is all and all I got to depend upon. Oh, God! and take charge of me once more time—on the road, out in the field, up to the fireside; Oh, God! to the well. Lord, I ask you tonight, take charge of my house whilst I leave. Friendly Master, make peace and love till I come back to home. And I ask you, Jesus, oh, God! be with me once more time; so when I come down to Jordan, oh, Lord, I want to cross over Jordan for meself and not for another. Oh, God! this evening, Lord, I didn't expect to be on this side till now; but you is—you is a good captain. You hold to the helm. Oh! I ask you, Lord, when you see me done knock about on Edisto from church to church, from class to class, oh, God! let me die with me right mind, for meself and not for another.

Send It Now, Lord (1951)

{William H. Pipes}

[This prayer was offered by a minister at a wake for a deceased Christian man in Macon, Georgia.]

"Oh, Gawd, we come this evenin' beared down wid' the sorrows of this worl'. We come as paupers to Thy th'one o' grace. We been down in the valley o' the shadder, an' our hearts is heavy this evenin,' Lord. Thou's done thundered fo'th Thy will. Thou's done took from our mist one o' Yo' lambs. Thou's done took a good brother who's done lived his 'lotted time an' died, Gawd, like we all mus' die. Ummmmmmmmmmmmm. Thou's done come into this house o' sons an' Yo' wid Yo' own han', Yo' own grat han', Gawd— Ummmmmmmmmmmmmm—Thou's done dashed down the vessel outa what Yo' po'ed life into them. Thou's done took a father an' a gran'-father. Thou's done beared down hearts. Thou's done put burdens on 'em. Thou's done whupped 'em wid stripes. 'Member dese hearts, great Gawd. Relieve 'em. You know when t' sun's been a-shinin' too long an' the earth's all parched an' barren, You sen's Yo' rain, Lord. You relieve the earth. When wars rage, like the one ragin' now,[1] an' mens dies an' makes widders an' orfins, den, in Yo' own good time, Gawd—Yo' precious time Ummmmmmm—You sen's peace. You takes the burden off'n the hearts o' nations. An' You promise', Father, by the sweetflowin' blood o' Jesus, to rescue the perishin', suckle the needy, give health to the ailin'. . . ." He [the minister] did not pause at a piercing scream from Jamie. [She is shouting.] His extended fingers worked spasmodically, as if each had a life, independent of him. ". . . An' sen' balm to the hearts o' sufferin'. Sen' it now, Lord. Let it flow like the healin' waters o' Gilead, an' ease the burden o' dese hearts broken by the fulfillin' o' Yo' almighty will. Amen."

---

[1] A reference to either World War II or the Korean War.

Thank Thee for Everything (1951)

{William H. Pipes}

Dear Lawd, we come befo' Thee and ask Thee ter stand by us. Thank Thee for ev'rything Thou's did for us. Christ, assemble between these four walls; git in the hearts uv men and women, boys and girls. Thou art God an' God alone.

Since the last time we's bowed, we's done things what we ought not uv done, an' we's left things undone what we ought uv done. Rule over Heaven and earth; rule over these people down here, the sick an' afflicted and weary. And bind us one to another.

Go with that one who gwine to preach de greater life today. Ask You to 'member the church. Brang us to pray. Lawd, have mercy on us.

Now, Lawd, when it come our time to die, pray You receive us into Thy kingdom an' give our souls a resting place *Amen.*

Thou Have Widen the Way for Us (1951)

{William H. Pipes}

[An anonymous minister offered this sermon from a pulpit some-where in Macon, Georgia.]

We thank Thee this morning for the opportunity extended towards us. Thank Thee that Thou hast saw fit to have us continue here in Thy vineyard to work out our soul salvation. Thank Thee that Thou hast left a written record, guide, and assurance that we have at Thy right-hand-side a friend, a friend-in-deed; at Thy right-hand-side a scarred Savior; at Thy right-hand-side a mediator and redeemer—but standing to receive our souls.

Thou have widen the way for us. We're knowed by our acts as did the disciples. They knowed Him by breaking of bread, giving livin' circumstance; to those we does meet, may we realize by our acts (by being born again) become living witness of Him.

Paul said to the Corinthians, brotherin, that—that "He came at Pentecost; and last of all, I saw Him myself." May we see 'im in our conversion and may we see 'im as we go about our daily occupation.

Now we pray Thee, bless the man of the hour. The Man of God. The one that Thou hast at present in this foreign part of the vineyard. When we are called from here to another world, Jesus did promise to sinner on cross, may we kneel at Thy feet and cry, "Redeemer!" Amen.

I Let Go of My Accumulations (1951)

Howard Thurman

My ego is like a fortress.
I have built its walls stone by stone
To hold out the invasion of the love of God.

But I have stayed here long enough. There is light
Over the barriers. O my God—
The darkness of my house forgive
And overtake my soul.
I relax the barriers.
I abandon all that I think I am,
All that I hope to be,
All that I believe I possess.
I let go of the past,
I withdraw my grasping hand from the future,
And in the great silence of this moment,
I alertly rest my soul.
As the sea gull lays in the wind current,
So I lay myself into the spirit of God.
My dearest human relationships,
My most precious dreams,
I surrender to His care.
All that I have called my own
I give back. All my favorite things
Which I would withhold in my storehouse
From his fearful tyranny,
I let go.
I give myself
Unto Thee, O my God. Amen.

O God, I Need Thee (1951)

Howard Thurman

I Need Thy Sense of Time
    Always I have an underlying anxiety about things.
    Sometimes I am in a hurry to achieve my ends
    And am completely without patience. It is hard for me
    To realize that some growth is slow,
    That all processes are not swift. I cannot always discriminate
    Between what takes time to develop and what can be rushed,
    Because my sense of time is dulled.
    I measure things in terms of happenings.
    O to understand the meaning of perspective
    That I may do all things with a profound sense of leisure—of
        time.

I Need Thy Sense of Order
    The confusion of the details of living
    Is sometimes overwhelming. The little things
    Keep getting in my way providing ready-made
    Excuses for failure to do and be
    What I know I ought to do and be.
    Much time is spent on things that are not very important
    While significant things are put into an insignificant place
    In my scheme of order. I must unscramble my affairs
    So that my life will become order. O God, I need
        Thy sense of order.

I Need Thy Sense of the Future
    Teach me to know that life is ever
    On the side of the future.
    Keep alive in me the forward look, the high hope,
    The onward surge. Let me not be frozen
    Either by the past or the present.
    Grant me, O patient Father, Thy sense of the future
    Without which all life would sicken and die.

The Prayer of Florence's Mother (1952)
{James Arthur Baldwin}

Her mother had taught her that the way to pray was to forget everything and everyone but Jesus; to pour out of the heart, like water from a bucket, all evil thoughts, all thoughts of self, all malice for one's enemies; to come boldly, and yet more humbly than a little child, before the Giver of all good things. Yet, in Florence's heart tonight hatred and bitterness weighed like granite, pride refused to abdicate from the throne it had held so long. Neither love nor humility had led her to the altar, but only fear. And God did not hear the prayers of the fearful, for the hearts of the fearful held no belief. Such prayers could rise no higher than the lips that uttered them.

Around her she heard the saints' voices, a steady, charged murmur, with now and again the name of *Jesus* rising above, sometimes like the swift rising of a bird into the air of a sunny day, sometimes like the slow rising of the mist from swamp ground. Was this the way to pray? In the church that she had joined when she first came North one knelt before the altar once only, in the beginning, to ask for forgiveness of sins; and this accomplished, one was baptized and became a Christian, to kneel no more thereafter. Even if the Lord should lay some great burden on one's back—as He had done, but never so heavy a burden as this she carried now— one prayed in silence. It was indecent, the practice of common niggers to cry aloud at the foot of the altar, tears streaming for all the world to see. She had never done it, not even as a girl down home in the church they had gone to in those days. Now perhaps it was too late, and the Lord would suffer her to die in the darkness in which she had lived so long.

The piano stopped. All around her now were only the voices of the saints.

"Dear Father"—it was her mother praying—"we come before You on our knees this evening to ask You to watch over us and hold back the hand of the destroying angel. Lord, sprinkle the doorpost of this house with the blood of the Lamb to keep all the wicked men away.[1] Lord, we praying for every mother's son and daughter everywhere in the world but we want You to take special care of this girl here tonight, Lord, and don't let no evil come nigh her. We know You's able to do it, Lord, in Jesus's name. Amen.

---

[1] This is an allusion to Exodus 21:6.

Lead Me, Guide Me (1953)

Doris Akers

I am weak and I need Thy strength and pow'r,
To help me over my weakest hour,
Let me thru the darkness Thy face to see,
Lead me, oh Lord, lead me.

Chorus:
Lead me, guide me along the way,
For if you lead me I cannot stray,
Lord, let me walk each day with Thee,
Lead me, oh Lord, lead me.

Help me tread in the paths of righteousness,
Be my aid when Satan and sin oppress.
I am putting all my trust in Thee,
Lead me, oh Lord, lead me.

I am lost, if you take your hand from me,
I am blind without Thy Light to see,
Lord, just always let me Thy servant be,
Lead me, oh Lord, lead me.

Part V

The Civil

Rights Ethos

1956–1980

A Prayer for a College Woman (1956)

William Lloyd Imes

O God, whose Son was born of a woman.
Look upon me with loving kindness and plenitude of mercy.
Help me to adore Thee in spirit and in truth,
And to learn how Thou hast ever brought beauty and radiance and
    joy into our world
Through the life and ministry of womanhood.
Especially commended unto Thy care
Is the womanhood on this college campus.
Help me as a college woman to be filled with eagerness to learn
The disciplines of mind, heart, and soul.
Help me in conduct and in character to reflect the best traditions of
    the Christian heritage.
In decisions, make me thoughtful and exact;
In temptations, keep me strong and pure;
In conflicts, make me just and wise;
In habits, filled with the ministry of human kindness and concern for
    all Thy children;
In the arts and sciences, give me skill to enrich our common fund of
    learning,
And to crown it with loveliness and dignity that shall give it highest
    worth.
So shall my life be a center of order, a mirror of beauty, and a ministry
    of comfort.

A Pastoral Prayer (1956)

Martin Luther King, Jr.

O God, our Heavenly Father, we thank thee for this golden privilege to worship thee, the only true God of the universe. We come to thee today, grateful that thou hast kept us through the long night of the past and ushered us into the challenge of the present and the bright hope of the future. We are mindful, O God, that man cannot save himself, for man is not the measure of things and humanity is not God. Bound by our chains of sins and finiteness, we know we need a Savior. We thank thee, O God, for the spiritual nature of man. We are in nature but we live above nature. Help us never to let anybody or any condition pull us so low as to cause us to hate. Give us strength to love our enemies and to do good to those who despitefully use us and persecute us.[1] We thank thee for thy Church, founded upon thy Word, that challenges us to do more than sing and pray, but go out and work as though the very answer to our prayers depended on us and not upon thee. Then, finally, help us to realize that man was created to shine like stars and live on through all eternity. Keep us, we pray, in perfect peace, help us to walk together, pray together, sing together, and live together until that day when all God's children, Black, White, Red, and Yellow will rejoice in one common band of humanity in the kingdom of our Lord and of our God, we pray. Amen.

---

[1] This is an allusion to Matthew 5:44 and Luke 6:27–35.

A Prayer for Freedom (1957)

Raphael Philemon Powell

Oh, God of nations, of peoples,
And of all creation,
Grant us freedom from fear
Of the white man's domination.
Grant us freedom from want
Of the world's production.
Grant us full enjoyment
Of the earth's fruition.

Give us free minds
To speak without fear.
Destroy tyranny, cruelty,
And the oppression, we bear.
Grant us freedom to worship
No God of color.
Let us worship the spirit,
The living God forever.

Grant us the knowledge
That the first requirement for freedom
Is to know ourselves.
This knowledge is to know
The right symbol of our identity.
The symbol of our identity is a name.
It is the name which identifies us
As men, as persons, as human beings.

Oh God, enlighten our minds
With new vision to see
That the respect of a people
Is vested in a name.
Oh Lord, inspire us to know that
The name is the soul of a people;

That the name, the soul,
And the man are one.

For when Jesus called forth
Lazarus from the dead,
The soul of Lazarus, the man,
Arose and returned to life.
Oh God, Almighty, help us to see
That with the name, Negro,[1]
We can hardly win freedom,
Because there is nothing
In the name, Negro,
To inspire men to freedom.

Lord, urge us to see
That the name, *African* has all
The requirements for freedom.
Our Father, incite us to know
That the name we are called
Must be the *right* name.
Oh Lord, quicken us to know
That the right name is, *African*.

Lord, let us call forth
From the dead,
The right name, *African!*
And sleeping souls will arise,
And return from the grave
Of the low, servile name, Negro.
For Negro has lain in the grave
For over three centuries,
It is now decayed and rot with evil.
It smells of the ghost of hate,
Of malice and race prejudice.

---

[1] The author included this footnote: "The word Negro is capitalized herein only to avoid questions about its fitness during this prayer."

Oh Lord, let us not be lazy
Of tongue and speech
Like mumbling babes.
Teach our tongues to say,
African-American.[2]
Guide our hands to write,
African-American.
Let us respect ourselves
As African-Americans, and
The world will respect us
For our existent potentiality;
For the power, the reality,
That's in the name, African.

Oh Lord, endow us
With the insight to know
That Negro is a slave name.
Oh Lord, grant us freedom to be men.
To stand the test to be our best!
Remove from us, the name, Negro.
Destroy its cancerous roots,
Implanted in us by the use of bad language.

By cunning and deception,
The white man by his language
Has deceived us, enslaved us,
And *made* us Negro.
But we know by thy creation,
That God made *man.*[3]
And God has not changed him;
Therefore, *God's man* is not Negro
He remains, a *man.*

---

[2] The author included this footnote: "Note: Not Afro-American, but African-American is the right name."

[3] The author included this footnote: "Genesis 1:26, 2:7. Bible history of the Genesis creation proves that God created no animal or being called, Negro. Rev. R. P. Powell's coming book, *Dr. Maketa's Solution of the Race Problem* explains the word Negro in detail."

Enlighten us to see the difference
Between man and Negro.
Grant us freedom
To transform ourselves
From Negro to man.

Oh God, grant us understanding
To know ourselves,
As the legitimate heirs
To the rich land of Africa.
Inspire the ministers with wisdom
To know that our people
Who were brought from Africa
Were not, and are not Negroes.
That they were, and still are, Africans.

Arouse thy ministers to preach
That in God's creation,
There was no Negro.
Oh God, infuse us with wisdom
To be proud of the name, African.
Move us with boldness of self-expression
To reclaim the name, African.

Grant us the vision to see
That freedom will come,
That liberty will come,
That justice will come, and
That civil rights will come
By the redemption of Africa;
And that our children, yet unborn,
Will again rule Africa.

Lord, show us that the way to freedom
Is by the control of land.
Then grant us freedom
To think of Africa
As the land for our inheritance.
Awaken us to discover that our ancestors

Were not Negroes,
But always were, Africans.

Lord, grant us freedom
To understand that like
The Chinese and Israelis,
We must have our own homeland,
But we seek no total return
Back to Africa.
America is our present home,
And we are here to stay;
While we encourage and support
The redemption of Africa.

Africa, whose Egypt
First gave to the world,
A civilization.
Africa, whose great fathers
Were the first to rule the earth.
For Thy Word has declared
That we ruled by King Rameses.[4]

History records that we governed
By King Thotmes, King Akhenaton,
King Tut-ankh-amen,
King Solomon, and by others.
Then, the white man had no power!

Oh God, thou didst bless
Our graceful women
As royal Queens and Princesses
To rule great empires by Queen Tiyi,
Queen Nefertiti, Queen Hat-Shepsut,
The Queen of Sheba, Queen Cleopatra
By Isis, mother of Horus,
And others.

---

[4] The author cited Exodus 1:11.

Our Father, we thank thee,
We praise thee, we magnify thee,
For the world's first
Virgin Mother and Child,
Isis and Horus[5] who originated in Africa.
Lord, stimulate us to know the truth
That royal and noble Africans,
Although partly enslaved today,
Were the first Queens and Kings,
The first Emperors and Presidents,
The first Leaders and Ministers
Of the world.

Lord, we who were first rulers
And now ruled by white savagery,
We, who first governed
Are now governed by white barbarity.
Show us Lord, the way to freedom.
Lead us, quickly lead us to victory.
Grant us again the power to rule,
Incite us to rule ourselves.
And may we never rule with vengeance,
For vengeance to the Lord belongs.

Oh God, make clear our eyes to see
That the name, *African* is the foundation-stone
Which we were taught to reject,
But Africa will be our chief protection, yet.
For by her recognition, we shall be free;
'Til then, there's much to regret.
Oh Lord, redeem our rightful name, *African*,
Which unwittingly, we spurn and neglect.

---

5 The author included this footnote: "Isis and Horus were the first Virgin Mother and Child known to the world. This means that the very same principle, the Christ, which was in the beginning, the Word, was first manifested to the world in Egypt, Africa, as Horus and his mother, Isis. The same idea of a Christ and mother, later came to be known as Jesus and Mary. In our time, we know that Jesus and Mary are not myths. Then, we should realize that in the time of our Egyptian ancestors, Horus and Isis were not myths."

Confound the deceitful tricks of
The oppressors who have misled us,
Brain washed us, and caused us,
Our right name to refuse.
Grant us understanding that to be free,
The slave name, Negro must go,
And we must use the right name, *African,*
Which demands the respect of nations.

Lord, let us know that
In our effort to gain freedom,
We must be recognized
By a name that is meaningful.
Teach us to respect our person
By identifying ourselves
With the right name, *African.*
Oh God, help us, transform us,
Renew our minds with the excellence
Of our dignified, African ancestors.

Lord, we beseech thee, open our eyes,
Let us see that the name, Negro
Relates only to color.
And that we are not just a color.
Oh God, thou hast blessed us
With a land, Africa,
and we need its name
As a symbol of unity,
Because it unites us to the land.

With unity and land, we have
The basis for freedom.
Lord, grant us the sense
To be proud of the land,
Where our people will be free
From racial discrimination,
From burning crosses,
And from school segregation;
From the threats and bombs

Of the Ku Klux Klan,
From the violence of *white citizens.*

Lord, grant us understanding,
And our children's children
Will find freedom
In the rich, bright land of Africa.
Oh Lord, our God; break down
The Steel curtain of race prejudice.
Protect our school children
From vicious attacks,
Save us from the cunning of
The *white citizen's* plots,
Save us from the villainy
Of the white mobs.

Oh God, grant us peace and security.
Save us from the hypocracy
Of men and governments
Who proclaim a free world,
While they keep us enslaved.
Oh Lord, if they deny
That they enslave us, speak for us.

Speak by thy thunder and lightning.
Speak by thy winds and tornados,
Speak by thy hurricanes,
Add to their bereavement.
Speak by thy floods and earthquakes,
For thine is the power.

Oh Lord, if they deny our enslavement,
We ask them, "if we have freedom,
Why a civil rights legislation,
Why a commission against discrimination,
Why a partial supreme court's decision,[6]

---

[6] The author included this footnote: "A court decision or a law which a court or legislature leaves without effective means of its execution is only a partial, halfway procedure which might never become effective."

Why a pilgrimage of our people
To Washington, to pray for our freedom?

Oh God, frustrate their politics,
Have mercy upon our oppressed people.
Give us courage and strength to endure.
Oh Lord, behold the tyrants in their pride!
They set fire to our houses
They bomb our churches
They destroy and bomb our homes,
With prejudice they insult us,
They persecute us,
They shoot and murder us.
How long will this white man oppress us,
Oh Lord, how long?

They frighten us, they terrorize us,
They come to us with covered, white faces,
They taunt us with the lynch rope
and the fiery cross,
While we pray by thy words;
Words like those which the lad, David,
Said to the giant, Goliath.
"Thou comest to me with a sword,
A spear and a shield,
But I come to thee
In the name of the Lord."[7]

Oh God, see the white boasters
Who use their color
As a vestment of power.
See the brazen-faced *white citizens*
Who use their national strength
To crush us, loyal African-Americans.
Oh, God, how self-exalted they stand,
In control of the national resources!

---

[7] The author cited I Samuel 17:45.

They discharge us from our jobs,
They expose us to the mobs,
They drive us from our homes;
They make us refugees
And we answer with our prayers—
Prayers mingled with sobs.
Oh Lord, how mighty they seem,
How cruel, how mean,
Those white clans who refuse to gin
Our farmer's cotton,
While perplexed, we reply with a prayer.

How might stand the white bankers,
Who refuse to furnish our people
With loans for their crops!
Oh Lord, behold our predicament
In Africa and in America,
See our plight in the South.
Some white store keepers
Have cut off our food supplies,
Some white mortgagors have threatened
To foreclose the mortgage
On the homes of our people.

The white Merchants have organized,
They have fixed the prices of goods.
Some white southerners
Have raised the price of bread
Which African-Americans must buy.
But for the truth that
Thou art the bread of life,
We would surely die.

For when they should serve bread,
They threaten us instead
While, our weapon is a prayer.
But, Lord God, thou art not mocked.
Our prayers shall not return void.
For thy Word has declared,

"Pride goeth before destruction,
And a haughty spirit before a fall."[8]

Our Father, teach us how to pray
Until the power of thy spirit
Impregnates us with the sense,
To re-create for ourselves,
A United States of Africa.
His wonders to perform.

Then, let us not ask, "how and when?"
We shall promote and have,
A United States of Africa.
But let us ask ourselves,
"Why look to Africa?"
The answer, Lord, thou knowest,
That after 338 years in America,
We still lack our freedom,
We are still enslaved.

But prayer will change things,
And the right will prevail.
For the Lord has heard our prayer.
He will answer, He will set us free,
And we shall have freedom
In these United States,
Through a United States of Africa.

Our God, thou hast made us heirs
To a land of great resources,
A land of wealth and riches
Where we'll have the sovereign right
To coin our own money.
A land with mines of gold and diamond,
Where we shall have respect and honor.
Where we shall have dignity and power,
Where we shall have peace and prosperity.

---

[8] The author cited Proverbs 16:18.

Guide us, Lord, direct us
To the security of its free abode,
Safe from race prejudice.
And our people shall attain the highest
In soul, in mind, and in body.
Our Father, we thank thee for the vision,
To see that a new world is coming,
That God is changing things,
In Africa, in America,
And in all the world.

Not as citizens, but like aliens
We are treated; for with impunity,
They debate our civil rights
In privy councils, and in meetings
To which we are not invited.
Lord, thou hast seen
the abuses we daily suffer.
The liberty to go and come freely,
We are denied.
The trains, the buses,
We could not in peace ride.
Then, thou didst send us brave leaders.

They preached to us, prayed with us,
They guided and organized us.
Martin Luther King and his group
Planned a passive resistance movement.
They started a bus boycott,
They made us refuse to ride
The white man's buses
They urged us to walk,
And they armed us
With the weapon of a prayer.

Our walk was long and weary,
Our feet were tired and sore,
But our prayer was answered.
Lord, thou didst make a change,

And we ride the buses again,
But not by the order,
"Go to the rear!"
We ride, but the injustice continues,
And our gallant leaders,[9]
Made a Prayer Pilgrimage
To pray for our freedom.

Protect us by thy grace
From the disgrace of selfish nations
Which have denied us our civil rights.
Our Father, most mighty,
All powerful God,
Let the Prayer Pilgrimage Day,
May 17th, 1957 be a day
Of Memorial for future generations,
And we shall ever commemorate
The day of our pilgrimage,
When we marched to Washington
With a prayer in our hearts.

Deliver us from the evil plots
Of the council of public officials
Who by their false concept of man's color,
Who by their false idea of white superiority,
Who by their racial prejudice,
Who by their tricks and politics,
Have denied our human rights.
In spite of their treachery,
Give us, we pray, our civil rights.

Oh God, most mighty, save us;
Redeem us, preserve us

---

[9] The author included this footnote: "Rev. Thomas Kilgore, A. Philip Randolph, Roy Wilkins, Rev. Henry Grant Jones, Dr. J. H. Jackson, Rev. Adam Clayton Powell, Rev. Thomas Harten, Dr. Sandy F. Ray, Rev. Martin Luther King, and our ministers from all over the country."

By thy mighty hand.
Thou wilt strengthen us,
Thou wilt uplift us,
Thou wilt enable us to endure
'Til race prejudice and hate
Shall be no more,
And we will earn our civil rights
And live in peace and freedom forever,
    Amen!

Prayer for Teacher (1958)

{James Mercer Langston Hughes and Arna Wendell Bontemps}

Dear Lord,
Bless our dear Teacher.
Give her the brightest crown in heaven.
Give her the whitest robe that can be given.
Put golden sandals on her feet, and let her
Slip and slide up to the throne of Master Jesus. Amen.

The Eighth Psalm (1958)

Charles Eric Lincoln

O Lord, how perfect is Thy name,
In all the earth how great Thy fame!
Above the heavens Thou didst set
Thy glory, gracious Lord, and yet
Out of the mouths of babes calls Thee
Thy strength to still the enemy!

When I behold Thy heavens so grand,
The moon and stars at Thy command,
Lord, what is man that Thou shouldst heed
His call, or visit with his seed?
Near angels Thou has fixed his stead,
Honor and glory crown his head.

O'er all Thy works man rules complete.
All things Thou placed beneath his feet:
Birds of the air, beasts of the field,
The fish that swim the seas must yield.
O Lord, our Lord, how great Thy name!
Throughout the earth, how wide Thy fame!

A Prayer for Love (1958)

Charles Eric Lincoln

Lord, let me love; let loving be the symbol of grace that warms my
    heart, of grace that warms my heart;
And let me find Thy loving hand to still me, to still me when I
    tremble
At Thy command to love all humankind.
Lord, let me love, though love may be the losing
Of ev'ry earthly treasure I possess.
Lord, make Thy love the pattern of my choosing.
And let Thy will dictate my happiness.

I have no wish to wield the sword of power,
I want no man to leap, to leap at my command;
Nor let my critics feel constrained to cower, feel constrained to cower
For fear of some reprisal at my hand.
Lord, teach me mercy; let me be the winner
Of ev'ry man's respect and simple love.
For I have known Thy mercy, though a sinner.
Whenever I have sought Thy peace above.

Lord, let me love the lowly and the humble,
Forgetting not the mighty, the mighty and the strong;
And give me grace to love those who may stumble, to love those who
    may stumble,
Nor let me seek to judge of right or wrong.
Lord, let my parish be the world unbounded,
Let love of race and clan be at an end.
Let ev'ry hateful doctrine be confounded
That interdicts the love of friend for friend. Amen.

Bless Those Who Teach (1961)
John Malcus Ellison

Almighty Father, we bless Thee for children, for youth, and for all who fill our institutions of learning. Reveal to them the glory and beauty of life. Enable them to rise to their opportunities. We implore Thy blessing, O God, on all the men and women who teach the youth of our nation. May they revere the young lives, clean and plastic, which have newly come from Thee. Gird these teachers for their task, and save them from loneliness, discouragement, the numbness of routine, and all bitterness of heart. In all things draw us to the mind of the Great Teacher, in whose name we pray. Amen.

Rekindle Our Sense of Wonder (1961)
John Malcus Ellison

Thou, who art the eternal God and our Father, hast set before each of us an untraveled way full of beauty and mystery, and calling for courage and the spirit of adventure. Grant us Thy kindly light to lead us onward. To the youth of this day in all nations, give us a vision of Thy purpose for their lives; and to us who are older, grant a return of the wonder which was the glory of our youth and which as we beheld it brought Thy light into our hearts. Oh, let not the wonder fade or the light become darkness, lest we lose our way. In His Name. Amen.

We Cast Ourselves Upon Thee (1961)
Jesse Jai McNeil

Almighty and everlasting God, our heavenly Father, whose mercy and lovingkindness are know to all who trust in Thee: We thank Thee for Thy unfailing promises to us Thy children. Generation after generation seek Thee, and are found of Thee. We cast ourselves upon Thee, and are supported by Thee. We live secure in the sure and certain fulfillment of Thy precious promises. Thou has promised, O God, that while the earth remaineth, seed-time and harvest, and cold and heat, and summer and winter, and day and night shall not cease. We praise Thy Name for these manifestations of Thy unfailing providence.

In the midst of sorrow or joy, sickness or health, adversity or prosperity, grant, we beseech Thee, that we may never lose sight of Thee. And when the storms of confusion and uncertainty overtake us, speak peace to our soul, O blessed Lord, and enlighten our mind with Thy Holy Spirit. Lighten our burdens by strengthening our spirit. Keep us strong and give us courage.

And when the ways of our common life would tend to discourage and to embitter us, give us the grace and the patience to maintain a loving and a confident spirit; through Jesus Christ our Lord. Amen.

Brother Ezekiel Prays Besides
Hetta's Deathbed (1966)
{Margaret Abigail Walker Alexander}

Brother Ezekiel held the [two-year-old] child down close to her mother's face and said, soothingly, "It's your mama, Vyry, say hello to your maw." The child spoke, "Mama," and then she whimpered. Hetta fell back on her pillows and Ezekiel handed the child to Mama Sukey, who quickly took her outside into the night air.

After a moment Brother Ezekiel spoke again to the dying and exhausted woman.

"Sis Hetta, I'm here, Brother Zeke, it's me. Can I do something for you?"

"Pray," she rasped, "pray."

He fell on his knees beside the bed and took her hand in his. The night was growing darker. Despite the full moon outside, spilling light through the great oak and magnolia trees, inside Granny Ticey had lighted a large tallow candle. It flared up suddenly, and eerie shadows searched the corners and crowded the room. Brother Ezekiel began to pray:

"Lord, God-a-mighty, you done told us in your Word to seek and we shall find; knock and the door be open; ask, and it shall be given[1] when your love come twinklin down. And Lord, tonight we is a-seekin. Way down here in this here rain-washed world, kneelin here by this bed of affliction pain, your humble servant is a-knockin, and askin for your lovin mercy, and your tender love. This here sister is tired a-sufferin, Lord, and she wants to come home. We ask you to roll down that sweet chariot right here by her bed, just like you done for Lishy,[2] so she can step in kinda easy like and ride on home to glory. Gather her in your bosom like you done Father Abraham and give her rest. She weak, Lord, and she weary, but her eyes is a-fixin for to light on them golden streets of glory and them pearly gates of God. She beggin for to set at your welcome table and feast on milk

---

[1] See Luke 11:9–13.

[2] Lishy is used here as the colloquial name for the Prophet Elijah, who, according to II Kings 2:11, was carried up into heaven in a chariot of fire.

and honey. She wants to put on them angel wings and wear that crown and them pretty golden slippers. She done been broke like a straw in the wind and she ain't got no strength, but she got the faith, Lord, and she got the promise of your Almighty Word. Lead her through this wilderness of sin and tribulation. Give her grace to stand by the river of Jordan and cross her over to hear Gabe[3] blow that horn. Take her home, Lord God, take her home.

And the sobbing women listening to him pray breathed fervent amens. When Brother Ezekiel got up from his knees he put the hand of Sis Hetta on her cover. But she no longer seemed to hear what he was saying.

---

[3] Gabe is a colloquial name for the archangel Gabriel. In African-American readings of Revelation 8–10, the trumpet or voice of the seventh angel shall be sounded at the end of time, when "the mystery of God should be finished, as he hath declared to his servants the prophets." See Revelation 10:7, which alludes to the vision of the Prophet Daniel in Daniel 8:15–27.

Vyry's Prayer in the Wilderness of Reconstruction (1966)
{Margaret Abigail Walker Alexander}

Before she realized where she was going she found herself deep in the woods. Around here there was a chapel-hush. She heard birds softly and sweetly singing, but most of all she felt the silence of the thickly soft carpet of pine needles under her feet, and looking up she could faintly see the blue sky in thin scraps of light through the interlacing of tender young leaves and green pine needles. She found herself a rock, and instead of sitting down she dropped to her knees. Instinctively she began to pray, the words forming on her lips at first in a halting, faltering, and half-hesitant fashion, and then rushing out:

"Lawd, God-a-mighty, I come down here this morning to tell you I done reached the end of my rope, and I wants you to take a-hold. I done come to the bottom of the well, Lord, and my well full of water done run clean dry.

"I come down here, Lord, cause I ain't got no where else to go. I come down here knowing I ain't got no right, but I got a heavy need. I'm suffering so, Lord, my body is heavy like I'm carrying a stone. I come to ask you to move the stone, Jesus. Please move the stone! I come down here, Lord, to ask you to come by here, Lord. Please come by here!

"We can't go on like this no longer, Lord. We can't keep on a-fighting, and a-fussing, and a-cussing, and a-hating like this, Lord. You done been too good to us. We done wrong, Lord, I knows we done wrong. I ain't gwine say we ain't done wrong, and I ain't gwine promise we might not do wrong again cause, Lord, we ain't nothing but sinful human flesh, we ain't nothing but dust. We is evil peoples in a wicked world, but I'm asking you to let your forgiving love cover our sin, Lord.

"Let your peace come in our hearts again, Lord, and we's gwine try to stay on our knees and follow the road You is laid before us, if You only will.

"Come by here, Lord, come by here, if you please. And Lord, I wants to thank You, Jesus, for moving the stone!"

A Child's Prayer (1966)
{Otho B. Cobbins}

An 8-year-old girl's mother had not left her bed for months. Broken hearted, she read promises of answers to prayer from her New Testament, then asked, "Mother, can Jesus make you well?" "Yes, my child, but it's not His will. I'm in such agony I can't talk to you; go and play." The child went and thought and prayed, then returned with the words of assurance: "Mamma, I'm going to try Jesus once more. He says ask, and I'm going to ask Him. Now, Mamma, pray with me." Kneeling she prayed, "O Jesus, dear good Jesus, I have no happy days since she has been sick these three months. She's so sick she can't talk to her little girl. She loves you and her little girl loves you." Suddenly she rose to her feet, and clapping her hands, cried, "He will, Mamma, He will." The lady had not moved her hands for months. Immediately she rose from her bed healed and able to go about and attend to her household duties, praising God.

A Prayer for African American Peoplehood

(1968)

Albert B. Cleage, Jr.

Heavenly Father, we thank thee for the opportunity of coming into thy house. We thank thee for our new understanding of the teachings of thy Son, Jesus Christ. We thank thee for knowledge that we are sustained and supported by thy strength and thy power. Be with us in everything we do in our efforts to unite and come together, in our efforts to fight against the enemy who would destroy us. Be with us in the difficult task of uniting and building a black brotherhood which has meaning in terms of today's world. We pray to thee with a sense of confidence in the future. The things which must be done, we will do. Sustain and support us as we go about our task. Amen.

The Hasty Word (1969)

Howard Thurman

We have turned aside from the tasks and the duties and the responsibilities which involve us day after day to present ourselves with as much confidence and faith as we can muster, hoping that in Thy presence and in the great quietness of this waiting moment we might find the measure of our deep and inner peace without which the enterprise of our private lives cannot be fulfilled. We share with Thee all of the meaning that we have been able to garner out of the days of our living. We see as if by a flash of blinding light the meaning of something which we have done; the hasty word, the careless utterance, the deliberate act by which another was injured or confused, the decision to do what even at the time we felt was neither the right thing nor the thing which we were willing to back with our lives. All of these things crowd in upon us, our Father. We want to be sure that what we say in Thy presence and what we feel in Thy presence will be honest and clear and sincere. As we look at this aspect of our lives, there is only one moving request which we make and that is for forgiveness: forgiveness for the sin, for the wrong act, for the bad deed; forgiveness, our Father. We do not know altogether what it is that we want beyond this. We see our lives, the goals which we have set for ourselves. And as we wait now in the quietness, these goals are weighted or held in tender balance before Thy scrutiny and Thy caring, and we see them in a new light. And we trust that somehow as we move into the tasks that await us, the radiance which we sense now will cast a long glow to guide us in tomorrow's darkness.

We are mindful also of all kinds of needs in the world. Those needs which are close at hand and about which we have had some superficial concern, which we have met casually out of the richness of our own sense of surplus. There are other needs at which we have not dared to look, our Father, because we fear what our response to such needs might make us do or become lest we find all of the careful plans of our lives upset and the goals which we have put in focus thrown out of line or discarded, because as we look into the depths of certain needs we cannot ever be ourselves in happiness and peace again; this is too costly for us. Yet, our Father, as we wait here, these needs move before us. We hear the cry and the anguish of the destitute, of the hungry, of the hopeless, of the despairing. We cannot be deaf, but we don't know what to do. We don't know how to give and not destroy ourselves. O God, deal with our disorder with redemptive tenderness so that we, as we live our tomorrows, may not be ashamed of Thy grace that has made our lives move in such tranquil places. These are all the words we have. Take them and let them say to Thee the words of our hearts and our spirits.

We Don't Know How (1969)
Howard Thurman

We find it very difficult, our Father, to bring to a point of focus all of the fragmentation and divisiveness of our lives. We ask Thee to draw upon Thy long experience with Thy children, and out of this special wisdom and understanding, to interpret the words which we say to Thee in our prayer. We are overwhelmed by our great inability somehow to manage the imperfections of life, the imperfections of our own private lives, the clear insight which suddenly becomes dim and often disappears at the moment when we are sure that we could act upon it; the good deed which we express and which, as it leaves us, wings on its way to fulfill itself in another's life, in another's need. And as we watch, we are horrified at the way in which something goes wrong and the good deed is not a good deed in the way in which it works, and we are thrown back upon ourselves. We don't know how to manage the imperfections of our lives, the imperfections of so many expressions of our lives.

We have brooded over nature. We have understood here and there some of its inner mandates, and we have been able to translate these mandates into expressions of machinery and objects, and we have learned how to operate these machines and to make these objects, created out of our insights, expressions of our intent. We have made these things into servants to obey our minds and our wills and then, suddenly, we are faced with radical and quick and devastating breakdown! Something goes wrong, we do not know what, and there is mindless violence and destruction. We don't know how to manage the imperfections of our lives.

Now we wait for the fateful moment when once again we ourselves as a nation will begin learning, with more finesse and accuracy, to kill, to destroy. And we feel, some of us, that the only way to survive is to do this, and some of us are sure that this is but to hasten the end of the age.

How to manage the imperfections of our minds and our spirits, our thoughts, even our intent? O God, we don't know how. We don't know how. We don't know how. Take all the outcry of our anguish, all the sin and brokenness of our faltering selves and hold them with such sureness that we learn from Thee.

Give Me a Clean Heart (1970)

Margaret Pleasant Douroux

Give me a clean heart so I may serve Thee.
Lord, fix my heart so that I may be used by Thee.
For I'm not worthy of all these blessings.
Give me a clean heart and I'll follow Thee.

I'm not asking for riches of the land.
I'm not asking for the proud to know my name.
Please give me, Lord, a clean heart, that I may follow thee.
Give me a clean heart, a clean heart and I will follow thee.

(Sometimes) I am up and sometimes I am down.
Sometimes I am almost level to the ground.
Please give me, Lord, a clean heart, that I may follow thee.
Give me a clean heart, a clean heart and I will follow thee.

Memorial Prayer at Howard University in Memory of Dr. Martin Luther King (1970)
Smallwood Edmond Williams

Eternal God, in the name of the Lord Jesus Christ, we would thank Thee today that Thou hast honored the purpose of our gathering. We thank Thee for sending unto us, this Nation, and the world our great departed leader, Dr. Martin Luther King, Jr., the late possessor of unique gifts, dignity, graces, and eloquence of rare beauty. He was profoundly inspiring and challenging to his generation. The potency of his personality was marked by social progress, moral, and ethical reform.

Thou sent him to us as Thou sent Moses to Egypt to deliver the Hebrew people from slavery and bondage. We sincerely pray that the rich heritage of his philosophy may continue to inspire our Nation and Race to develop a social order of love, equality, brotherhood, compassion for black people, poor people, socially disinherited people, with dignity and justice for all people.

May the torch of non-violence which he held so high continue to burn brightly in spite of the gross darkness that is covering our world today. May we never permit his dream to be an impossible dream. May we never surrender to the enemy which he fought so courageously, so bravely, and heroically to the end.

In his dwelling place among the immortals, grant that there be no future postponement, procrastination, and delay of the righteous demands that he made on the American establishment for a regeneration of our Society.

> "Minorities since time began
> Have shown the better side of man,
> And often in the list of time
> One man has made a cause sublime."

In His Name. Amen.

A Prayer for a Positive Attitude (1972)
Leon H. Sullivan

Now, great God, give us thy power to believe in ourselves, and in what we can do, and in what we can be, and in what we are. May the grace of Jesus Christ be with us all. Amen.

Good Friday Declarations of Awareness (1972)
M. Moran Weston

O God, we acknowledge we do not see clearly, nor fully understand: open our eyes and our perception.

O God, we acknowledge we have too often been unwilling to march on the seat of power to cleanse church, government and the marketplace from corruption which defiles man and defies God.

O God, we acknowledge, we have too often been unwilling to take a stand and keep it no matter what the cost:

> *grant us wisdom, grant us courage*
> *for the facing of this hour.*[1]

O God, we acknowledge we have too often been unwilling to face the agents of corrupt power without fear or flinching: grant us the moral power to hold our ground.

O God, we acknowledge we have too often retreated and given ground under the backlash of the Establishment; we have too often run away and deserted those called by God to lead the eternal confrontation of injustice and evil:

> *grant us wisdom, grant us courage*
> *for the living of these days.*

O God, we acknowledge that too often we have failed under cross examination on the witness stand; too often we have lost our nerve when prosecutor, witnesses, jury, and judge have conspired with a blood-thirsty mob to render a verdict of "guilty" and a sentence of "death":

---

[1] This quotation is from Harry Emerson Fosdick's great hymn titled "God of Grace and God of Glory," which can be found in most Protestant hymnals.

grant us wisdom, grant us courage
lest we miss thy kingdom's goal.

O God, we acknowledge that too often we have refused to become involved, we have sought refuge from the battle by being a sightseer or spectator: may we be inspired to follow the example of Thy chosen ones who have been involved until the bitter end, even at the cost of their life.

O God, we acknowledge that too often we have not had confidence in Thy power to bring light out of darkness, good out of evil; by faith we believe through Thy chosen one Jesus the Carpenter, People's Leader, Chosen One, Prisoner, Defendant, Condemned Man and Confident Man, that good will indeed overcome evil, love overcome hate, and life overcome death.

[May we] go forth into the world with courage and confidence, [and] be ready to confront evil without retreating, knowing that men and women, young and old, chosen and called by God will receive power to stand fast against evil, and to triumph day by day.

Benediction (1973)
William Lee Ransome

Almighty God, we thank thee for the hours we have spent on this campus. Every now and then when the way seems dark, you give us a little sample of what is better further along. We have been encouraged this week by the fact that what we have received is a sample of that which is waiting for those who hold out and prove faithful to the end. We are like the ox who is pulling the load up the hill, and about to give out; when the driver gets out of the ox cart and carries a little food up the hill—the oxen know the food is up there, by faith they pull harder. We are gonna pull harder now. We are gonna cut more deeply. We are gonna believe more firmly. We are gonna hold more assuredly, because one thing you told Peter, "that the gates of hell will not prevail against the church."[1]

Help us to go back now. When Samson wanted to burn down the wheat fields of the Philistines, he got a hundred or so foxes and tied their tails together. He struck one match and lighted all those fiery tails and turned them loose among the wheat fields of the Philistines. When the foxes got through, the enemies of God didn't have nothing to feed on.[2] We've been tied together here this week.

The Servant of God has lighted our hearts with the candle of Thy Word. He's turning us loose now! We're going out into the world, and we're gonna burn down hell and the kingdom of Satan in this age!

May the grace of God and the sweet communion of the Holy Spirit and the peace that passeth all understanding, abide with us until that same Jesus, who went into the first airship, manned by two pilots, ascended out of sight, and the angel said, "In like manner He's coming again."

And when He comes, when He comes, all those looking for Him

---

[1] See Matthew 16:13–19 (KJV).

[2] See Judges 15:1–5.

by faith will be with Him and shall never separate from that Holy Church.

Where shadows never fall, calendars never bedeck walls, funerals are never had, and parting is no more.

On the sea of glass, we will retire. Palms of victory in our hands,[3] we will wave to Him who shall reign forevermore.

---

[3] See John 12:12–13.

Lord, Help Me to Hold Out (1974)

James Cleveland

Lord, help me to hold out,
Lord, help me to hold out,
Lord, help me to hold out
    until my change comes.

My way may not be easy
You did not say that it would be.
But if it gets dark,
I can't see my way,
You told me to put my trust in Thee,
    that's why I'm asking You.

Lord, help me to hold out,
Lord, help me to hold out,
Lord, help me to hold out
    until my change comes.

Lord, help me to hold out!
Lord, help me to hold out!
Lord, help me to hold out!
Lord, help me to hold out!
Lord, help me to hold out!
Lord, help me to hold out!

I believe that I can hold out!
I believe that I can hold out!
I believe that I can hold out,
    until my change comes.

Dear Jesus, I Love You (1976)

Walter Hawkins

Dear Jesus, I love you.
Dear Jesus, I love you,
You're a friend of mine.
You supply my every need.
My hungry soul You feed.
I'm aware You are my source
From which all blessings flow,
And with this thought in mind
I know just where to go.

The Prayers of Our Grandmothers (1977)

Jesse Louis Jackson

Last, there is a prayer tradition that emerges from the black church. My grandmother doesn't have any money, doesn't know anything about a balance sheet, but she knows the worth of prayer. My grandmother doesn't have any education, she can't read or write, but she's never lost. She knows the worth of prayer. She's never taken a course on nutrition at the university and can't read the directions of Betty Crocker, but she's a chemist in the kitchen. She knows the worth of prayer. To the world she has no name, and she has no face, but she feels she has cosmic importance because there's a God she communicates with in heaven who is eternal. And so she knows that every boss is temporary, that every rainy day is temporary, that every hardship is temporary. She used to tell me, "Son, every goodbye ain't gone. Just hold on; there's joy coming in the morning." I used to wonder how she made it. I went back and got one of those old prayers they used to pray down in Long Branch Baptist Church. I don't know whether or not you can read all six hundred pages of *Roots*[1] or not. I hope you understand Kunta Kinte. I hope you understand some of the African terminology, but there's a tradition that we've kept that hasn't been on NBC or CBS or ABC, and UPI and AP haven't picked it up. These are our roots, and they run underground today.

> I thank Thee, Lord, for sparing me this morning, for the blood running warm in my veins, for the activity of my limbs and the use of my tongue. I thank thee, Lord, for raiment and for food, and, above all, I thank Thee for the gift of Thy darling Son, Jesus, who came all the way from heaven down to this low ground of sorrow, who died upon the cross that "whosoever believeth upon him should not perish but have everlasting life."[2] Our Lord, our Heavenly Master, we ask Thee to teach us and guide us in the way we know not. Give us more faith and a bet-

---

[1] See Alex Haley, *Roots* (Garden City, NY: Doubleday, 1976).

[2] See John 3:16 (KJV).

ter understanding and a closer walk to Thy bleeding side. I have a faith to believe, Lord, that you are the same God that was in the days that are past and gone. Thou heard Elijah pray in the cleft of the mountain;[3] Thou heard Paul and Silas in jail;[4] Thou heard three children in the fiery furnace.[5] I have a faith to believe that you once heard me pray when I was laying and lugging around the gates of hell with no eye to pity me and no arm to save me. Thou reached down your long arm of protection, snatched my soul from the midst of eternal burning. Thou placed a new song in my mouth. Thou told me to go and you would go with me, to open my mouth and you would speak to me. For that cause, Lord, we call upon you this hour. And we call upon Thee; we ask you don't go back to glory, neither turn a deaf ear to our call, but turn down the kindness of a listening ear. Catch our moan and our groan, and take them home with you in the high heavens. We plead bold one thing more, oh Lord, if it is Thy glorious will, I pray Thee, O Lord, our Heavenly Master. We ask Thee to search our hearts, tie the reins of our mind, and if Thou see anything laying and lugging around our hearts that not your right hand planteth and neither is pleasing to Thy sight, we ask Thee to remove it by the brightness of your coming; cast it into the sea of forgiveness, where it will never rise up against us in this world, neither condemn us at the bar of judgement, if it's Thy will. Oh God, our Heavenly Father, we ask Thee to make us a better servant in the future than we have been in the past. We thank Thee, our Heavenly Father; won't you have mercy. Please remember the sick and the afflicted, the poor and those in hospitals, bodies racked with pain, scorched with parch and fever. Have mercy on them, if it's Thy glorious will.

This is our tradition; these are our roots. "Come by here, Lord," somebody said, "come by here." Not songs with complicated lines but songs that the salt of the earth can sing. Not only "Lord, come by

---

[3] This biblical reference is unclear. Perhaps the allusion is to Elijah's flight from Jezebel's attempt to have him killed. He goes to a cave in Mount Horeb and has a momentous encounter with God's Spirit. See I Kings 19:9–15.

[4] See Acts 16:25–40.

[5] Daniel 3:8–30.

here," but I got a mother down in Georgia and I want you to go by there, oh Lord, won't you come by here. I heard somebody else say, well, Lord, I'm gonna wait. I gonna wait 'cause I can't do nothing 'til you come. I'm gonna hold on to your unchanging hand. Then long before they knew about Jesus, in the Old Testament, they say we know you can part the waters and you can come to us in the midnight hour. The church has been our rock in a weary place. The church has been our foundation in ages past.

Help Me, Lord, to Stand for the Kingdom (1978)

James Alexander Forbes, Jr.

O Lord, here we stand. We've heard the experience of Peter and John and then we've heard the experience of that John who was on the Isle of Patmos. We see the handwriting on the wall. Times are going to get tough. Lord, we've committed ourselves to the Kingdom. To-night we want to rededicate. We want to rededicate, and say Lord, "Here I am, send me." Some folks may not like me. I may lose my job. I may be called first one thing and another. But Lord, help me to know how to be wise. Don't make a fool out of me unless you let me be a fool for Christ's sake.

Lord, teach us how to bear witness. Teach us how to be sensitive. Teach us where we are to stop. We can't be everywhere. Take us by the hand, and lead us to the temples that you'd like us to stop by. Let us see the lame men and women that you would want us to help. Then give us the strength to get up on our feet. Enable us to declare with all that is within us that the Kingdoms of this world must become the Kingdoms of Jesus Christ.

Lord, help us. Help us, Lord. Help me, Lord. Help me in my post of duty. I'm a teacher, Lord; help me as a teacher. Lord, I'm a preacher. Sometimes the powers that urge me to compromise are very strong. But help me, Lord, to stand up for the Kingdom.

Lord, there are pastors here who are trying to serve, who are trying to love, who are not about anything radical. But in our day, Lord, just to be a Christian encourages others to view them in a negative light. Lord, be with them. Be with them as they return with a dedication to your cause. While we wait here, Lord, I don't know how you are going to be with us in these days. Some people have their own notions of how you anoint your people. Some want outward demonstrations. Some want inward demonstrations. But, Lord, it matters not to me how you are going to be with us. I just want you to come and be with us.

Lord, fill us with the inward light. Give us, like you gave many Quakers, the powers of the spirit to bear witness in trying times. Lord, give us a Pentecostal power to somehow clean out the carbon in our hearts so that we might run with joy and enthusiasm. Lord, any way you want to bless us, bless us. Bless us in the midst of quietness. Bless us in the midst of noise. Bless us with an inward penetration, or with an outward demonstration, of your presence. But however you do it, Spirit of the living God, fall afresh on each one of us. Lord, break up our kingdom. Melt down the fragments, then mold us, Lord; and then fill us with the Spirit of the living God. Fall afresh upon us while we stand right here in this chapel tonight, do something for us. Do something for us that makes us know that you are still real. Do something for us that lets us know we're not alone. Do something for us, Lord, that sends us on our way fully confident that the power of God is more than a match for the enemy.

Lord, sustain us, lead us, and guide us. And when we get low, lift us; and when we get wrong, correct us. And when we go out on the deep end, give us a life raft to bring us back to the shore. But Lord, be with us and stand by us. And your name which is worthy to be above all other names shall have all the praise. We ask for these blessings in the name of the One whose Kingdom shall have no end. Amen.

Pray for the Christian Family (1978)

Fred C. Lofton

Thou who art the Giver of families and family life, we beseech Thee to hear our prayer and Thanksgiving. We are thankful for our family. Mother laid a firm foundation for our family and our lives. Our parents believed in the love of God and the sustaining power of God through the storms and stresses of life. By fervently believing in Thee, they imparted to us a religious heritage as solid as the "Rock of Ages." Our sisters and brothers were taught the meaning of prayer in their personal and collective lives. Every day in our home was lived in constant prayer and meditation. Mother inbred us with a love and appreciation for the Church. Its lofty hopes and aspirations propelled us onward and upward.

Mutual love and cooperation were instilled in us early as children. Each, O God, knew he had a place, a role, an individual responsibility to the welfare of our home and corporate lives. Our relationships were fostered by mutual respect, love, and admiration for the skills and talents of each other.

O dear Father, I thank Thee for the skillful and tactful manner in which strife and ill-will were prevented in our home. Jesus knew every feud and argument. Believing in Him completely, we submitted our problems to Him. His revolutionary tactics always made us more willing to give than to receive, more willing to love than to hate, more willing to forgive than to be forgiven, more willing to see the mote in our own eye than the beam in another's eye, more willing to give the cloak than to keep it, more willing to go two miles than just one, more willing to suffer than to inflict pain, more willing to learn than to presume to know.

We were taught, O Father, never to forget Thee. Things were always placed before Thee. Our commitments to ourselves always were considered after we had committed all we had to Thee. We sought Thy will and purpose for our lives.

And finally, Lord of hosts, we are thankful for the closeness in our homes which never allowed us to forget some wayward pilgrim along life's journey. In the stresses and strains of life, we were taught to serve Thee better by serving our fellowman. So in all kinds of weather our shelter became a haven for ships tossed at sea.

In His name. Amen.

You Know the Purpose of Our Gathering, Jesus (1980)

James Brown

Our Father who art in heaven
Hallowed be thy name
Thy kingdom come, Lord
Let thy holy and righteous
Will be done on this earth
As your will was already done in heaven
Give us Lord this day
As our daily bread
You forgive those who have sin
And trespass against us
 Amen
Lead us not into sin neither temptation
But, please deliver us from evil
 Yes!
O Lord that thine may be our kingdom
We expecting your kingdom to be
Poor sinner glory
 O yeah!
Master Jesus, hear me
Another one of you servant
Bow this evening, Jesus
 Bow yes
 My Lord!
Sin anguished and bended
 Bended knees
Master, it's no lower
Could I come this evening
 No!
Excepting my knees are down at the floor
 Floor.
Guilty heart within
Crying guilty and already condemned
 Condemned.

Crying to you this evening Jesus
For mercy
Yeah
Uh hum
While mercy can reach
As you say the foxes of the forest
Yes
Got hole
And then the birds of the air has nest
Yes!
Master, we are poor son of man
Pray now!
No where to lay down weary head
Yeah!
Father we down here this evening
O yeah!
Heavenly Father
Asking for your mercy
While mercy can reach us
Yes, oh yeah
Father, while traveling over the mortal
Vineyard this afternoon
We ask you to please drop water here
Yes.
Don't leave us alone to oneself
Uh uh.
Neither in the hands of the wicked man
Ah yeah!
Lead us though in the tempting of old Satan
Oh yeah!
Have mercy if thou, on us so please.
We are here this evening, Jesus
Oh yeah
We can't do nothing without you
Uh huh
Come Holy Spirit, Heavenly Dove
Oh yeah
With all thou quickening power
Power!

Kindle the flame of our Savior love
    Yeah!
In these cold hearts of ours
    Cold
Master, look how we are graveling here below
    Oh yeah!
Trying to find our earthly toys
    All right
Master, our poor soul can't find a goal
    Yeah
But we trying to reach an eternal joy
    Joy
Have mercy, if thou only so please
    So please
And then, then my God
    My Lord
While traveling from Jericho maybe going to
Jerusalem
    Uh hum
We want you to come in this building
    Yes
One more time
Want you to touch us this evening Jesus
    Yes
Realize this evening Father
    Oh yeah
We are nothing but a chafe before the wind
    Before the wind
We get raindrop in the morning just as
Bloom of the lily
By noon we cut off wilt and die
    Die!
Have mercy, if thou only so please
    O yeah
And then, then my God
    My God
You know the purpose of our gathering
Jesus
    Yes

We ask you to please strengthen us
Oh yeah.
We are weak
And build us where we are tearing down
Tearing down
Here we are trying to celebrate this twentieth
Anniversary, Jesus
Oh yeah
Give us faith that will not shrink
Mercy!
But oppressed by every folding
And then, then my God
Then, my God!
We ask you to look at the leaders
Oh yeah!
From one to another Jesus
Oh yeah!
Make them ushers of sound judgement
Yes.
Then truly devoted to God
We realize heavenly Father
Yes
From, from July last gone
O yeah
What trouble have I seen
Yes
What conflict have I bear
Oh yeah
Sometime I ben fighting within
Yeah
And fear without
Since I assembled last.
Yes!
Then, then my God
My God!
I want you to bless each and every usher
Jesus
Uh hum
Help them to please hold out and hold on

Yes

Help them to follow building a household of God
  Oh yes!

And then, then my God
    Yes Lord!
    Then!

Help them not to wear a uniform
To be seen
But only to be a child of God
    God!

Help them to say:
I want to be the child of God
    Pure heart!

And then, then I want my sins forgiven
    Oh yeah!

Want my spirit meek and mild
    Uh hum

I want to get to heaven when I die
    Oh yeah!

Do show me Lord, thy way.
    Oh yeah!

And then guide me on thy road
    Oh yeah!
    Oh Lord

And then, then my God
Never to let me go astray
    Astray

Until I get home to thee
    Yes Lord!

And then, then heavenly Father
    Oh yeah

Look at Reverend Pinckney one more time
    Oh yeah!

Who is going [to] unfold the word of eternal truth
    Oh yeah!

Want you to please, dear Jesus
Give him a silver trumpet
    Uh huh!

He can coax and call some more ushers into this fold

Oh yes!
And then, then, then my Master
   My Lord!
Look at the mistress of ceremonies, Jesus
   Oh yeah!
Want you to plant her deep down in the soil Master
   Oh yeah!
Where she'll never be rooted by the storm of life
   O yeah!
Then, then my God
   My God
Want you to look at [New] Jerusalem [A.M.E.
   Church] one more time
   Oh yeah!
Help them to say:
Jerusalem my happy home
   Yes! Yes Lord!
So never dear to me
   Oh yeah!
And then, then Jesus
   Uh huh!
Then, then Lord
   Amen!
When, Master Jesus
   Oh yeah
Me too got to pull off mortal
   That what you got to do
   Oh yeah!
Put on mortality
Because then Jesus
Going down by the river of Jordan
   Jordan
Gonna stake my sword in the golden sand
   Oh yeah
Because Master Jesus
   Master Jesus!
Wouldn't had to study war no more.
   Oh yeah!
And then Lord

Lord!
I can hear her say
Must I be that judgement bar
All right
Must I be
Answer in thy day
Oh yeah!
Every vain or idle thought
And for every word I say
Say now!
For every secret of my heart
Oh yeah!
Will shortly be made known
And then Lord
Then Lord!
I will go home and get
My just resolve
Oh yeah!
For all that I have done
Done!
And when, Lord
My Lord
Want you to meet me Jesus
Somewhere Lord, Job declare:
O yeah!
The wicked must cease in trouble
Trouble!
And my soul have rest
Rest
Tis thy servant's prayer, Master.
Amen.
Amen! Amen!
Yeah! Yeah! Sir!
All right!

A Prayer before the Everlasting Fountain

(1980)

Gardner Calvin Taylor

Our Father and our God, we open now our very souls before Thee, for something within us craves food which the bread of this world cannot satisfy. We would slake our thirst at the everlasting fountain.

We thank Thee for all Thou hast done for us, for the way Thou hast shepherded us and provided for us all this journey through, for family and friends and the fulfillment of daily work. Above all, for Jesus Thy Son, our Lord.

We lift before Thee our nation, so splendid in possibility, so stricken and uncertain in this moment of its history. Give us again the vision of a nation under God, moving to be what Thou wouldest have us be and to do what Thou dost bid us do. We pray for all political prisoners and, indeed, for all who languish in cells anywhere. Likewise we hold up before Thee those who have come within sight of the grave. Sustain them. Bless our young people seeking to find the point and purpose of their lives. Bless all who are here and those who worship with us beyond this visible company.

Bless this Church and Thy churches everywhere. Put on Thy churches' lips the old Gospel of Bethlehem and Galilee and Calvary's resurrection morning. Come Thou among us. Set the fires of God burning afresh in our hearts.

Let the words we utter here with our mouths and the thoughts we think with our hearts, be acceptable in Thy sight, O Lord our strength and our Redeemer.

Through Jesus Christ our Lord we make our petition—Amen.

The Classic African-American Folk Prayer (1981)

{Melva W. Costen}

Almighty! and all wise God our heavenly father! 'tis once more and again that a few of your beloved children are gathered together to call upon your holy name. We bow at your footstool of mercy, Master, to thank you for our spared lives. We thank you that we are able to get up this morning clothed in our right mind, for Master, since we met here, many have been snatched out of the land of the living and hurled into eternity. But through your goodness and mercy we have been spared to assemble ourselves here once more to call upon a Captain who has never lost a battle. Oh, throw round us your strong arms of protection. Bind us together in love and union. Build us up where we are torn down and strengthen us where we are weak. Oh, Lord! Oh, Lord! take the lead of our minds, place them on heaven and heavenly divine things. Oh, God, our Captain and King! Search our hearts, Master, as far as the east is from the west. Now Lord you know our hearts, you know our heart's desire. You know our down-setting and our up-rising. Lord you know all about us 'cause you made us. Lord! Lord! One more kind favor I ask you. Remember the man that is to stand in the gateway and proclaim your Holy Word. Oh, stand by him. Strengthen him where he is weak and build him up where he is torn down. Oh, let him down into the deep treasures of your word.

And now oh, Lord, when this humble servant is done down here in this low land of sorrow: done sitting down and getting up: done being called everything but a child of God; oh, when I am done, done, done, and this old world can afford me no longer, right soon in the morning, Lord, right soon in the morning, meet me down at the river of Jordan, bid the water to be still, tuck my little soul away in that low swinging chariot, and bear it away over yonder in the third heaven where every day will be Sunday and my sorrows of this old world will have an end, is my prayer for Christ's my Redeemer's sake and amen and thank God.

The Plea of a Raped Woman (1982)
{Alice Walker}

Dear God,

He act like he can't stand me no more. Say I'm evil an always up to no good. He took my other little baby, a boy this time. But I don't think he kilt it. I think he sold it to a man an his wife over Monticello. I got breasts full of milk running down myself. He say Why don't you look decent? Put on something. But what I'm sposed to put on? I don't have nothing.

I keep hoping he fine somebody to marry. I see him looking at my little sister. She scared. But I say I'll take care of you. With God help.

A Prayer for Healing (1983)

Richard Daniel Henton

God in heaven, we thank Ya because healing is the children's; because you're the answer to all our problems; and you're the cure for our ills. And as we look to Thee tonight, we don't have to tell you to go nowhere. You're already there.

You're omnipotent. That is to say, you're all powerful.
You're omniscient. That is to say, you're all knowing.
You're omnavision. You see everything.
You're omnaglory. The whole earth is full of your glory.
And in the name of Jesus, I pray that those that are sick,
 that's suffering
 and tired of being sick
 and tired of the pain
 and tired of the shots,
  Gawd, my Savior,
 tired of one operation after another,
 Stretch out your hands in the Name of Jesus!

Jee-sus! My friend in God. Touch now! Touch now! Touch the fever! Touch the cancer! Touch that tumor! [Touch] that malignant growth!

Heal that blood pressure! Heal that heart condition! Heal that consumption—the tuberculosis! Heal the hemorrhoids! In the Name of Jesus.

Devil, I come against you in the Name that you cannot stand [against]—the Name that's above everything. It cries out against you. You're a defeated foe. Christ overcome ya. You're a defeated foe. He bruised your head with his heel. You enemy of righteousness. You snake in the grass. I come against you. The birch of the Cross. The blood of Jesus prevails against you.

Heal now in that hospital room, in that bedroom. Heal now, in the Name of Jesus. Let the pain subside. Give a miracle of healing. Give a miracle of healing.

Stop that man from groanin'.
Stop that woman from moanin'.
Heeealll! by the wound in your side.
Healll! for your glory tonight.

Yeahhh! Thou balm in Gilead. You're a balm in Gilead. And we call Your Name because earth has no sorrow that heaven cannot heal. Heal! Let virtue go-out-on-ether-waves! Let healing virtue go in every hospital. Let the healing virtue go out.

> Heeealll!
> Saaave!
> Lift!
> Healll!
> Move oppression!
> Lift the Burden.
> Move obsession!
> Move possession! in Jesus' Name.

Let the hand of God be over the city. Let the hand of God be over every home and every hospital.

> Some-boddy. Some-body is looking for a miracle.
> You're a miracle worker.
> You're a wonder worker.
> Yeahh!
> Yess!

You're a wonder worker! In Jesus' Name[,] I'm lookin' for it. I prayed. We agreed. We believe You because I heard You say in Your Word "If two on earth would agree as touching anything that shall ask it shall[,] it shall be done."

We thank You. We thank You. We thank You for the victory. We thank You for the answer. We thank Ya for healin'. We thank You for the answer. We thank Ya for healing. We thank Ya for salvation! Ha! Yeahh!

Glory to God Wonderful Jesus. Haya [glossolalia ensues]. Ha! Wonderful Jesus. Let Your Name be exalted. Let Your Name be exalted. Let Your Name raise in the hearts of the people. Lift Your people everywhere. Let the weak say that I'm strong. Let the discouraged say I'm gonna make it in the Name of Jesus.

Yeahh! Wonderful Son of God. Hallelujah. It is so. It is so. It is so. Thank You, Jesus. Hallelujah. Somebody say "How do you know it is so?" I'm gon' tell Ya why I know it's so. [Rev. Henton then starts singing, "Something really happened and I know, He touched me and He made me whole."]

O God, Slow Us Down (1983)

George Thomas

O God, slow us down and help us to see that we are put in charge of our lives, but with thy help. Help us to get in tune with the rhythm that makes for life.

We keep moving, even though we know that we are made to center down, as well as to be actively engaged in the business of life. We compete for things and make those things more important than they ought to be. We eat what we ought not to eat. We neglect and misuse our bodies. We fail to discipline our minds and to be still and know that thou art God and that we are the temple of the Most High. Yet we often complain about our misfortunes and our hard luck, when at times it is we who are guilty of disregard.

Help us to know that we can be broken by life only if we first allow the victory of evil over our spirits.

May our hope and strength and faith be grounded in you; and may we recall the strength of our model, our brother and your Son. Amen.

Thank You for Each One of Them (1984)

William Townsend Crutcher

Our Father in Heaven, we come at this hour to express our sincere thanks for another year. We are thankful that you have spared these lives, and that you have brought them all the way through another year.

We pray that, as they conclude this old year and begin a new one, they will find joy, that they will find happiness, that they will find grace sufficient to take care of their needs. Our Father, we thank you for each one of them.

We thank you that they are still *here,* that they can still *hear,* that they are still able to *feel,* that they are still able to *walk,* and that they are still able to *talk.* We just want to thank you for these blessings as well as others.

Oh God, bless them. Bless their homes that they may continue to live in your light. Bless each one here this morning, as well as those who were unable to come. Enable us to do the things that you would have us to do.

And oh God, great God, we just thank you! We thank you Jesus! You have been so good to us! You have brought us such a long way. You lifted us up when we were down! You healed our sick bodies! You brought us a very long way. We want to thank you for it. You have fed us, and kept us from being hungry. You have opened doors that were closed in our face. We want to thank you for it this morning.

And, oh God, we don't know whether we will be here another year or not! We can't depend on that. But we know that wherever we are, that where you are, everything will be all right! We want to thank you this morning, our Father. Take our hands and lead us on. We ask in your name. Amen.

Lord, We Didn't Come Here to Stay (1984)

{Wyatt Tee Walker}

No self-respecting black pray-er would think of closing a prayer in a service of worship without clear mention of last things. As preaching is eschatological, so is praying, perhaps more so.

"Now Lord, we know that we didn't come here to stay always. We know this earth is not our home. We're just pilgrims making our way through this waste howling wilderness. One day soon and very soon you're going to send your angel to fetch us one by one. You promised us that if we'd be faithful, you'd have a crown waiting for us. I want my crown. I want to be in that number that John saw, coming from the north, south, east and west—that number that no man can number.[1] We don't mind dying Lord; if this earthly tabernacle shall dissolve, Paul said we got another building not made with hands, eternal in the heavens.[2] I want to be in that number! I want to go to that land where Job said the wicked shall cease from troubling and the weary shall be at rest.[3] Every day will be Sunday; no more good-byes, just howdy, howdy. I want to be in that number. I want to see the Blessed Lamb upon the throne.[4] We'll sing in the heavenly choir:

> All hail the power of Jesus name
> Let angels prostrate fall
> Bring forth the royal diadem
> And crown Him, crown Him
> Crown Him, Lord of all.

"Oh, I want to be in that number. I want to hear your welcome voice say, 'Well done.' Grant unto us a resting place in your kingdom and we'll give you honor, praise and glory throughout ceaseless ages. Amen. Amen."

---

[1] See Revelation 7:9 (KJV).

[2] See II Corinthians 5:1 (KJV): "For we know that if our earthly house of this tabernacle were dissolved, we have a building of God, an house not made with hands, eternal in the heavens."

[3] Job 3:17 (KJV).

[4] See Revelation 7:10–17.

A Benediction for a Church Ground Breaking Service (1989)
Benjamin Stanley Baker

And now, O God, we know that there is no other foundation that can be laid other than Jesus Christ. As co-laborers with Him[,] let us now have a mind to do Your work, to build this edifice for Your honor and glory that men and women who are in the darkness may come to the light, and those in the storm may come here as a refuge. Keep us in Your care[;] and as we depart from each other[,] may we never depart from You. In Jesus' name we pray. Amen.

Trying to See the Light (1989)

James Arthur Baldwin

Lord,
    when you send the rain,
    think about it, please,
    a little?

Do
    not get carried away
    by the sound of falling water,
    the marvelous light
    on falling water.

I
    am beneath that water
    It falls with great force
    and the Light

Blinds
    me to the light.

A Peace and Affirmation Prayer (1989)

Johnnie Colemon

What [should] we do about peace? We can speak positive words. We can pray together. On your bulletin here, the first thing we have is peace for ourselves because everything must begin with me. Jesus said, "My peace I give unto you."[1] In the silence of my soul[,] I would claim peace. All is peace and harmony in my world, for God in me i[s] the Lord of Peace. I am the consciousness of God in action. I am always at peace. My mind is poised, serene and calm.

In this atmosphere of peace and good which surround me, I feel a deep abiding strength and freedom from all fear. I now sense and feel the love and beauty of His Holy presence. Day by Day, I am aware of God's love. All that is unlike God falls away. I see God manifesting in all people.

I know that as I allow this inner peace to flow through my being, I am a channel for peace, blessing mankind. I consciously dwell in the love and peace of God. Jesus Christ is here and now raising me, raising us to His consciousness of oneness with God and all people. Our prayer is for peace for all our world leaders[,] and for all nations through the power of Jesus Christ.

I am inspired to speak words of wisdom, words of life, words of health, words of love for the world and the nations. The Christ mind is the inspiration and guide for the leaders of our United States, for all nations everywhere, and they make wise and loving decisions through the Christ Mind. World leaders, you are united in thought, purpose, and understanding, and inspired to right action for the good of all mankind. [A]nd we know that peace is now being established wherever peace is needed.

Oh Thou kind Father-God, unite all. There are no separate nations in reality. All men belong to one country. All men belong to one nation. The White light surrounds all people everywhere. The peace of God which passeth all understanding fills my mind, fills the minds

---

[1] See John 14:27 (KJV).

of the world leaders, fills the minds of people everywhere. Thank You, Father, for Thy peace. It is done according to Thy perfect Law; and that Law is established in the hearts of mankind everywhere. Dear Lord, make us an instrument of Thy peace. Thank You, God. Amen and amen.

Lord, I'm Willing (1989)

Genna Rae McNeil

Lord, it's more than I'll ever understand,
how I am preserved by thy hand.
But then there's only two things required of me:
to be faithful (because I've been set free)
and to be willing to be used by Thee.
So Lord I come willing to be used by Thee.

Refrain:
Lord, I'm willing.
Lord, I am willing your will and way to see.
Lord, I'm willing. Lord, I'm willing
Lord, I'm willing to be used by Thee.

'Though sometimes I don't feel worthy,
consecrate me. I'm saved, I'm not the same.
'Though the world may under-rate me,
dedicate me so I'll be wholly changed.

Lord, I'm willing. Here I stand.
Lord, I'm willing. Take my hand
and keep me by thy grace,
so I can run this race.

A Plea for Divine Presence (1989)

J. Alfred Smith, Sr.

Older than the morning stars that twinkled in the blackness of night's first birth, the rotation of the axis of time, bring us into the freshness of your mercy and the newness of your presence. We come to you today with heartfelt gratitude, not with mixing Judas paint with Judas praise in order to cover our hypocrisy. Some of us come to you with triumph over tragedy. Others of us come with enduring pain suffered from shameful defeat in an inescapable battle of life. Some of us feel like going on and others of us feel like giving up. But to you we come just as we are. Whether we are winners or losers, we know that you love us one and all. Greatest of the Greatest, you know just how much we can bear. We all come to commune with you:

> The tireless champion;
> The tired loser;
> The retired forgotten ones;
> We all come to be consistently corrected and comforted by
>   you.
> We come counting our lost.
> We come confronting our crises.
> We come as citizens of cities controlled by crime.
> We come chilled by the cold of cowardice.
> Great God Almighty:
> Commune with us conscience clean.
> Caress us with the cradle of compassion.
> Consecrate us with courageous convictions.
> Control us with Christlike concerns.
> Great Physician Powerful:
> Pardon us with the conscience of peace.
> Place us in paths of productivity.

Practice the perfection of healing upon those who are physically, emotionally, or spiritually sick.

This is our humble plea, we present in the precious Name of the prince of peace, Jesus Christ, our priceless priest. Amen.

An Altar Prayer (1989)
Jeremiah Wright, Jr.

With every heart turned toward God we come, Lord. [F]irst of all just to thank You this morning—to thank You for all Your blessings. [We come] to thank You for the opportunity of having some kneeling space [in order to have] a time to be alone with You in communion. [We come] to thank Thee for the joy and privilege of being with Your children in the House of Worship. [You have enabled us to join] in the Christian's most beneficial exercise . . . of talking friend with friend.

Lord, Thou has searched us and known us. We cannot come before You with any pretense this morning. We come open, [indeed] naked before the One who knows all about us. And as we sit or kneel, we realize that You see us worts and all. We are covered up with Sunday-go-to-meeting clothes and make-up and jewlry[;] but we realize that before You all the scars, the pain, and the *isness* of who we are is made evident before Thine eyes.

We thank You for not treating us like we've treated You, Lord.

We thank You for watching over us over this [past] week[.] [We thank You] for being a doctor in a sickroom [.] [We thank You] for opening up a way to provide a job for somebody who did not know how they were going to feed [their] family.

Lord, we thank You for watching over us last night[.] We thank You for the food we eat and the clothes on our backs. We thank You for loved ones and for family. We thank You most of all this morning for JESUS, the one who helps us hold on when we don't feel like it, the one who helps us keep on knowing that we are not moving all by ourselves.

And Lord, [as] we're holding hands[,] make our hearts touch one another as our hands are touching [as we seek] to be bound by Thy love[,] and bound to Thy precious bleeding side. [Yes] Lord, help us to be Your church outside this building [as we are now touching with heartfelt love inside this building.]

[Now] bless, Lord[,] the visitor within our gates. Bless the one who is making a decision about life and about Eternal Life in terms of accepting the call. You've been tugging and prodding and pulling them, and they have resisted[.] Lord, You know[,] and we know[,] that the Holy Spirit leads and draws them[.] [A]nd we just hold them up to You to continue to work with them.

[We ask you to] [b]less those homes that are coming apart at the seams. Bless those parents who wait anxiously for children to turn around toward an old Rugged Cross. Bless all Your people, Lord. You know our needs[;] and You never promised us to give us everything we say we wanted. But we thank You for supplying all our needs[,] and for having an answer to the prayers lifted up to You right now on the way already[.] Lord, we thank You.

Then, when we have done all You've assigned our hands and hearts to do[.] When it's Your turn to call and our turn to answer, Lord[;] [w]hen You meet us down at the River Jordan and bear us safely on the other side[,] we will be careful to give Your name the praise for we realize that *all* of these prayers are offered in Your name.

All of our blessings You give us in [that precious] Name[,] and [all] the petitions You give us are offered in [that precious] Name. And [yes,] we pray right now in the Name of Jesus, in the Name of Jesus[.] Let the Church say "Amen." Say "amen" again. One more time, my Father's children. Arise and know that He hears and answers prayer.

O God of Love, Power and Justice (1990)
James Alexander Forbes, Jr.

O God of love, Power and Justice, who wills the freedom and fulfillment of all your children. We thank you for the constancy of your loving kindness and tender mercies toward us. Especially on this day as we celebrate the birthday and life of your servant and prophet, Dr. Martin Luther King, Jr. We are reminded that in every age you raise up seers and sayers and doers of justice. We marvel at the way by which you shaped a young black boy from Georgia into a towering figure of his time—to awaken the conscience of the nations, to rekindle a passion for freedom, equality, and peace; to redirect the traffic of human affairs from the back alley of bigotry toward the grand concourse of courage and compassion. We stand in awe at the marvelous networking by which you built a movement around a man of vision. It included blacks and whites, Protestants, Catholics, and Jews, conservatives and progressives, rich and poor, business and labor. This "coalition of conscience" dedicated itself to the proposition that the American dream of freedom and equality could be made real through courageous action in a spirit of love, in pursuit of human dignity for all. This dignity includes all who suffer from homelessness, joblessness, purposelessness, carelessness, hopelessness.

Because our needs are so great today, and your care so constant, we know that you are rebuilding the network of compassion around new visionaries who you have assembled for this hour. Surprise us with the discovery of how much power we have to make a difference in our day:

—A difference in the way citizens meet, greet, respect, and protect the rights of each other.

—A difference in the breadth of our vision of what is possible in humanization, reconciliation, and equalization of results in our great city.

—A difference in the way government, business, and labor can work together, for justice and social enrichment.

—A difference in our response to the needy, and a difference in our appreciation for those who give of themselves for the surviving and thriving of our beautiful people.

Use this season of celebration to spark new hope and stir up our passion for new possibilities. Make compassion and the spirit of sacrifice to be the new mark of affluence of character. Strengthen us to face reality and to withstand the rigor of tough times in the anticipation of a bright side beyond the struggle. Inspire, empower, and sustain us until we reach the mountaintop, and see that future for which our hearts yearn.

This is our fervent and sincere prayer. Amen.

Dear God, If You Please (1992)

Matthew L. Watley

Dear God, if you please, let me be paranoid.
I know this sounds like the strangest request.
But it's the only thing can fill this void.
And until it is fulfilled, I'll find no rest.

It seems today that the world is against me,
The only reason being that my skin is black.
I try to convince myself this just isn't true,
Yet all of the evidence shows it as fact.

I see poor education and unequal chances.
I see people mistreated—their skin like mine.
I am told these things don't really exist,
But I just don't think they're all in my mind.

Why then would I still not believe?
Because I'd lose all my hope, I'd lose all faith.
If I accepted my suspicions simply as truth,
Then wouldn't this world be an evil place?

So God, you must see the need for me to be paranoid,
Then this world really wouldn't be so bad.
Then all that I see is not a true picture.
Lord, let me be paranoid so I know I'm not mad.

Dear God, My Son Prays (1992)
William Donnel Watley

Dear God, my son prays for healthy paranoia concerning the social ills that he sees and feels as a young black person. I pray for holy restlessness and sensitivity to the racism that still affects the lives and impacts the aspirations of your children of the African sun. As we view human sin at work in the world, we pray for wisdom to discern that you created a good earth and that out of one blood you have made all nations to dwell upon the face of the earth.

As we fight the good fight of justice and righteousness against racism and other sins, we pray that we will keep before us the original intent of creation and that we will not replace old tyrannies with new ones. In the midst of our struggles help us to always be able to see beauty and your image in others who may be different from us.

We pray for passion regarding those things that ought not to be. Save us from complacency—the proverbial "I have arrived" syndrome—that cuts off our compassion and empathy for others who have not yet been able to overcome the battering they have received by sin and the vicissitudes of life. Deliver us from the temptation to shut ourselves up in our own little corner of the world, being content with whatever modicum of comfort and security we have been graced to achieve.

God, grant us sensitivity without cynicism, righteous indignation devoid of bitterness, the wisdom of the serpent without its craftiness, the gentleness of the dove without its naiveté. Then, Lord, help us to direct all of this passion that we feel into meaningful action, we pray. Amen.

O God, Death Is All Around (1992)

William Donnel Watley

This prayer is Watley's response to the following poem, "Death," which was written by his son, Matthew L. Watley:

> Death stands at the gates of the hereafter
> As a sentry shrouded in fear and power,
> Guarding the entrance to eternal joy and laughter
> And haunting the people as they cower.
>
> For he knows that he will meet all of them
> And it won't be so grim.
> He knows that all want to come within,
> Though none want to see him.
>
> There he stands, that terrible sentry,
> Denying and inviting people entry;
> The helpless people he haunts and taunts,
> Taking from life those he wants.
>
> But there is a word of hope about our fate
> To save us from death's cruel ways.
> It is that he just stands at the gate,
> But death won't last always.
>
> For upon entry there is life
> Free of grieving, sorrow, and strife
> Where happiness lies in store,
> Meeting loved ones who have gone before.

O God, when I first read the poem on death, I asked myself, *Isn't this a strange subject for a young man to write about? Why is my son writing about death?* Then I looked at this world and his life and I understood why.

O God, death is all around. In the midst of life, death is present.

Death strikes down our young people before they really have a chance to live. Death, in the form of street violence, gang wars, drive-by shootings, and muggings over leather jackets and gold chains, takes away the flower of our youth while it is still in bud. Fatal encounters and death-dealing outbursts emerge from arguments over trifles. Death comes in slow form to those who have fallen victim to the drug scourge. Death is seen on the big screen in the theater and on the small screen in the home. Deaths are reported daily in the news.

More personally, my son has seen some of his peers buried. He has seen me as pastor bury church members whom he has known for most of his life. So death is a subject that he would reflect on.

However, as I read his poem, I noticed his lack of fear and the hope born of faith. I praise you for the hope that is ours as believers, the hope that now lives within the heart of my son. As a parent I pray that you would keep my children as they daily walk through mean streets. O God, hold them in your hands. Keep them from hurt, harm, and danger and bless them with long life that they might glorify you and fulfill their potential. This is my daily, heartfelt prayer that I lift before you. O God, have mercy. In Jesus' name, amen.

O God, I Get So Tired of Racism Wherever I Go (1992)

William Donnel Watley

O God, as a black man, I get exceedingly tired and so filled up with confronting and fighting racism, that formidable foe. It passes its poison from one generation to another. It has polluted all of the wellsprings of the nation's institutional life. More widespread than the drug scourge, more explosive than nuclear weapons, more crippling than germ warfare—racism has washed up on the shores of every nation of every continent.

O God, I get tired of racism wherever I go—abroad and at home. From stores that let me know that I have gotten "out of place"; from looks of fear that my black manly presence engenders in some; from small insults to major offenses; from polite, subtle, condescending paternalism or maternalism to outright, open hostility; from insulting jokes about my intelligence to curiosity about alleged black sexual prowess; from caricatures and stereotypes to the "you are the exception" syndrome—racism rears its many heads and shows its various faces all the time.

Yet as I bow before you, O God, I pledge to you, to my ancestors who sacrificed greatly so that I might enjoy whatever rights and privileges—however limited or circumscribed—are mine to experience, and to my children and to their children that I will keep up the noble fight of faith and perseverance. I will not go back to the back of the bus. I will not accept the invincibility of racism and the inviolability of its mythical sacred precepts.

I know that greater is the One that is in me than the one that is in the world. May that Spirit's presence and power direct and inspire me now and evermore until victory is won for my people, and all people, and until the kingdoms of this world become the kingdom of our Lord and of his Christ. Amen.

I Call Upon Your Name, Lord Jesus (1993)

Leroy Davis

This evening,
    O Heavenly Father,
        I come to You in humblest manner that I know.
I come,
    Lord Jesus,
        with a humble heart and a bowed head.
I come,
    Lord Jesus,
        because I'm standing in the need of prayer.
I call upon Your name,
    Lord Jesus,
        because I know no other name to call.
I come tonight,
    O God,
        asking that if You will, Lord Jesus, to have a blessing
        upon us right now.
Lord Jesus,
    bless the ones that are here under the sound of my weak voice.
Now Lord Jesus,
    for we know that the road is rough and rocky down here.
But just help us,
    Lord Jesus.
For afterwhile,
    Lord Jesus,
        we won't have to come in this building no more.
We'll be where we can praise Your name,
    Lord Jesus.
Where every day will be Sunday and the Sabbath will have no end.
And when we, too,
    Lord Jesus,
        must quit the walks of life,
We're asking that,

if You will,
    Lord Jesus,
to give us a place in Your Kingdom
    where we can praise Your name forever.
    Amen.

We Need Thee, Lord Jesus, As Never Before (1993)

Fred C. Lofton

Let us share in the gift of giving, the moment of prayer. This the House of Prayer for all people, and Lord Jesus, there are moments in our lives when we want to steal away. We want to get away from the clatter of our world and we want to find a quiet place where we can talk face to face with Thee. Our slave forefathers and mothers found the need and discovered a place where they could steal away, and forget the burdens of the world, the lashes on their backs, the crosses in their hearts.

We steal away this morning, Lord, for in many ways we are still like them. We are free, our Father, physically, but mentally we are still slaves. We do not believe in Black doctors, Black lawyers, Black financiers, Black teachers, Black preachers, Black businesses. We are still, our Father, mentally enslaved, believing that White is right. Show us that Thou hast a purpose for us, that Thou hast called us into existence to use our talents and our skills for the building of Thy kingdom on earth, that we have a rich legacy and a rich heritage that we can be proud of. We're stealing away this morning, Father, because we need to. Our Black manhood is being tested on every side. More of our sons are in jail than in college; more and more of our daughters are having children out of wedlock and boasting and bragging about it.

Have mercy on us, Lord. We're stealing away because the Black community seems to be under siege again—dope running rampant in our community; hoodlums and thugs have frightened our women; our churches are being broken into; houses are being burglarized; and we seem, our Father, to be destined to destroy ourselves. We need Thee, Jesus. Have mercy on us. And those of us who have made it out of the ghetto have forgotten about the rest of us still in the ghetto. Is there a Balm in Gilead?[1] Is there a word from the Lord for those at the bottom of the ladder? Is there a word? Is there a healing word, a word of hope?

---

[1] See Jeremiah 8:18–22.

We need Thee, Lord Jesus, as never before. We need Thee in our nursing homes and with those who are sick and shut-in and afflicted. We steal away for the burdens of the world cannot satisfy our spiritual yearnings. We need to share in the fellowship of the redeemed, to walk with one another, and to hear a healing word and a helping word from one another. Help us to care, to share and to dare. Teach us how to be strong and how to be brave, stalwart soldiers of the cross.

Anoint Thy servant this morning, Lord, in the midst of agony, to speak a word to Thy people. The sheep look up in hope, O Lord, that the undershepherd would hear from the Chief Shepherd and will have a word for the children of color, the children of oppression, the disinherited and dispossessed. We have stolen away, Jesus, from our communities. Let this moment not be in vain. And when we leave from this Holy House, may we feel a new kinship with those who know the Lord, who have walked in Jerusalem just like John. In Your blessed Name, Lord Jesus, when You came down the mountain from Your prayer retreat, You went back out unto the world to heal and to provide a word of hope. Help us to be that healing instrument this week out there for some boy or some girl, some man or some woman. In Your blessed Name and for Your sake we pray this morning. Amen and Amen.

A Pastor's Prayer for a Son on Drugs (1993)
Lloyd Preston Terrell

Most heavenly Father, I come to you, first saying, "Thank you for letting me rise to a new day." I thank you for being merciful to me and my family. Thank you for watching over us while we slumbered in the cool of the night. Lord, I thank you.

Father, I am asking you to please look down from heaven and help the son of a heartbroken mother. His name is Joe, Lord. You know him, and you know that "crack" has possessed his mind and body. Lord, please deliver him from the demon of drugs. Loose him from Satan's grip. Restore him to manhood and a good life. Satan has robbed too many Black men of character, employment and self-respect. O Lord, I am not just praying for Brother Joe, I'm praying and asking your help for a good many men and women. Lord, please deliver Brother Joe just as you delivered Jonah from the belly of the whale.[1] I thank you, Father, in the name of your Son, Jesus. Amen.

---

[1] See Jonah 1:15–2:10.

A Pastor's Prayer for Those in Prison (1993)

Lloyd Preston Terrell

Heavenly Father, please look down and have mercy on 650,000 Black men and thousands of Black women who are in prison. Help them, dear Jesus, to experience hope and renewal. Empower us as a church to reach out and minister to their needs. Let each of us remember that we, too, have experienced a form of imprisonment. But through your grace, we have been set free. In the precious name of Jesus. Amen.

I Must Tell Jesus (1993)

Nancy Lynne Westfield

"I must tell Jesus all of my trials;
I cannot bear these burdens alone;
In my distress He kindly will help me,
He ever loves and cares for His own;
I must tell Jesus! I must tell Jesus!
I cannot bear my burdens alone;
I must tell Jesus! I must tell Jesus!
Jesus can help me, Jesus alone."[1]

Loving Savior and Ever Present Friend, we thank you this morning for the opportunity to pray for ourselves and for others. We know that no prayer goes unanswered. We trust you Lord, and we love you. We know that you will be steadfast—Oh thank you Jesus.

We acknowledge that our hearts are heavy because the truth of the Gospel is as yet squandered. Some of your poor children are not yet listening; some pathetic souls are unable to hear; and others are simply unwilling to comply. And so we pray this morning for those who are spiritual paupers:

- Persons who are destitute, penniless, without the necessities to sustain a home, or a table, or a bed. [Please] motivate us to share all that we have with those who have nothing.

- Persons whose very souls are impoverished—lacking in love, showing no kindness—compel us to reach out to these scrooged[2] persons loving them into humanness.

We pray for the poor persons who are only able to find comfort in the hollow pleasures of hedonism. Oblige us away from envy, and toward the setting of an example of righteous living.

---

[1] This famous hymn, "I Must Tell Jesus," written and composed by Elisha A. Hoffman, is sung widely among African-American congregations.

[2] The author invented a word here by adding -*ed* to the word *scrooge,* which means "a miserly person," and using it as an adjective.

We pray for the needy persons whose barren imaginations are cracked and splintered. Entreat us to risk challenging them. Teaming with them, let us dare to cooperate into your vision.

We pray for the destitute persons who are trapped in the violence of stalking and slaying victims as an acceptable occupation. Turn our bystander mentality into tangible acts of justice at any price.

Lord, there are depleted persons who selfishly never take time for renewal [while] seeking to be *indispensable*. Teach us how to quiet their raging egos, and to give healing balm to the wounds of low self-esteem.

We pray for those who do shoddy work in their jobs because they feel unvalued, unseen, disrespected. Grant that we who are their co-workers may no longer tolerate being shortchanged.

Oh Lord we pray this morning as poor people—knowing that ours is the kingdom of God. You promised that the poor in spirit shall be filled; that the poor shall laugh.[3] We thank you and we rejoice!

In all the complexity of living, grant us simplicity to love those who are our enemies. Let us do good [while] hoping for nothing in return. In all the power struggles, family member to family member, city to city, nation to nation, help us realize that the greatest power is shown not in might, but in selflessness.

Lord, there are people in our church community who need your tender mercy. . . .[4] We ask you to bless each of them. We ask that you bless their families and those who care for them. We ask that you energize our church to surround the poor and the needy with love and attention, and the kind of faith that heals, and redeems, and transforms lives.

All these things we ask in the name of Jesus who listens to all trials; who in our distress kindly helps us; who himself prayed to God saying:

Our Father who art in heaven,
Hallowed be thy name.

---

[3] An allusion to Luke 6:20–21 (NRSV).

[4] The ellipses denote the deletion of the names of members of the congregation who were being prayed for at that time.

Thy kingdom come,
Thy will be done,
  On earth as it is in heaven.
Give us this day our daily bread;
And forgive us our debts,
  As we also have forgiven our debtors;
And lead us not into temptation,
  But deliver us from evil.[5]
For thine is the kingdom and the power
  and the glory, forever. Amen.[6]

---

[5] Matthew 6:9–13 (RSV).

[6] Although it is placed in a textual note, this last sentence is not included in the main text of either the Revised Standard Version or the New Revised Standard Version. But it is included in most other translations.

A Prayer For Liberation That Leads to Liberating Love (1994)

Frank Madison Reid III

O God, who is a father to the fatherless, a mother to the motherless, and a friend to the friendless, we come seeking fellowship with your power and peaceful presence.

In a culture filled with divisiveness, disconnectedness and domination, we pause for a moment of centered-cosmic Christian connection that will bring wholeness and healing to ourselves and our world.

We take time right now to worship you, to adore you, to magnify you, and to praise your holy name. In the words of the psalmist, "We lift up our eyes unto the hills from whence cometh our help, our help cometh from the Lord."[1]

O God, liberate us *from* the domination of individual and institutional violence. Liberate us *for* the ministry of deliverance to the captives within and without.

Liberate us *from* a self-centered spiritual materialism and liberate us *to* serve the present age. Liberate us *from* building our kingdoms and liberate us *for* the Kingdom of God.

Now God, we thank you for your liberating love which redeems us, restores us, and revives and resurrects us. We thank you for the gift of love you gave us in Jesus Christ. We thank you that it is because of your divine liberating love that we are able to *serve,* to *stand* and have this moment of prayer strengthened for the journey of this day. Amen.

---

[1] Psalm 121:1–2 (KJV).

A Lenten Prayer (1994)

Obie Wright, Jr.

"Thine, O Lord, is the greatness, and the power, and the glory, and the victory, and the majesty: for all that is in heaven and in earth is thine; thine is the kingdom, O Lord, and thou art exalted as head above all."[1] Like a potter, You scooped up clay, soiled Your hands with it, pressed, patted, and pounded it, and breathed into lowly dust the breath of divinity. The sun and moon praise You, the stars of light praise You;[2] having tumbled from Your wondrous fingertips they forever sing, as they shine, the hand that made us is divine.

O God, our Father in heaven, our Mother on earth as in heaven, You love us with an everlasting love; You hold us, and never loosening hold, You are molding and making us still. Forgive our ingratitude, our tardiness to worship You as the center of our unbroken praise. God, our All Supply, free us from the agitation of self-absorption. May we hear Your gentle voice saying to us now, "Be still, and know that I am God."[3]

Lord Jesus, be to us the power of God unto salvation. Give us stout hearts to hang tough with the hopes of the prophets. Embolden us with "a passion for the possible."[4] Make us zealous for Your kingdom's goal of mutual service and mutual bliss, with every barrier broken down, and You, dear Lord, whose name is Love, abiding with us always as the only power and presence in our lives.

Spirit of holiness, prod us, rebuke us, charm and enchant us until our minds are stayed on the Beloved Community. Lift us up—put running in our feet, clapping in our hands. Lord, make us free, make us whole, fill our voices with the sound of the genuine. Make us ready to testify:

---

[1] I Chronicles 29:11 (KJV).

[2] This is a paraphrase of Psalm 148:3.

[3] Psalm 46:10 (KJV).

[4] See William Sloane Coffin, *A Passion for the Possible: A Message to U.S. Churches* (Louisville, KY: Westminster Press/John Knox Press, 1993).

Done made my vow to the Lord and I never will turn back,
I will go, I shall go, to see what the end will be.
Done opened my mouth to the Lord and I never will turn back
I will go, I shall go, to see what the end will be.[5]

Strong Son of God, our Healing Wisdom, we give thanks for the glorious promise of new beginnings. Thank You for apostles of sensitiveness who have walked among us with the listening ear that hears beyond a sister's faults, a brother's failures, the child within crying for acceptance, and for "new hands for holding on." Thank You for men and women, children and youth, of every race, nation, and creed who have trod paths of undiscourageable good will, and "with new eyes for seeing,"[6] let their light shine in the midnight of warring madness. Thank You for those whose feet have been shod with the justice that triumphs over rivalry for selfish gain. For all travelers of the road less traveled who have led us in Your righteousness, and made plain Your way before our faces, we give You praise and thanksgiving.[7]

God of all good life, on our journey toward Easter, cleanse our hearts of every desire to mimic the violence of wrongs that befall us. Save us from becoming the evil we hate. Save us from denial of abuses which daily crucify Christ afresh. Drive away the chilling cold, the wintry frost, of numbing detachment from others' pain, and our own hurts, also. Breathe, O breathe Your empowering Spirit into the troubled hearts of Your children who wish they could wish to love but cannot.

Creator of our bodies, Father and Mother of our spirits, O how we yearn to see You and our Friend Jesus face to face. Precious to us are

---

5 Pastor Wright was quoting what John Lovell has called "the best of the 'vow songs' " produced in the crucible of enslavement. This quotation is from Lovell's magisterial study of the African-American spirituals, *Black Song: The Forge and the Flame: The Story of How the Afro-American Spiritual Was Hammered Out* (New York: Macmillan, 1972), 323.

6 This phrase, as well as the earlier "new hands for holding on," is taken from Fred Kaan's hymn titled "Help Us Accept Each Other" (1974). See hymn no. 560 in *The United Methodist Hymnal* (Nashville, TN: United Methodist Publishing House, 1989).

7 See Psalm 5:8 (KJV).

the Christ-like influences, and the whispered encouragement to keep on keeping on, of souls whom we have loved long since and lost awhile. What a morning it will be when we mingle our voices with theirs, and with all the souls invisible, and adoring angels in a mighty chorus of unending wonder. My Lord, what a morning when You shall crown us with the crowns You are holding now above our heads. Chastise, charm and enchant us until we have grown tall enough to wear them.

Hear our prayer, in the name of Jesus, the Shining Way, the Truth, and the Life. Amen.

Why, Jesus?! (1989)

{Jeff Stetson}

Rev. Wilcox: This church has never before been so full and, yet, I as your pastor, have never felt this empty. In these past few days, I have prayed for the strength and the courage that would enable me to deliver a message to you of love and hope built out of ashes of despair and upon the dead bodies of these four innocent little girls. . . . I have screamed to Jesus the question, "Why," and I have listened for a response that could help me here today but, my brothers and sisters, perhaps my heart was too weak, or my faith not strong enough, for no response came. . . . And, so, I stand before you this afternoon, still waiting, still asking, "Why," still praying for *faith* which has been severely tested by the sacrifice and blood of our delicate young children who should be here to dream, to laugh, to discover, to learn, to experience, to wonder, to do *all* of the things that children have a *right* to do, protected from the insanity of a world driven *mad* by the hatred and evil of men who deny Jesus as quickly as they accept faith. (He looks carefully and slowly at his congregation.) I know, some of you are here with violence and revenge in your hearts. (He points to some members.)

You young brothers dressed in the militancy of our times sitting in anger, backs erect, jaws tightened, fists clenched, ready and willing to correct that which can never be corrected. What do I say to you to change your minds, to touch you with a greater vision, to turn you again from thoughts of destruction and lead you toward the road of compassion and forgiveness? What do I say, sweet Jesus, to these grieving parents, who want only to hold their children again, to guide them to safety, to protect them from the wickedness that destroyed them in the place where we worship your father, murdered them in the very house of God! What can I say to this congregation, who suffers with them, who now fear for their own children, who may be the next to be violated on this hallowed? (He seems desperate and lost.)

Dear Lord, master of life, what can you say to me, that will restore a purpose to what I do, and a belief in what I speak to these your devoted servants? I have never asked you for a sign before, I have never *begged* you to answer questions that my faith was once strong enough to push aside. But, Jesus, I *was not ready* for this test. I was not prepared for this, your greatest challenge. I cannot go on without an answer to this question which burns a hole inside of me, that shakes my very foundation, that makes me curse restraint, and has given me cause to doubt my own capacity to believe. WHY, IN THIS HOUSE, WHERE WE OFFER OUR DEVOTION TO YOU? WHY, THESE CHILDREN WHO WANTED ONLY TO SERVE YOU, THAT PRAYED TO YOU WHILE THEIR PRECIOUS LIMBS WERE BEING BLOWN APART AND CRUSHED BENEATH THE WEIGHT OF FALLEN DREAMS AND BROKEN PROMISES? WHY!? Why, in your holy and sacred name did you allow barbarism and evil to enter this church and make a mockery of *all* that we hold dear, to shatter goodness, to destroy hope, to torture the faithful who now live only to mourn the dead? WHY, TAKE OUR CHILDREN AND LEAVE US MEMORIES OF WHAT COULD HAVE BEEN BUT NO LONGER CAN BE? Why death instead of dreams, why lifelessness instead of laughter, why sorrow instead of the serenity of our children's smiles? WHY!? (His voice and spirit are now all but broken.)

Why these children, who never had a chance to let life touch them fully, to know the answer of life before confronted with the question of death? Why? (He searches his congregation for an answer that does not come.)

Do you have an answer? . . . Do *any* know why we are gathered in this place? . . . You? . . . Or you? . . . Sisters, is there no hint of an answer? . . . Brother, is there no clue? . . . No whisper to silence the wonder? . . . Then, are we not surely lost? (He lifts his head to heaven, cries softly, then screams.)

Why?

Afterword: A Scholar's Benediction

[DEDICATED TO CORNEL WEST, MY PRECIOUS BROTHER, WITH
UNDYING LOVE AND SOLIDARITY]

Thou who grants clarity, thank you for permitting us to have access to the archives of Thy grace and truth. Even though our finiteness limits the duration and thoroughness of our visits, we give you praise for your openness. How kind of you, Precious One, to replenish our souls within the unfathomable library of conversations that you have had with others in the past. When we yearned for the convenience of a catalog, you reminded us of the preciousness of privacy. When we envied the deeper intimacy that other researchers seemed to have had with you, you did not scold us. You beckoned us to come closer, nay, to go further into the immense sanctuaries of divinity.

We reluctantly accepted this primal invitation. The night of our ignorance and fears, however, so enshrouded us with the seeming impossibility of such exacting mimesis that the profanity of our expectations eclipsed the bright promise of your edification. As we searched for the peculiar citations of your presence, the fugitive, indeed rationalistic, footnotes of our species deluded us into thinking that scholars of spirituality are morticians rather than trustees of a living spiritual endowment. Then our hearts felt the sudden infusion of memories when we too once grasped the swift butterflies of divine insight.

Lord, why do these thoughts, these imaginings, these echoes, these tracings of past conversations seem so incomplete, so lacking in a sense of *real presence* for many? Can it be that the psychic dislocations of our time so offend us that we choose to be *in absentia*? Whatever the reasons for the complexity of reality, one reality is that far too many of us do not miss you. We yearn to feel your presence. But do not comprehend the nature of this absence which we often call "emptiness." We have been absent from you for so long that we either never knew, or have forgotten, that the soul must be nurtured and nourished. Spiritual malnutrition besets us. We have become the servants of an instant gratification that is devoid of both thought and purpose. We are hurriers with narcissistic agendas who refuse to look for you in the groans, joys, and plight of the poor. Our fetish for civility voids such contemplation. We look for you in our narrow conceptions of beauty rather than in the fierce ambiguity of sublimity. The ugliness that informs this predilection is disarming.

Malfeasance, malice, and even murder have become scandalous dog-ears in the macabre texts of the newest versions of barbarity that bedevil the twentieth century. We ask, "Do this infanticide and genocide that daily mock the sanctity of the human body constitute the endnotes of these texts?" Maybe, maybe not. But we do know that a vast caldron of nihilism and self-hatred rages in our bosom because of past and present unrequited wrongs. It permeates, and sometimes even severs, the precarious sinews of our communities. Your archives reveal past prayers that engaged the creeping issues of theodicy that threaten to sour our covenant with Thee. Only you know how many of your black children are angry with you. Like Cain, it is easier to kill Abel than to admit anger with our Divine Parent. Some of us scream, "Why do you favor Abel, especially when Abel has more than he needs?" Your silence pains us. Our souls demand justice. Perhaps it is a fool's errand. But Abel's spiritual heirs feel compelled to defend your character before the scandalous pomposity of the judgment bar of human reason. Some of them even edit anthologies in an effort to index the prayerful moods and practices of those who believed in your reality in the midst of explicit and unrepentant racism. May such books become a library of hope for those who believe, want to believe, and even those who deny your reality. May these prayers be a testimony to the aristocracy of a faith that believes in the endurance of your self-predication even in a postmodern world.

Lord, the search for two centuries of the prayers of our forebears offers a profile of the trials, defeats, and triumphs of often unheralded martyrdom. Many of our spiritual forebears assumed that prayer is a form of spiritual combat against the profane absurdities of racism that curse your divinity by confusing it with the perversities of tribal privileges and rites. Has the sense that prayer is a signal way to rally our tempestuous selves around the anchorage of your incomparable love been lost? Much work lies ahead if we are to answer this interrogative. Such questions require much analysis, research, time. The tragic consequences of our alienation from you are manifold. But none is greater than our captivity to a busyness and profanity that devalues visits to your archives. We find it too inconvenient to wait on Thee. Grant us the desire to celebrate the sacrament of waiting.

Despite our lingering infidelities, our souls faintly feel the sound waves of your movements. This is why we yearn to resonate with the music of your spheres. When we attune ourselves to your sacred cosmic score, we discover that your joyous sounds simultaneously contain inaudible noises of your desire to commune with us. Some of us can still hear the strong echoes of that African-American gospel song registering its arresting query:

> Somebody's knocking at your door, Somebody's knocking at
> your door;
> O sinner, why don't you answer? Somebody's knocking at your
> door.
> Knocks like Jesus, Somebody's knocking at your door;
> Knocks like Jesus, Somebody's knocking at your door.[1]

This becomes too much for our little minds to comprehend, and our little bodies to absorb. The pulsating rhythms of your insistent knocking disturb our contrived equilibrium. We respond by lurching toward the faint hope that you will go away, and return only when we want you. Such postponements encourage us to look for you in the wrong places, in inappropriate ways, and for unrighteous reasons. We confess that we are afraid of you. You insist on the subordination of our insubordinate nature and culture. So we deny our pending deaths by erecting monuments of shame: hatred for those who are different from us; pleasure in the technologies of destruction and selfishness; indifference to how banal evil has become; petty public and private envies that spawn the delusion that there can be justice without love, and love without justice.

Sweet Spirit, grant us the faith to resist our resistance to Thee!

O God, God, I pray that you will bless us with a mighty increase in the gift of prayer in every culture, race, and nation on this abused planet. Liberate us for service in the ministries of word, deed, and sacrament. May we rediscover our oneness in the unyielding, yet often belittled, fact of the diversity of creation. Bless those who pray

---

[1] *The New National Baptist Hymnal,* 4th ed. (Nashville, TN: Triad Publications, 1978), hymn no. 484.

to the One who is able to knead, shape, and bake us into a wholesome and holistic spiritual bread that can become a sacrament worthy for our children to partake.

For more than two centuries, in the shadow of an imperial democracy, when they "couldn't hear nobody pray," you allowed prayer to thrive among a despised and rejected people. They faced the terrors of their history by courageously believing in the power of your regime to ultimately subdue the malicious habitus that denied their humanity. They blessed your reality and your Name by their determination to love themselves, each other, as well as their enemies. Many were faithful even unto death. They kept saying and singing and praying, "For thine is the kingdom and the power and the glory, forever. Amen." Amen!

Contributors

Akers, Doris (1923–) is one of the great gospel music composers, arrangers, and performers who have gained prominence since the 1940s. Akers herself acquired widespread visibility during the integrationist mood of the 1950s and 1960s, when she founded the first racially integrated choirs in Los Angeles. These choirs partly distinguished themselves by their devotion to African-American gospel music. Out of hundreds of songs she has composed, and several she has recorded, her best-known compositions include "Lead Me, Guide Me" (1953), "You Can't Beat God Giving" (1957), and "Sweet, Sweet Spirit" (1962).

Albert, Octavia Victoria Rogers (1853–1890?) attended Atlanta University to prepare for the work of a Christian teacher and later became a strong and notable lay worker in the Methodist Episcopal Church, North. She is remembered among scholars as one of the earliest African-American collectors and anthologists of slave narratives. This interest culminated in her *The House of Bondage or Charlotte Brooks and Other Slaves* (1890), which consists of seven largely religious narratives of Louisiana freedwomen.

Alexander, Margaret Abigail Walker (1915–) is a distinguished poet, novelist, and former professor and administrator at Jackson State University in Jackson, Mississippi. She is perhaps best known for her famous poem "For My People," as well as for her best-selling Civil War novel, *Jubilee* (1966), which won the Houghton Mifflin Literary Award as well as many other honors.

Allen, Richard (1760–1831) became the most prominent founder and first bishop of the African Methodist Episcopal Church. Shortly after the American Revolutionary War, he began preaching in the Delaware River Valley. By 1786 Allen and Absalom Jones were holding prayer meetings among Africans in Philadelphia. Out of these meetings grew a religious mutual aid society, known as the Free African Society, as well as the African Methodist Episcopal Church and later the first black Episcopal congregation. When Allen, Jones, and William White were pulled from their knees in the sanctuary of the predominantly white St. George's Methodist Episcopal Church in Philadelphia, a sufficient number of African Americans galvanized to form their own congregation and build their own edifice. By 1816 Allen, Jones, Daniel Coker, and others had founded several black Methodist congregations, which agreed to form the first African-American denomination, the African

Methodist Episcopal Church. Allen was a skillful and effective organizer for various efforts to unify African Americans to struggle against slavery and racism. A small posthumous collection of his extant writings was titled *The Life, Experience, and Gospel Labors of the Rt. Rev. Richard Allen, To Which is Annexed The Rise and Progress of the African Methodist Episcopal Church in the United States of America* (1833).

Baker, Benjamin Stanley (1948–) is pastor of the New Light Baptist Church (Detroit, Michigan) and former pastor of the Antioch Baptist Church (Houston, Texas). His books include *Special Occasions in the Black Church* (1989).

Baldwin, James Arthur (1924–1987) was a boy preacher who spent his life, outside of institutional religious settings, exegeting the presence of the divine in both expected and unexpected places. He was a prodigious and sterling African-American belletrist whose existentialist plays, essays, novels, short stories, poems, and principled activism inspired lovers of literature as well as many who constituted the intellectual and spiritual phalanx of both the Civil Rights and Black Power movements. Among his numerous books the ones that portray his spiritual quest include *Go Tell It on the Mountain* (1952), *The Fire Next Time* (1962), *Just Above My Head* (1979), and *The Price of the Ticket* (1985).

Baumfree, Isabella. See Sojourner Truth.

Bibb, Eloise Alberta Veronica (1878–1927) was a social worker and active worker in Catholic organizations in Los Angeles. She wrote special interest articles for newspapers and poetry for various magazines. Her notable collection of poetry is *Poems* (1895), published when she was just seventeen.

Binga, Anthony, Jr. (1843–1919) was a prominent minister in the Consolidated American Baptist Missionary Convention (1865–1879) as well as a missionary and teacher. But he is best remembered for his work among the African-American Baptists in Richmond, Virginia, and various moral and social reform movements such as the Temperance Movement. Besides numerous pamphlets, he published *Sermons on Several Occasions* (1889) as well as *Binga's Addresses on Several Occasions* (1901?).

Bontemps, Arna Wendell (1902–1973) was the distinguished librarian of Fisk University between 1943 and 1965. He was a prominent poet, novelist, historian, anthologist, bibliographer, and collector of African Americana as well. Besides *The Book of Negro Folklore* (1958) he coedited *The Poetry of the Negro* (1949) with Langston Hughes.

Botkin, Benjamin Albert (1901–?) was a distinguished European-American folklorist. He excerpted several of the slave narratives that were gathered from the labors of the Works Projects Administration. This famous New Deal project employed interviewers to gather the personal narratives of ex-slaves who were still living in the 1930s. Botkin's anthology, *Lay My Burden Down: A Folk History of Slavery* (1945), is still in print. He also directed the recording of *Negro Religious Songs and Services,* which can be found in the Library of Congress.

Brawley, Benjamin Griffith (1882–1939) was a distinguished professor of English at Morehouse College who also served as its dean (1912–1920). He served briefly as pastor of Messiah Baptist Church (Brockton, Massachusetts) after his ordination in 1921 and then taught at Shaw and Howard universities. Among his numerous books one in particular discloses his rather private spirituality: *A History of the English Hymn* (1932).

Brooks, Walter Henderson (1851–1945) served several prominent Baptist congregations primarily in Virginia before being called to the pastorate of the famous Nineteenth Street Baptist Church (Washington, DC) in 1882. He served this congregation for sixty-three years. He was a distinguished religious leader, able poet, disciplined writer, and tireless Christian leader. His best-known religious book, at least among scholars, is *The Pastor's Voice: A Collection of Poems* (1945).

Brown, Diana (unknown) was an African-American woman who resided on Edisto Island, South Carolina, and whose prayer was recorded and transcribed by Lorenzo Dow Turner. Turner conducted his research for *Africanisms in the Gullah Dialect* in the 1930s and 1940s. See Lorenzo Dow Turner.

Brown, James (unknown). See Patricia Jones-Jackson.

Cameron, James (1914–) is the founder, president, and director of America's Black Holocaust Museum (Milwaukee, Wisconsin). He is also the author of *A Time of Terror* (1982).

Campbell, Lucie Mae (1885–1963). See Lucie Mae Eddie Campbell Williams.

Cleage, Albert Buford, Jr. (1911–) is the founder and bishop of the Pan African Orthodox Church. He was ordained in the United Church of Christ, was one of the early leaders of the Black Theology Movement, and advanced the concept and practice of Black Christian Nationalism. His books include *The Black Messiah* (1968), *Myths About Malcolm X* (1968), and *Black Christian Nationalism: New Directions for the Black Church* (1972).

Cleveland, James (1932–1991) was the most famous male black gospel singer of the mid-twentieth century. A minister and composer as well, he was pastor of New Greater Harvest Baptist Church (Los Angeles, California) and founding pastor of Cornerstone Institutional Baptist

Church (Los Angeles). He founded the Gospel Music Workshop of America, organized the Southern California Community Choir, and sang with several famous African-American gospel music groups, such as the Cravans, Gospelaires, and Roberta Martin Singers, as well as the great Mahalia Jackson. He composed hundreds of gospel songs, including "God Specializes" and "He's Using Me," recorded over seventy record albums, and received many music awards, including several Grammy Awards.

Cobbins, Otho B. (1895–1972) was a bishop of the Church of Christ (Holiness) between 1945 and 1947. He had an extensive career as a public secondary school educator and is best known as the editor in chief of the compilation of documents known as *The History of Church of Christ (Holiness), U.S.A., 1895–1965.*

Coker, Daniel (1780–1846) [born Isaac Wright] was one of the first ministers of the African Methodist Episcopal Church. He was elected as the first bishop of the church on 16 April 1816 but declined to serve in favor of Richard Allen. There was some apparent dissension about having a light-skinned African American, such as Coker, serve as the first bishop. In addition, Coker fell victim to unrecorded calumnies that led to his official ouster from the church on 17 April 1818. Two years later he found himself sailing to West Africa as a missionary under the auspices of the Maryland Colonization Society, which was affiliated with the American Colonization Society (ACS). The ACS, formed in 1817, promoted and supported sending free African Americans back to their ancestral continent. They believed that this would serve the twofold purpose of homogenizing North America with those of European descent and creating a beachhead for "Christian civilization" in Africa. After the beginning of the annual meetings of the National Negro Convention in 1830, most African Americans opposed the work of the ACS. Coker wrote the *Journal of Daniel Coker, a Descendant of Africa* (1820).

Colemon, Johnnie (192?–) is the founder of the Universal Foundation for Better Living, a denomination associated with the religious movement known as New Thought, which emphasizes positive thinking as a way of life and a gateway to divinity. She was ordained by the Unity Church, the largest denomination of this movement, in 1956, and organized Christ Unity Temple (Chicago), which became the first predominantly African-American Unity congregation in the United States. By 1978 she had more than 1,000 members. She developed a television ministry in 1981 called *Better Living with Johnnie Colemon.* Christ Unity Temple had become Christ Universal Temple by 1985, and claimed more than 3,500 members with a multimillion-dollar edifice, a school, and extensive television facilities.

Corbett, Maurice Nathaniel (1859–192?) was a politician, government worker, and poet. He served in the North Carolina state legislature after Reconstruction, was a delegate to numerous political conventions, and was a clerk in the United States Census Bureau and then in the Government Printing Office in Washington, DC, until his health failed him in 1919. He is best remembered for his collection of poetry, *The Harp of Ethiopia* (1914).

Costen, Melva Wilson (1933–) is the Helmar Nielsen Professor of Worship and Music at the Interdenominational Theological Center in Atlanta, Georgia. She is the author of *African American Christian Worship* (1993).

Crummell, Alexander (1819–1898) was the most distinguished African-American Episcopal priest of the nineteenth century. He was very active in the Abolitionist Movement and often promoted African-American self-help and unity in sermons, general public addresses, and publications. Between 1848 and 1853, he studied at Queen's College, Cambridge University, and left England in 1853 to do missionary work for the Church of England in Liberia. In 1861 he was appointed to the faculty of the new Liberia College at Monrovia but was dismissed from this post in 1866 because of differences with the college's administration. He returned to the United States in 1873, settled in Washington, DC, and formed St. Luke's Episcopal Church, from which he retired in 1894. He spent his rather brief retirement years teaching at Howard University (1895–1897) and organizing the American Negro Academy, whose membership included about forty notable African-American intellectuals, such as W. E. B. Du Bois and Paul Laurence Dunbar. His books consist of collections of sermons and addresses, including *Relations and Duties of Free Colored Men in America* (1861), *The Future of Africa* (1862), *The Greatness of Christ* (1882), and *Africa and America* (1891).

Crutcher, William Townsend (1905–1989) was born in Stevenson, Alabama, and between 1935 and 1989 he served as pastor of the Mount Olive Baptist Church, Knoxville, Tennessee. He was the major civil rights leader in Knoxville and the focus of Merrill Proudfoot's *Diary of a Sit-in*. He wrote a pamphlet titled *A Bus Ministry Manual: A Guide for National Baptist Churches* (1976).

Cullen, Countée Porter (1903–1946) was a distinguished poet, novelist, anthologist, and secondary school teacher who was adopted at an early age by the Reverend Frederick A. Cullen, pastor of the Salem Methodist Church in Harlem. Cullen was a major figure in the Harlem

Renaissance. Some of his best writings were recently anthologized in *My Soul's High Song: The Collected Writings of Countée Cullen, Voice of the Harlem Renaissance* (1991).

Dabney, Elizabeth J. (?–1967), often called affectionately Mother Dabney, deliberately guarded details of her early life. She believed that only spiritual knowledge of Jesus is important. A native of Virginia, she became a legendary spiritual leader in Philadelphia, where she and her husband, in obedience to a vision from God, formed the Garden of Prayer Church of God in Christ. In the midst of a worship service led by Bishop O. T. Jones, Sr., Mother Dabney was "filled with the Holy Ghost," experienced the healing of her body from tuberculosis, as well as an abscess that ran continuously, and spoke in Italian. Mother Dabney once received a vision that she should covenant with God to pray every day at the church at nine o'clock in the morning for three years and to fast seventy-two hours per week for two years. She obeyed. Many people came to her for prayer and healing.

Dandridge, Raymond Garfield (1882–1930) was a poet, painter, and decorator. He is best known for his collection of poetry, *The Poet and Other Poems* (1920).

Davis, Leroy (unknown), a man in his thirties, the son of C. T. and Mattie Davis of Giddings, Texas, was apparently a member of the St. John Progressive Baptist Church of Austin, Texas, when Dr. Pitts recorded and transcribed this prayer. See Walter F. Pitts, Jr.

Dett, Robert Nathaniel (1882–1943) was a distinguished educator and musician who taught most of his career at Hampton Institute (1913–1932), where he organized the Hampton Choral Union, and the Musical Arts Society. But his greatest acclaim came as the conductor of the famed Hampton Institute Choir. He was a significant African-American composer whose arrangements of Negro spirituals helped to canonize them as an original American contribution to African and Western music. His most famous work beyond his arrangements of Negro spirituals include "Juba" from *In the Bottoms Suite* for piano (1913) and "Listen to the Lamb" for mixed voices.

Dorsey, Thomas Andrew (1899–1993) is deservedly called the Father of Gospel Music. Through his scores of pioneering gospel songs, often both composed and performed by himself, Dorsey became the major leader in revolutionizing African-American religious music. Michael Harris in his excellent biography characterized Dorsey's music as "the gospel blues." Dorsey believed that the groans and moans of African-American social pain were invitations for the Holy Spirit to be a colaborer in the crucible of spiritual rebirth. Dorsey and his cohorts inspired those who found themselves in the absurd belly of Jim and

Jane Crow. Not only did he organize his own gospel choir at the Pilgrim Baptist Church in Chicago but he also joined forces with Sallie Martin in 1932 to form the National Convention of Gospel Choirs and Choruses and established the Thomas A. Dorsey Gospel Songs Music Publishing Company.

Douglass, Frederick (1817–1895) was the most prominent African-American leader of the nineteenth century. He was born into slavery and escaped at the age of twenty-one. He discovered his oratorical and literary gifts on the platforms and in the periodicals of the Abolitionist Movement and was a lay preacher in the African Methodist Episcopal Zion Church. His classic autobiographies were recently reprinted and anthologized in *Autobiographies: Narrative of the Life of Frederick, an American Slave; My Bondage and My Freedom; Life and Times of Frederick Douglass* (1994).

Douroux, Margaret Pleasant (1941–) is a distinguished composer, arranger, and publisher of gospel music, hymns, anthems, and spirituals. Founder and president of the Reverend Edward A. Pleasant Publishing Company, she has three notable musical recordings, "Revival from the Mount" (1970), "The Way of the Word" (1982), and "Signs of Advent" (1987). Her book publications include *About My Father's Business* (1977), *Christian Principles That Motivate and Enhance Education Among Black Children* (1979), *Why I Sing* (1983), and *Find the Kingdom* (1985).

Drake, John Gibbs St. Clair (1911–1992) was a distinguished professor of anthropology and sociology at universities including Dillard, Roosevelt, Chicago, Boston, Columbia, Liberia, Ghana, and Stanford. Two of his most significant publications are *Black Metropolis* (1945) and his two-volume magnum opus *Black Folk Here and There: An Essay in History and Anthropology* (1990).

Du Bois, William Edward Burghardt (1868–1963) even in death is the most influential African-American public intellectual of the twentieth century. As scholar, professor, poet, novelist, journalist, author, Pan-Africanist, and human rights activist, he used his towering intellect and longevity to inspire several generations to press for a just society. Among his writings, *The Souls of Black Folk* (1903) stands as a momentous classic.

Dunbar, Paul Laurence (1872–1906) was a poet and novelist of great prominence. A subtle but poignant critique of the plight of African-Americans can be detected in his verse, written in both standard English and dialect. His writings include several collections of poetry, such as *Oak and Ivy* (1893), *Majors and Minors* (1895), *Lyrics of a Lowly Life* (1896), and *Lyrics of the Hearthside* (1899), as well as several novels. Perhaps *Sport of the Gods* (1902) is his best-known novel.

Ellison, John Malcus (1889–1979) spent most of his adult life as an educator. He founded and was principal of a high school, held professorships at Howard and Virginia Union universities, and served as president and then chancellor of Virginia Union. He was the author of *Tensions and Destiny* (1953), *They Who Preach* (1956), and *They Sang Through the Crisis: Dealing with Life's Most Critical Issues* (1961).

Ferrill, London (c. 1789–1854), a house joiner by trade, was born into slavery. At an early age, he answered a call to be a preacher of the Gospel to enslaved and freed Africans in Hanover County, Virginia. He pursued the same course shortly after arriving in Lexington, Kentucky. In 1821 the white First Baptist Church of Lexington, with the blessing of the Elkshorn Baptist Association, ordained Ferrill. With the assistance of a salary supplement from the town council, Ferrill formally organized the First African Baptist Church of Lexington, which had been meeting as an auxiliary of the white First Baptist Church since 1786. At the time of his death, he had the largest congregation in Kentucky.

Forbes, James Alexander, Jr. (1935–) is senior minister of Riverside Church and Harry Emerson Fosdick Adjunct Professor of Preaching at Union Theological Seminary. He is the author of *The Holy Spirit and Preaching* (1989).

Gilbert, Ralph Mark (1899–1956) served as pastor of Pilgrim Baptist Church (South Bend, Indiana), Second Baptist Church (Dresden, Canada), and most prominently First African Baptist Church (Savannah, Georgia) from 1939 until his death. He was a prolific writer and producer of religious plays, distinguished preacher, and courageous fighter for civil rights in the 1930s and 1940s. Most of his personal papers are in the possession of his wife, Mrs. Eloria Sherman Gilbert, who resides in Manhattan.

Hammon, Jupiter (1711?–1800) is known as "the first published" African-American enslaved poet. He lived, wrote, and died a slave. His sense of earthly and divine determinism brought him, and many others in his age, a great measure of theological comfort. He was deeply affected by the piety of eighteenth-century Calvinistic evangelicalism. A long overdue, kinder, and more contextual reading of his writings can now be found in Sondra A. O'Neale's *Jupiter Hammon and the Biblical Beginnings of African-American Literature* (1993).

Hawkins, Walter (1949–) is the founding pastor of the Love Center (Oakland, California), which he organized in 1975. Although the congregation is an independent Pentecostal church, Hawkins was ordained by the Church of God in Christ. He is best known as a widely acclaimed composer and performer of African-American gospel music.

In 1979 he received a Grammy Award for best soul gospel performance. His albums "Love Alive I" and "Love Alive II" were best-sellers.

Haynes, Lemuel (1753–1833) was a soldier in the Revolutionary War, Congregationalist minister, and the first African American to receive an honorary Master of Arts degree. He was ordained in 1785 and preached to predominantly white congregations for most of his ministry, especially the First Congregational Church (Rutland, Vermont), which he served between 1788 and 1818. His strong Calvinist convictions are evident throughout his many writings. The best single source of his writings is Richard Newman, ed., *Black Preacher to White America* (1990).

Hays, Stephen (unknown) was a minister who served in upstate New York when he overheard "A Slave Woman's Prayer" (1816). See "Notes on Sources."

Haywood, Garfield Thomas (1880–1931) was the first presiding bishop of the Pentecostal Assemblies of the World (PAW). One of the central beliefs of this denomination is the "Jesus Only" doctrine, which teaches that, since salvation comes "only" through Jesus Christ, baptism can only be administered in "the name of Jesus." Haywood's skills as a writer, poet, and songwriter can be seen in his compilation of PAW hymns titled *The Bridegroom Songs*.

Heard, Josephine Delphine Henderson (1861–1921) taught in African-American schools in South Carolina and Tennessee before she married Bishop William Henry Heard of the AME Church in 1882. Although she was not a notable poet either during her lifetime or now, her poetry in *Morning Glories* (1890) advocates moral, spiritual, and personal uplift. These Victorian sentiments were quite prevalent among African-American church people in her day.

Henton, Richard Daniel (1933–), a powerful preacher, is the founder and pastor of the Monument of Faith Evangelistic Church, an interdenominational congregation on the southwest side of Chicago. He organized the Full Gospel of the Word of God Association, a denomination of more than twelve churches. The more than 2,000 members of Henton's congregation do not include the considerable radio and television audience that listen to and view his Sunday morning program, *The Breakthrough Hour*.

Holly, James Theodore (1829–1911) was consecrated the first missionary bishop of Haiti for the Episcopal Church in 1874. He was an avid advocate of African-American emigration to countries ruled by Africans and author of several theological and scholarly articles; he wrote *Manuel de Théologie Dogmatique ou Résumé des Chefs de la Science Sacrée à l'Usage du Clergé De l'Eglise Orthodox Apostolique en Haiti* (1879).

Hughes, James Mercer Langston (1902–1967) was a famous poet, novelist, playwright, anthologist, columnist, and translator who was often called the Poet Laureate of Harlem. He kept the passion and excellence of the literary and intellectual revival of the Harlem Renaissance vibrant, especially after the death of James Weldon Johnson in 1938. His literary output was both prolific and brilliant. Rather than enumerate his writings, I suggest reading Arnold Rampersad's two-volume biography: *The Life of Langston Hughes* (1986, 1988).

Imes, William Lloyd (1889–1966) was a Presbyterian minister of national stature who was the pastor of several congregations. He is best remembered for his pastorate at the St. James Presbyterian Church in Harlem (New York) between 1925 and 1943. His publications include *Integrity: Studies in the Book of Job* (1939), *The Way of Worship in Everyday Life* (1947), and *The Black Pastures, a Pilgrimage in Two Centuries* (1957).

Jackson, Jesse Louis (1941–), an ordained minister associated with the National Baptist Convention, USA, Inc., emerged in the 1970s as the most prominent leader of the African-American Civil Rights Movement. The Reverend Dr. Martin Luther King, Jr., appointed Jackson to head the Chicago Office of the Southern Christian Leadership Conference's (SCLC) Operation Breadbasket, a grassroots social development organization that focused on the use of economic boycotts to force the revitalization of economically depressed African-American communities. Jackson later became national director of the SCLC Operation Breadbasket. He transformed this organization into People United to Save Humanity (PUSH) and became its first national president. Well over six books have been written about Jackson's phenomenal public career. He is the author of *Straight from the Heart* (1987). He is presently National President of the Rainbow Coalition.

Jackson, Rebecca Cox (1795–1871) was a rather obscure African-American eldress of a colony of black female Shakers in Philadelphia until Jean Humez published a critical edition of her writings. Jackson's writings grant privileged access to the world of dreams, visions, and conversations with God that were quite prevalent among religious African-Americans. This spiritual legacy is still alive.

Jacobs, Harriet Ann (1813–1897) was a famous fugitive slave whose *Incidents in the Life of a Slave Girl* (1861) became one of the classic published slave narratives of the nineteenth century. Jacobs used the voice of Linda Brent, the narrator and heroine of her remarkable autobiography, to disclose the excruciating trials and unexpected humanity that defined her life.

Jea, John (1773–1818?) was a sailor, itinerant Methodist minister, and hymn writer. See Graham Russell Hodges's excellent anthology

Black Itinerants of the Gospel: The Narratives of John Jea and George White (1993).

Johnson, James Weldon (1871–1938), the son of an African Methodist Episcopal minister, became prominent in the literary revival known as the Harlem Renaissance, which thrived in the 1920s and 1930s. His urbane insight and sterling gifts as a belletrist and editor were placed in the service of both the Harlem Renaissance and the Civil Rights Movement. His tireless work and skill as a reigning savant of African-American culture, baptized in a disciplined agnosticism, often eclipsed his deep sensitivity to the spirituality of his forebears. He was always more critical of institutional religion than of African-American spirituality per se. His famous depiction of African-American folk sermons in *God's Trombones* (1927) blessed his spiritual roots and gave focus to the African-American sermon as a significant literary genre.

Jones, Absalom (1746–1818) was the first African-American ordained to holy orders in the Episcopal Church. He was a stalwart cohort of Richard Allen in the founding of both the Free African Society and the African Methodist Episcopal Church. Instead of remaining in either the Methodist Church or Allen's Bethel Church, Jones began holding meetings of his own on 1 January 1791. This self-styled African Church met for three years before deciding to join the Episcopal Church. The new parish was received into the Diocese of Pennsylvania on 17 October 1794, and became the St. Thomas African Episcopal Church. Jones was not ordained until 1804. St. Thomas, however, grew from 246 members in 1794 to 427 in 1795. Like its sister African churches of various denominations throughout the Northeast, St. Thomas was led by Jones in being a community church that offered mutual aid and leadership in protest endeavors against racist causes such as that of the American Colonization Society. Although only a few of Jones's writings are extant, his exemplary piety, pastoral faithfulness, and moral integrity were legendary. See Richard Allen.

Jones, Charles Price (1865–1949), one of the great spiritual geniuses of African-American Christian history, was the founder and first bishop of the Church of Christ (Holiness), which originated in the holiness revivals that blessed the Mount Helm Baptist Church (Jackson, Mississippi) during the 1890s. Jones and his famous cohort in this endeavor, Charles Harrison Mason, organized many African-American congregations toward an emphasis on realized rather than "progressive" sanctification. Jones, however, did not endorse speaking in tongues as a major sign of realized sanctification when it became prevalent in the pentecostal impulse that grasped his friend Mason.

Among Jones's many contributions to African-American spirituality, his hymnal, *His Fullness* (1906), stands as a landmark.

Jones, Singleton Thomas Webster (1825–1891) was one of the great, and most beloved, bishops of the African Methodist Episcopal Zion Church. His literary elegance enhanced his preaching gifts. Although forgotten or overlooked by many historians of Christian homiletics, he should be counted as one of the great preachers of the nineteenth century. His piety was exemplary without being sentimental. His gifts as a church politician are evident in his *Jones's Handbook on the Discipline of the A.M.E. Zion Church,* and some of his sermons and addresses have been anthologized. See Singleton T. Jones, *Sermons and Addresses of the Late Rev. Bishop Singleton T. Jones, D.D., of the African M.E. Zion Church, with A Memoir of His Life and Character Written by Rev. J. W. Smith* (1892).

Jones-Jackson, Patricia (unknown) taught at Howard University while completing her fine study of the culture of the Gullah people. See her *When Roots Die: Endangered Traditions on the Sea Islands* (1987).

Jordan, Lewis Garnett (1858–1939) became the first corresponding secretary of the Foreign Mission Board of the National Baptist Convention, USA, in 1896, after serving several pastorates and offering exemplary service in various endeavors. He later became historiographer of his beloved National Baptist Convention. His most popular and influential book is *The Baptist Standard Church Directory and Busy Pastor's Guide* (1929), but his other books have exerted considerable influence in recent scholarly interpretations of the history of African-American Baptist denominationalism and foreign missions. They include *Up the Ladder in Foreign Mission* (1901) and his compilation of documents *Negro Baptist History, 1750–1930.*

King, Martin Luther, Jr. (1929–1968), the martyred prophet of the Civil Rights Movement, reluctantly accepted leadership of the Montgomery Improvement Association in December 1955 in its effort to desegregate public transportation. Out of his brooding jeremiads, King stubbornly advocated and embraced nonviolent resistance as the best way to depose white supremacy. His spiritual struggles and insights fired the imagination of America. For the only book-length selection of his publications, see James Melvin Washington, ed., *A Testament of Hope: The Essential Writings of Martin Luther King, Jr.* (1986). The definitive collection of King's writings is being developed by Professor Clayborne Carson at Stanford University. See Clayborne Carson et al., *The Papers of Martin Luther King, Jr.* This is a projected twelve-volume collection, and volume 1 is now in print.

Lawrence, George (unknown), a prominent African-American abolitionist in his day, was involved in resisting the American Colonization Society's attempt to encourage and support African-American migration to Africa. He apparently later changed his mind and actively encouraged African-American migration to Haiti. See Floyd Miller, *The Search for a Black Nationality* (1975).

Lawson, Robert Clarence (1883–1961), was an esteemed pastor and bishop who founded several Pentecostal denominations, including the Pentecostal Assemblies of the World. In 1919 he founded the Refuge Church of Our Lord in New York City. By 1923, while pastor of this congregation, he started his famous New York radio broadcast; founded the Southern Pine School in North Carolina; and organized a new denomination, Church of Our Lord Jesus Christ of the Apostolic Faith, for which he established churches in St. Louis, Missouri, and San Antonio, Texas. He was noted for accenting the power of prophecy. Uncharacteristic of many Pentecostal ministers, Lawson's preaching emphasized the need for social, economic, and political justice. He was a prolific writer of tracts and books, and wrote the lyrics for several hymns and gospel songs.

Lee, Jarena (1783–?) was the first female minister in the African Methodist Episcopal Church. Her deep spirituality and fervent devotion to the Gospel are best known through her spiritual autobiography *Religious Experience and Journal of Mrs. Jarena Lee, Giving An Account of Her Call to Preach the Gospel* (1849).

Lincoln, Charles Eric (1924–) is a distinguished professor of religion and culture emeritus at Duke University. He is the author of numerous books, including *The Black Muslims in America* (1961), *The Black Church Since Frazier* (1974), a book of poetry, and an award-winning novel, and coauthor, with Lawrence H. Mamiya, of the much acclaimed study *The Black Church in the African American Experience* (1990).

Lofton, Fred C. (1928–) is pastor of the Metropolitan Missionary Baptist Church (Memphis, Tennessee). He has served as a chaplain and professor at Owen College (Memphis), dean of students at Morehouse College (Atlanta, Georgia), and pastor of the First African Baptist Church (Columbus, Georgia). His books include *When We Pray* (1978); *Help Me Somebody!* (1988), and *A Crying Shepard: A Therapy of Tears, Altar Prayers Delivered at the Metropolitan Baptist Church, Memphis, Tennessee* (1993).

McGirt, James Ephraim (1874–1930) was a prolific poet and somewhat successful businessman. He published *McGirt's Magazine* (Philadelphia). In addition to publishing other lesser known writers, this race journal often printed McGirt's own poetry, articles, and stories which advocated racial progress.

McGuire, George Alexander (1866–1934) was ordained an Episcopal priest. He founded and became the first bishop of the African Orthodox Church in 1921. This denomination was associated with Marcus Garvey's Universal Negro Improvement Association (UNIA). He promoted racial pride. In 1924, he urged African Americans at a convention of the UNIA to incinerate representations of a white Christ and a white Madonna, and to worship a black Christ and a black Madonna. Soon, however, a personality conflict between Garvey and McGuire developed, and by 1925 McGuire led the African Orthodox Church to break with the UNIA.

McNeil, Genna Rae (1947–), the daughter of Jesse Jai McNeil, is professor of history at the University of North Carolina, Chapel Hill. She is the author of *Groundwork: Charles Hamilton Houston and the Struggle for Civil Rights* (1983) and the former deputy general secretary for cooperative Christianity of the American Baptist Churches in the USA.

McNeil, Jesse Jai (1913–1965) served several prominent pastorates during a lifetime of Christian service. They included Spruce Street Baptist Church (Nashville, Tennessee) and Tabernacle Baptist Church (Detroit, Michigan). He also taught at Bishop College and California Baptist Theological Seminary, and served as director of publication for the Sunday School Publishing Board of the National Baptist Convention, USA Inc. His books include *As Thy Days, So Thy Strength* (1960), *Minister's Service Book for Pulpit and Parish* (1961), and *Moments in His Presence* (1962).

Mason, Charles Harrison (1866–1961) was the legendary first bishop of the Church of God in Christ, International, the largest African-American Pentecostal denomination. Elder Mason, along with two other Baptist colleagues, Elders Charles Price Jones and W. S. Pleasant, incorporated a holiness denomination in Memphis, Tennessee, in 1897, and called it the Church of God in Christ. After receiving the gift of speaking in tongues at the great Azusa Street Revival in 1906, Bishop Mason parted with Jones, who opposed this practice. By November 1907, Jones and his holiness followers formed the Church of Christ (Holiness) U.S.A. Mason was known for his stringent prayer life, and for his distinctive proclivity to offer public prayers that were an unusual combination of exhortation and prophecy. He was an open pacifist who opposed America's involvement in World War I, which aroused the attention of the federal government. A copy of the extensive FBI file on Bishop Mason is deposited in the DuPree Papers on the African-American Holiness-Pentecostal Movement at the Schomburg Center. Despite Mason's unwarranted detractors in the FBI, he is revered as a towering African-American shaman with remarkable, charismatic gifts.

Massie, William (unknown) is identified in *The Negro Journal of Religion* (November 1937) as "a recent graduate of Wilberforce University."

Mays, Benjamin Elijah (1895–1984) was one of the most distinguished and influential African-American educators of his generation. As president of Morehouse College, he was a powerful role model for young African-American men who sought to combine professional competence with civic virtue. He exemplified this in his own career as an ordained Baptist minister with a Ph.D. from the University of Chicago committed to achieving racial justice. His leadership in pressing for racial justice in the Student Volunteer Movement, YMCA, National Council of Churches, and the World Council of Churches was exemplary and legendary. Martin Luther King, Jr., attended Morehouse College during Dr. Mays's presidency. They became important collaborators. Dr. Mays's books include *The Negro's God* (1938), *The Negro Church* (1933), and his autobiography, *Born to Rebel* (1971).

Nichols, Lewis Ruffin (1857–1938) pastored noted African Methodist Episcopal Churches. He spent sixty-nine years in the ministry, mostly as pastor of Morris Brown AME Church (Charleston, South Carolina) and Emanuel AME Church (Charleston, South Carolina). He also sometimes served as a presiding elder. He was the father of Bishop D. Ward Nichols of the AME Church.

Nicholson, Joseph William (1901–?) earned a Ph.D. in sociology, and was an ordained minister in the Christian Methodist Episcopal Church. He and Benjamin E. Mays coauthored *The Negro Church* (1933).

Payne, Daniel Alexander (1811–1893) was elected a bishop of the African Methodist Episcopal (AME) Church in 1852. His deep piety and support for education were legendary. He was also the first notable scholar of his denomination. Indeed, he accepted an invitation in 1865 to serve as president of Wilberforce University and held this office until he resigned in 1876 in exchange for the less taxing position of chancellor of the university and dean of Wilberforce's seminary. Next to Richard Allen, Payne was the most prominent AME bishop of the nineteenth century. Although no critical biography has been published, his useful autobiography, *Recollection of Seventy Years* (1980), contains crucial insights and information about his life, his denomination, and African-American social and religious life in nineteenth-century America.

Peters, Phillis Wheatley. See Wheatley, Phillis.

Phillips, Charles Henry (1857–1951) was a bishop of the Christian Methodist Episcopal (CME) Church best known for his efforts to promote the publication work of his denomination by serving as editor of the CME's newspaper, *The Christian Index*. He also published the first history of his denomination, titled *The History of the Colored Methodist Episcopal Church in America* (1898).

Pipes, William Harrison (1912–) served between 1937 and 1956 as a noted professor of English and as an administrator at several African-American colleges, including the presidency of Alcorn University. He joined the faculty of Michigan State University in 1957. His books include *Say Amen, Brother!* (1951), and *Death of "Uncle Tom"* (1967).

Pitts, Walter F., Jr. (1947–1991) was an astute African-American anthropologist who conducted extensive field research in New York, Louisiana, California, Texas, the Dominican Republic, and Trinidad, in a valiant effort to advance our understanding of processes of African cultural retentions in the diaspora. His major book-length contribution to this endeavor is *Old Ship of Zion: The Afro-Baptist Ritual in the African Diaspora* (1993).

Plato, Ann (unknown) was a teacher in the "Colored" School associated with the predominantly black Fifth Congregational Church in Hartford, Connecticut. James Williams Charles Pennington, a famous African-American abolitionist, introduced Plato's miscellaneous collection of writings without offering any biographical information about her, nor did Plato offer any of her own. Researchers, including this editor, have been unable to find anything about Plato outside the suggestions offered in her miscellany *Essays; Including Biographies and Miscellaneous Pieces in Prose and Poetry* (1841). Pennington introduced this book as a repudiation of that "stupid theory" which argues that *"nature has done nothing but fit us for slaves, that that art cannot unfit us for slavery"* (xviii). Plato's poetic prayer in this anthology exemplifies the Romanticist evangelical piety that was prevalent among many urban New Englanders in the 1840s.

Popel, Esther Shaw (1896–?) is best known for her collection of poetry entitled *The Forest Pool* (1934).

Powell, Raphael Philemon (1899–) is an ordained Baptist minister who was born in Jamaica, British West Indies. He is the author of several books, inspired by his commitment to the philosophy of Marcus Garvey, including *The Human Side of a People and the Right Name* (1937), recently revised and retitled *The Invisible Image* (1979).

Ransome, William Lee (1879–1975) was pastor of the First Baptist Church, South Richmond, Virginia.

Reid, Frank Madison, III (1951–) is pastor of the 9,000-member Bethel African Methodist Episcopal Church (Baltimore, Maryland) and the author of *The Nehemiah Plan: Preparing the Church to Rebuild Broken Lives* (1993).

Robinson, William H. (unknown) was a Baptist minister best known by scholars for his contribution to the literature of the slave narratives. See his autobiography, *Log Cabin to Pulpit, or Fifteen Years in Slavery* (1913).

Samuels-Belboder, John Nathaniel (1876–1945) was born in British Guiana, educated in London, England, and at General Theological Seminary (New York), and served as rector of St. Margaret Episcopal Church (Dayton, Ohio) from 1915 until his death. He also served as chaplain to Episcopal students and lecturer in church history at Wilberforce University. He was a contributing editor of *The Negro Journal of Religion,* the official periodical of the Fraternal Council of Negro Churches.

Shackelford, Theodore Henry (1888–1923) was a Canadian-born African-American poet who spent most of his life in the United States, where his grandparents were African-American slaves. He was the author of *My Country and Other Poems* (1918).

Smalls, John Bryan (1845–1905) was a bishop in the African Methodist Episcopal Zion Church. His Holiness theology is reflected in several of his books, especially *The Human Heart Illustrated by Nine Figures of the Heart* (1898). He also published *Practical and Exegetical Pulpiteer* (1895) as well as *A Cordial and Dispassionate Discussion on Predestination, Its Scriptural Import* (1901).

Smith, Amanda Berry Devine (1837–1915) was a prominent Methodist evangelist and temperance worker. Until 1870 she focused on being a wife and domestic worker. She was married to Calvin M. Devine, who died fighting for the Union Army during the Civil War, and then to the Reverend James Smith of Philadelphia, who was an AME minister. During the 1860s she began following the Holiness teachings of Phoebe Palmer. With the death of her second husband and third child in 1869, she sought sanctification with persistence and power as never before. She began to speak in black churches in New York City and New Jersey in 1870, and by 1878 she had become a well-known personage in the Holiness Movement. She preached in camp meetings from Maine to Tennessee. Her sermons enthralled audiences not only in the United States but also in Great Britain, India, Liberia, and Sierra Leone. Her powerful spirituality is evident in her autobiography, *An Autobiography: The Story of the Lord's Dealings with Mrs. Amanda Smith, the Colored Evangelist* (1893).

Smith, James Alfred, Sr. (1952–) is senior pastor of the 4,000-member Allen Temple Baptist Church (Oakland, California). Among his many denominational and ecumenical accomplishments, he is a former president of the Progressive National Baptist Convention. Dr. Smith's pastoral genius, theological acumen, and powerful spirituality permeate his multifaceted ministry in the form of pacesetting engagements with the cutting-edge religious, political, economic, social, and intellectual forces concerned with the liberation of Africans in the diaspora.

Smith, Sallie (unknown). See Octavia Victoria Rogers Albert.

Stetson, Jeff (unknown) is an African-American playwright and screenwriter who resides in Los Angeles, California.

Stewart, Maria W. (1803–1879) was a popular abolitionist speaker and a Baptist who lectured on spiritual topics.

Stone, Orrin (unknown) is identified as a minister in South Carolina in the source from which his prayer is taken: Henry D. Spalding, *Encyclopedia of Black Folklore and Humor* (1990).

Stroyer, Jacob (1849–1908) was a former slave and AME minister who is best known for his autobiography, *My Life in the South* (1898), which offers many insights into slave life and culture before and during the Civil War. After the war, Stroyer, like many other ex-slaves, sought to overcome the ignorance slavery had imposed upon him. His quest for education was almost indistinguishable from his quest to serve God. He attended schools in Columbia and Charleston, South Carolina. In February 1869 he moved to Worcester, Massachusetts, where he attended evening schools and, later, the Worcester Academy. He was licensed as a local preacher in the AME Church, and was ordained as a deacon sometime later at Newport, Rhode Island. His bishop sent him to serve the AME Church in Salem, Massachusetts. While in Salem, Stroyer attended the Wesleyan School in Wilbraham, Massachusetts, and later pursued theological studies at Talladega College in Alabama.

Sullivan, Leon Howard (1922–) is the distinguished pastor emeritus of Zion Baptist Church (Philadelphia, Pennsylvania). He combined Booker T. Washington's advocacy of industrial education with the economic boycott tradition of more progressive African-American leaders. Sullivan historicized these strategies by arguing that they are stages in a process of capitalizing the African-American community rather than ends in themselves. His disciplined capitalism earned him considerable influence among American corporations, but his deep spirituality is often overlooked. Sullivan should be seen as an advocate of the moderate wing of the Social Gospel Movement, which equated material well-being with signs of the presence of the Kingdom of God on earth. This can be seen in his best-known books: *Build, Brother, Build!* (1969) and *Alternatives to Despair* (1972).

Tanner, Benjamin Tucker (1835–1923) was a distinguished bishop of the African Methodist Episcopal Church (AME) who was noted for his theological acumen and deep spirituality. His long tenure as editor of the denominational newspaper, *The Christian Recorder,* as well as the *AME Review,* placed these periodicals in the first ranks of the African-

American literary world. His openness to literary forms such as poetry, short stories, and novellas provided support and visibility to struggling African-American authors, who had few other outlets for their work. His theological conservatism, however, sometimes censored more radical political and theological expressions. He was also the father of the famous African-American artist Henry Ossawa Tanner, whose painting *The Thankful Poor* (1894) graces the cover of this book.

Taylor, Gardner Calvin (1918–) is senior pastor emeritus of the Concord Baptist Church of Christ (Brooklyn, New York), where he served for forty-two years. He is one of the greatest preachers in the history of Christianity. His intellect, wisdom, and oratorical genius have won him the affection and admiration of thousands of fellow preachers and believers, as well as far-flung devotees, who consider him the "Dean of American Preachers." He is the author of three books: *How Shall They Preach?* (1977), *The Scarlet Thread* (1981), and *Chariots Aflame* (1988).

Terrell, Lloyd Preston (1950–) is pastor of Franklin–St. John United Methodist Church (Newark, New Jersey) and the author of *Pray, Pastor, Pray!* (1993).

Thomas, George (1931–) is senior minister of the Congregational Church of Park Manor (Chicago). He has held several ministerial positions in the United Church of Christ, including St. Mark Congregational Church (Boston), Massachusetts Conference of the United Church of Christ, Riverside Church (New York), and the First Congregational Church (Atlanta, Georgia).

Thompson, Clara Ann (c. 1887–19?) and **Thompson, Priscilla Jane** (1882–1942) were part of a family of poets who are not well known beyond their writings.

Thurman, Howard (1900–1981) is best known as the premier African-American spiritual genius of the twentieth century. He was ordained a Baptist minister, and his first pastorate was the Mount Zion Baptist Church (Oberlin, Ohio). He was deeply influenced by the Quaker theology of Rufus Jones but ranged broadly and creatively through the spiritual, theological, and philosophical literature of Western culture. He served as professor of religion and director of religious life at Morehouse College and Spelman College, and dean of Rankin Chapel at Howard University (1932–1944). He worked with Albert Fisk to organize the Church for the Fellowship of All Peoples (San Francisco, California) between 1944 and 1953. In 1953 he accepted a call to become dean of the Daniel L. Marsh Chapel at Boston University, where he served until his retirement in 1965. He was a prolific and effective writer and one of the greatest preachers of this century. He published his autobiography, *With Head and Heart,* in 1980. His many deeply moving and influential books include *Jesus and the Disinherited* (1949), *The Luminous Darkness* (1965), and *The Search for Common Ground* (1971).

Tillman, Katherine Davis Chapman (1870–?) was one of the young, emerging African-American writers whom Benjamin Tucker Tanner promoted in the AME *Christian Recorder*. Much of her poetry would have been lost otherwise. She was a well-known worker in the AME Church and continued her faithful lay service after she married George M. Tillman, a minister in the Methodist Episcopal Church, North.

Tindley, Charles Albert (c. 1851–1933) was an ordained minister in the Methodist Episcopal Church, North, who is best remembered for his legendary preaching gifts and his pioneering hymnody. He was pastor of the East Calvary Methodist Episcopal Church (Philadelphia), now called Tindley Memorial Methodist Episcopal Church. After 1915 this congregation numbered more than 5,000 members. His music, however, touches the lives of millions of African-American Christians. His hymns include "We'll Understand It Better By and By," "Stand by Me," "Leave It There," and "Some Day." These hymns and more helped to shape gospel music. Tindley is counted as one of the premier founders of gospel music. See critical biographical articles on him in Bernice Johnson Reagon, ed., *We'll Understand It Better By and By* (1992).

Truth, Sojourner (c. 1799–1883) was a former slave who distinguished herself as an abolitionist, champion of women's rights (especially the rights of African-American women), and a powerful orator who devoted her gifts to advocating her causes and preaching her religious convictions. She changed her name from Isabella Baumfree to Sojourner Truth on 1 June 1843, as a declaration of her decision to be an itinerant preacher. She shares with Harriet Tubman the distinction of being one of the most famous African-American woman of the nineteenth century. Her legendary spirituality is canonized in the *Narrative of Sojourner Truth* (1878), an anecdotal autobiography which she dictated in the late 1840s—she herself was illiterate.

Turner, Lorenzo Dow (1895–1969) was a distinguished linguist who focused on the study of African languages in Africa itself, and especially among African-Americans. He taught at Fisk University and was professor of English emeritus at Roosevelt University (Chicago) when he died. His *Africanisms in the Gullah Dialect* (1949) maintains its place as a landmark achievement in the study of the retention of African culture and languages among African-Americans in the Sea Islands of South Carolina.

Walker, Alice (1944–) is a distinguished poet, novelist, and essayist who won the Pulitzer Prize in 1983 for her novel *The Color Purple* (1982), as well as other major prizes and awards for her poetry, such as the Lillian Smith Award for *Revolutionary Petunias and Other Poems* (1973), and a Richard and Hinda Rosenthal Award from the National Institute of Arts and Letters for her collection of short stories titled *In Love and Trouble: Stories of Black Women* (1973).

Walker, David (1785–1830) is best known for his famous *Appeal* (1829). We know that he was a resident of Cambridge, Massachusetts, before his death. His essay is a classic expression of prophetic African-American spirituality.

Walker, Margaret. See Alexander, Margaret Abigail Walker.

Walker, Wyatt Tee (1929–) is senior minister of the Canaan Baptist Church (New York). Besides his exemplary involvement in various liberation struggles, especially his memorable work as chief of staff of the Southern Christian Leadership Conference (1960–1964), he is a noted author and lecturer on African-American spirituality and church tithing. His several books on African-American spirituality include *The Soul of Black Worship* (1984), *Spirits That Dwell in Deep Woods* (1987), and *Spirits That Dwell in Deep Woods II* (1988).

Washington, James Melvin (1948–) is professor of church history at Union Theological Seminary (New York), adjunct professor of religion at Columbia University, author of *Frustrated Fellowship: The Black Baptist Quest for Social Power* (1986), and editor of *A Testament of Hope: The Essential Writings of Martin Luther King, Jr.* (1986) and *I Have a Dream: Speeches and Writings That Changed the World* (1992).

Watley, Matthew Lawrence (1973–) is presently an undergraduate at Howard University who plans to attend law school in preparation for a career in public policy. He is also president of the New Jersey Conference Young People's Division of the AME Church and coauthor of *Poems of a Son, Prayers of a Father* (1992) with his father, the Reverend Dr. William Donnel Watley.

Watley, William Donnel (1947–) is pastor of St. James African Methodist Episcopal Church (Newark, New Jersey). He is the author of several books, including *Roots of Resistance: The Nonviolent Ethic of Martin Luther King, Jr.* (1985), *Sermons on Special Days* (1987), *From Mess to Miracle* (1989), and *Singing the Lord's Song in a Strange Land* (1993).

Westfield, Nancy Lynne (1962–) until recently was the diaconal minister of Christian education at Riverside Church in New York. She is presently pursuing an Ed.D. degree at Columbia University.

Weston, M. Moran (1910–) is the distinguished rector emeritus of St. Phillips Episcopal Church (New York), where he served between 1957 and 1982. He also served as executive secretary of the Division of

Christian Citizenship, the National Council of the Protestant Episcopal Church, and as a professor at the State University of New York, Albany. Also known for his extensive achievements as a banker and advocacy of moderate- to low-income housing, he is the founder and chairman of the board of Carver Federal Savings and Loan Association. His published writings include *Social Policy of the Episcopal Church in the Twentieth Century* (1964) as well as *Who Is This Jesus!* (1973).

Wheatley, Phillis (c. 1753–1784) was the first African-American woman to become a published author when her *Poems on Various Subjects, Religious and Moral* (1773) appeared. Her deep Evangelical spirituality and earnest expression are reflected in her writings, which have most recently been critically anthologized by John C. Shields. Shields's excellent critical biographical sketch of Wheatley, whose married name was Peters, can be found in Darlene Clark Hine, *Black Women in America: An Historical Encyclopedia* (1993).

Williams, Lucie Mae Eddie Campbell (1885–1963) was a famous pioneer, composer, and performer of African-American gospel music. A Christian educator and tireless worker within the National Baptist Convention, USA, Inc., Campbell Williams is the subject of three excellent biographical essays by Horace Clarence Boyer, Luvenia A. George, and Charles Walker, which can be found in Bernice Johnson Reagon, ed., *We'll Understand It Better By and By* (1992).

Williams, Peter, Jr. (c. 1780 or 1786–1840) was a pioneer African-American Episcopal clergyman, abolitionist, and opponent of the American Colonization Society. Williams led a group of African Americans who attended Trinity Church in New York City in organizing what is now known as St. Phillip's Episcopal Church. The following year this congregation was consecrated by the Bishop of New York. Williams himself was not ordained until 1826. During 1833, Williams became deeply involved in organizing the American Antislavery Society. But he acquiesced to the requirement of his priestly vows to obey his bishop when, after a white mob burned the sanctuary and rectory of St. Phillip's Church in July 1834, his bishop instructed him to abandon his abolitionist activities.

Williams, Smallwood Edmond (1907–1992) was the founder and organizer of the Bible Way Church of Our Lord Jesus Christ of the Apostolic Faith (Washington, DC) in 1927. From 1934 to 1957, he was the General Secretary for Church of Our Lord Jesus Christ of the Apostolic Faith. In 1957 he became the Bishop of the Bible Way Churches Worldwide. His books include *Significant Sermons* (1970), and *This Is My Story* (1981).

Woods, Fannie (unknown). See William H. Robinson.

Wright, Isaac. See Daniel Coker.

Wright, Jeremiah, Jr. (1941–) is a distinguished pastor in the United Church of Christ (UCC) and has been senior minister of Trinity UCC since 1972. His powerful intellect and pastoral vision as reflected in his preaching and imaginative leadership are admired by many colleagues and followers. He has two published hymns: "God Will Answer Prayer" and "Jesus Is His Name." He is the author of *What Makes You So Strong? Sermons of Joy and Strength* (1993).

Wright, Obie, Jr. (1944–) has been professor of religious studies at North Carolina State University at Raleigh, as well as professor of theology at Howard University Divinity School (Washington, DC). He is presently pastor of the Ryland Epworth United Methodist Church (Washington, DC).

Wright, Richard (1908–1960) was one of the great literary figures of the twentieth century. As a prolific author, an existentialist, and an African-American expatriate, he might be described as an apostle of anguish. Abject poverty, a father who deserted his family, and a mother who suffered several permanently disabling paralytic strokes, constitute the primal pain of his childhood. This experience shaped his worldview, and is reflected in most of his writings and public pronouncements. The extreme, moralistic Seventh-Day Adventism of his maternal grandmother caused him to believe that Christianity is an agent of modern psychic and material oppression. This experience with familial and religious oppression deeply influenced his personality and led him to a life of faithful radicalism and independence. He identified with the African-American cultural nationalism of Marcus Garvey during the 1920s. But after the Great Depression began in 1929, his nascent Marxist analysis of American classism and racism led him to join the Communist Party in 1933. Unfortunately, Wright's prodigious political and social commentary often marred his public and literary reputation, especially during the cold war. Nevertheless, his major writings have become ensconced in the American literary canon with the inclusion of a critical edition of his *Black Boy (American Hunger), The Outsider, Lawd Today!, Uncle Tom's Children,* and *Native Son,* annotated by Arnold Rampersad, in The Library of America (1991).

Glossary of Terms

ah: [interjection used to express religious ecstasy][1]

ahmen: amen

ain't: are not

an': and

axed: asked

bar': bear

canniser: canister or cannon

chile: child

chillun: children

conneck: connect

cuss: curse

dan: than

dar: that

dat: that

de: the

dee: thee

deliber: deliver

dem: them

dere: there

dese: these

dey: they

dis: this

do': door

doubtin': doubting

dus': dust

dy: thou

dy: thy

ef: if

em: them

ennybody: anybody

erbuv: above

ergree: agree

erway: away

fer: for

fersake: forsake

f'om: from

fiah: fire

fiel': field

fo': for

fotch out: fetch out

froo: from

fur: far

furnis: furnace

Gawd: God

ghos': ghost

gib: give

gonna: going to

grape: grapeshot

han's: hands

heah: hear

heared: heard

hearn: heard

hoss: horse

ile: oil

jes: just

jestice: justice

jined: joined

kep': kept

kin: can

---

[1]For careful studies of religious ecstasy see the following books: I. M. Lewis, *Ecstatic Religion: An Anthropological Study of Spirit Possession and Shamanism* (Baltimore, MD, and Harmondsworth, Middlesex, England: Penguin Books, 1971) and Sheila S. Walker, *Ceremonial Spirit Possession in Africa and Afro-America: Forms, Meanings, and Functional Significance for Individuals and Social Groups* (Leiden: Brill, 1972).

knowed: knew
Lawd: Lord
lectrify: electrify
lef: left
luminate: illuminate
luv: love
magination: imagination
marster: master
mawnin': morning
moah: more
mutterin: muttering
'n': and
noint: anoint
nuffin: nothing
o': of
odder: other
ol': old
outen: out of
ovah: over
petual: perpetual
possum: opossum
powah: power
ribber: river
roun': around
sarvint: servant
secesh: success
seekin': seeking
shiel': shield
sinkin': sinking

sistah: sister
soggers: soldiers
sol': sold
sot: set
sperrit: spirit
sposed: supposed
stan': stand
tallah: tallow
telefoam: telephone
ter: to
tho: though
tote dem: carry them
tree: three
trufe: truth
trus': trust
tudder: another
tuh: to
turpentime: turpentine
ub: of
uh: an
weepin': weeping
we's got no: we do not have
whare: where
whatsomebedder: whatsoever
wheah: where
wid: with
wifin: within
yer: you
yere: here

Selected Bibliography

I. Contemporary Works on African-American Prayers

Aptheker, Herbert, ed. *Prayers for Dark People*. Amherst: University of Massachusetts Press, 1980.

Bishop, Shelton Hale. *The Wonder of Prayer*. Greenwich, CT: Seabury Press, 1959.

Bowyer, O. Richard, Betty L. Hart, and Charlotte A. Meade. *Prayer in the Black Tradition*. Nashville, TN: Upper Room, 1986.

Carter, Harold. *The Prayer Tradition of Black People*. Valley Forge, PA: Judson Press, 1976.

Costen, Melva W. "The Prayer Heritage of Afro-America." *Presbyterian Survey* (October 1984): 21–23.

———. "The Prayer Tradition of Black Americans." *Reformed Liturgy and Music* 15 (Spring 1981): 83–93.

Healey, Joseph G. "Adapting African Prayers in Black Liturgy." *Liturgy* 3 (Spring 1983): 55–61.

Henry, Kenneth. "Prayer and the Practice of Ministry: The Afro-American Heritage." *Impact* (1979): 11–31.

James, Willis Laurence. "The Romance of the Negro Folk Cry." *Phylon* 16/19 (1955): 15–30.

Lofton, Fred C. *A Crying Shepard: A Therapy of Tears, Altar Prayers Delivered at the Metropolitan Baptist Church, Memphis, Tennessee*. Winter Park, FL: Four-G Publishers, 1993.

———. *When We Pray*. Elgin, IL: Progressive Baptist Publishing House, 1978.

Mbiti, John. *The Prayers of African Religion*. Maryknoll, NY: Orbis Books, 1975.

Shorter, Aylward. *Prayer in the Religious Traditions of Africa*. London and New York: Oxford University Press, 1975.

Smith, J. Alfred, Sr. *A Prayer Wheel Turning: Selected Pastoral Prayers*. Morristown, NJ: Aaron Press, 1989.

Walker, Wyatt Tee. "Praying: The Strength of Black Worship." In Wyatt Tee Walker. *The Soul of Black Worship: A Trilogy—Preaching, Praying, Singing*. New York: Martin Luther King, Jr., Fellows Press, 1984. Pp. 27–43.

II. Major General Works on Prayer

Appleton, George, gen. ed. 1985. *The Oxford Book of Prayer*. Reprint, Oxford and New York: Oxford University Press, 1992.

Arintero, J. G. *Stages in Prayer*. Translated by Kathleen Pond. London: Blackfriars, 1957.

Baillie, John. *A Diary of Private Prayers*. New York: Charles Scribner's Sons, 1949.

Bloesch, Donald. *The Struggle of Prayer*. San Francisco: Harper & Row, 1980.

Bloom, Anthony. *Beginning to Pray*. New York: Paulist Press, 1970.

Boros, Ladislaus. *Christian Prayer*. Translated by David Smith. New York: Seabury Press, 1976.

Boulding, Maria. *Prayer: Our Journey Home*. Ann Arbor, MI: Servant Books, 1979.

Bounds, E. M. *Power Through Prayer*. Grand Rapids, MI: Zondervan, 1979.

Boutaud, Father. *The Art of Conversing with God*. Translated by J. D. Souza. Rome: n.p., 1959.

Brown, William Adams. *The Life of Prayer in a World of Science*. New York and London: Charles Scribner's Sons, 1931.

Brummer, Vincent. *What Are We Doing When We Pray? A Philosophical Inquiry*. London: SCM Press, 1984.

Buttrick, George Arthur. *Prayer*. New York: Abingdon-Cokesbury, 1942.

Douglass, James W. *Resistance and Contemplation: The Way of Liberation*. New York: Dell, 1972.

Ellul, Jacques. *Prayer and Modern Man*. Translated by C. Edward Hopkin. New York: Seabury Press, 1970.

Forsyth, P. T. *The Soul of Prayer*. 1916. Enlarged ed., London: Independent Press, 1952.

Foster, Richard J. *Prayer: Finding the Heart's True Home*. San Francisco: HarperSanFrancisco, 1992.

Gallen, John, ed. *Christians at Prayer*. Notre Dame and London: University of Notre Dame Press, 1977.

Gossip, Arthur John. *In the Secret Place of the Most High, Being Some Studies in Prayer*. 1946. Reprint, London: Independent Press, 1950.

Grou, Jean-Nicholas. *How to Pray*. Translated by Joseph Dalby. Greenwood, SC: Attic, 1982.

Guyon, Madame. *Experiencing God Through Prayer*. Edited by Donna C. Arthur. Springdale, PA: Whitaker, 1984.

Hallesby, Ole. *Prayer*. Translated by Clarence J. Carlsen. Minneapolis, MN: Augsburg, 1959.

Heiler, Friedrich. *Prayer: A Study in the History and Psychology of Religion*. Translated and edited by Samuel McComb with the assistance of J. Edgar Park. London and New York: Oxford University Press, 1932.

Hollings, M., and E. Gulick, eds. *The One Who Listens: A Book of Prayer*. New York: Morehouse-Barlow, 1971.

James, William. *Varieties of Religious Experience*. 1902. Reprint, Bergenfield, NY: New American Library, 1958.

Louf, A. *Teach Us to Pray*. Translated by H. Hoskins. Chicago: Franciscan Herald Press, 1975.

Maritain, Jacques, and Raissa Maritain. *Prayer and Intelligence*. New York: Sheed & Ward, 1943.

Martin, Bernard, trans. *Prayer in Judaism*. New York: Basic Books, 1968.

Merton, Thomas. *Contemplative Prayer*. Garden City, NY: Doubleday, Image Books, 1971.

Nédoncelle, Maurice. *The Nature and Use of Prayer*. Translated by A. Manson. London: Burns Oates, 1962.

Pittenger, Norman. *Praying Today*. Grand Rapids, MI: William B. Eerdmans, 1975.

Rahner, Karl. *On Prayer*. 1958. Reprint, Collegeville, MN: Liturgical Press, 1993.

Schmidt, Herman, ed. *Prayer and Community*. New York: Herder & Herder, 1970.

Schmidt, Joseph F. *Praying Our Experiences*. Winona, MN: St. Mary's Press, 1989.

Spong, John Shelby. *Honest Prayer*. New York: Seabury Press, 1973.

Sponheim, Paul R., ed. *A Primer on Prayer*. Philadelphia: Fortress Press, 1988.

Steere, Douglas V. *Prayer and Worship*. New York: Edward W. Hazen Foundation, 1938.

Stewart, George S. *The Lower Levels of Prayer*. New York and Nashville: Abingdon-Cokesbury Press, 1939.

Swanson, Kenneth. *Uncommon Prayer: Approaching Intimacy with God*. New York: Ballantine, 1987.

Ulanov, Ann, and Barry Ulanov. *Primary Speech: A Psychology of Prayer*. Atlanta: John Knox Press, 1982.

Vincent, Mary Clare. *The Life of Prayer and the Way to God*. Still River, MS: St. Bede's Publications, 1982.

von Balthasar, Hans Urs. *Prayer*. Translated by A. V. Littledale. New York: Sheed & Ward, 1961.

Ware, Timothy, ed. *The Art of Prayer: An Orthodox Anthology*. Compiled by Igumen Chariton of Valamo. Translated by E. Kadloubovsky and E. M. Palmer. London: Faber & Faber, 1966.

Weil, Simone. *Waiting for God*. Translated by Emma Crauford. New York: Harper & Row, 1973.

Notes on Sources

INTRODUCTION

Arendt, Hannah, *Eichmann in Jerusalem: A Report on the Banality of Evil* (New York: Viking Press, 1963).

Bercovitch, Sacvan, *The American Jeremiad* (Madison, WI: University of Wisconsin Press, 1978).

Berger, Peter L., *The Sacred Canopy: Elements of a Sociological Theory of Religion* (Garden City, NY: Anchor Books, 1967).

Booker, Robert J., *Two Hundred Years of Black Culture in Knoxville, Tennessee, 1791–1991* (Virginia Beach, VA: The Donning Company/Publishers, 1993).

Buber, Martin, *Eclipse of God: Studies in the Relation Between Religion and Philosophy* (New York: Harper, 1952).

Buckley, Michael J., *At the Origins of Modern Atheism* (New Haven: Yale University Press, 1987).

Carter, Stephen L., *The Culture of Disbelief: How American Law and Politics Trivialize Religious Devotion* (New York: Basic Books, 1993).

Clark, Kenneth B., *Prejudice and Your Child* (Boston: Beacon Press, 1955).

Coles, Robert, *The Spiritual Life of Children* (Boston: Houghton Mifflin Company, 1990).

Comer, James P., *Beyond Black and White* (New York: Quadrangle Books, 1972).

Cone, James H., *Black Theology and Black Power* (New York: Seabury, 1969).

———, *God of the Oppressed* (New York: Seabury Press, 1975).

Cose, Ellis, *The Rage of a Privileged Class* (New York: HarperCollins Publishers, 1993).

Cousineau, Philip, comp., *Soul: An Archaeology, Readings from Socrates to Ray Charles* (San Francisco: HarperCollins, 1994).

Cross, William E., Jr., *Shades of Black: Diversity in African-American Diversity* (Philadelphia: Temple University Press, 1991).

Crummell, Alexander, *Destiny and Race: Selected Writings, 1840–1898,* ed. Wilson Jeremiah Moses (Amherst, MA: University of Massachusetts Press, 1992).

DeVries, S. J., "Sin, Sinners," in *The Interpreter's Dictionary of the Bible,* vol. 4, ed. George Arthur Buttrick, et al. (Nashville: Abingdon, 1962), 361–376.

Douglass, Mary, *Purity and Danger: An Analysis of Concepts of Pollution and Taboo* (1966; reprint, Boston: Routledge & Kegan Paul, 1980).

Du Bois, W. E. B., *The Souls of Black Folk* (reprint, New York: Vintage Books/Library of America, 1990), 138.

Eagles, Charles W., *Outside Agitator: Jon Daniels and the Civil Rights Movement in Alabama* (Chapel Hill: University of North Carolina Press, 1993).

Edwardes, Charles, "A Scene from Florida Life," *Macmillan's Magazine* 50 (May–October 1884): 264ff.

Eliade, Mircea, et al., eds., *The Encyclopedia of Religion,* vol. 13 (New York: Macmillan Publishing Company, 1987), 426–465.

Ellison, Ralph, *Shadow and Acts* (New York: Random House, 1964), 112.

Erikson, Erik, "Evolutionary and Developmental Considerations" in *The Long Darkness: Psychological and Moral Perspectives on Nuclear Winter,* by Lester Grinspoon (New Haven: Yale University Press, 1986), 65–72.

Evans, Eli N., *The Provincials: A Personal History of Jews in the South* (New York: Atheneum, 1976), 297–298.

Evers, Mrs. Medgar, with William Peters, *For Us, the Living* (Garden City, NY: Doubleday, 1967).

Fanon, Franz, *Black Skin, White Mask,* trans. Charles Lam Markman (1953; reprint, New York: Grove Weidenfeld, 1967).

Fenn, Richard K., *Liturgies and Trials: The Secularization of Religious Language* (New York: Pilgrim Press, 1982).

Ferris, Theodore, *Book of Prayer for Everyman* (Greenwich, CT, 1962), vii.

FitzGerald, Frances, *America Revised: History Schoolbooks in the Twentieth Century* (Boston: Little, Brown, 1979).

Frady, Marshall, *Billy Graham: A Parable of American Righteousness* (Boston: Little, Brown, 1979).

Freud, Sigmund, *The Psychopathology of Everyday Life,* ed. James Strachey, trans. Alan Tyson (New York: W. W. Norton & Company, 1965).

Girard, Rene, *Violence and the Sacred* (Baltimore: Johns Hopkins University Press, 1977).

————, *Things Hidden Since the Foundations of the World* (Palo Alto: Stanford University Press, 1987).

Goodman, Nelson, "Prospects for A Theory of Projection," in *Fact, Fiction, and Forecast,* 4th ed. (1979; reprint, Cambridge, MA: Harvard University Press, 1983), 84–124.

Harrington, Michael, *The Politics at God's Funeral: The Spiritual Crisis of Western Civilization* (New York: Holt, Rinehart and Winston, 1983).

Hatch, Nathan O., *The Democratization of American Christianity* (New Haven: Yale University Press, 1989).

Hegel, G. W. F., *Phenomenology of Spirit,* trans. A. V. Miller (Oxford: Oxford University Press, 1977), 126–138.

Heschel, Abraham J., *The Prophets* (New York: Harper & Row, Publishers, 1962), esp. 221–231.

Horton, Walter Marshall, *Theism and the Modern Mood* (New York: Harper, 1930).

Howard-Pitney, David, *The Afro-American Jeremiad: Appeals for Justice in America* (Philadelphia: Temple University Press, 1990).

Howlett, Duncan, *No Greater Love: The James Reeb Story* (1966; reprint, Boston: Skinner House Books, 1993).

Hughes, Langston, ed., *The Book of Negro Humor* (New York: Dodd, Mead, 1966).

Hull, John M., *Touching the Rock: An Experience of Blindness* (New York: Pantheon Books, 1990), esp. 76–121.

Isenhour, Judith Clayton, *A Pictorial History* (Virginia Beach, VA: The Donning Company/Publishers, Inc., 1978), 179.

Jacoby, Russell, *Social Amnesia: A Critique of Contemporary Psychology from Adler to Laing* (Boston: Beacon Press, 1975), 3–4.

James, William, *The Varieties of Religious Experience: A Study in Human Nature* (1902; reprint, New York: The Modern Library, 1936), 476.

Jay, Martin, *Force Fields: Between Intellectual History and Cultural Critique* (New York: Routledge, 1993).

————, *Downcast Eyes: The Denigration of Vision in Twentieth-Century French Thought* (Berkeley: University of California Press, 1993).

Jung, Carl Gustav, "The Shadow," in *Aion: Researches into the Phenomenology of the Self* (1951), vol. 9 of *The Collected Works of C. G. Jung.* (Princeton, NJ: Princeton University Press, 1967).

————, *Modern Man in Search of A Soul,* trans. W. S. Dell and Cary F. Baynes (New York: Harcourt Brace Jovanovich, Publishers, 1933), 205.

Kovel, Joel, *White Racism: A Psychohistory* (New York: Columbia University Press, 1984).

Lemann, Nicholas, *The Promised Land: The Great Black Migration and How It Changed America* (New York: Alfred Knopf, 1991).

Levine, Lawrence, *Black Culture and Black Consciousness: Afro-American Folk Thought from Slavery to Freedom* (New York: Oxford University Press, 1977).

McDonald, Michael J., and William Bruce Wheeler, *Knoxville, Tennessee: Continuity and Change in An Appalachian City* (Knoxville: University of Tennessee Press, 1983), 152–153.

McKivigan, John R., *The War Against Proslavery Religion: Abolitionism and the Northern Churches, 1830–1865* (Ithaca: Cornell University Press, 1984).

Marcuse, Herbert, *Eros and Civilization: A Philosophical Inquiry into Freud.* (1955; reprint, Boston: Beacon Press, 1966), 232.

Martyn, Dorothy W., *The Man in the Yellow Hat: Theology and Psychoanalysis in Child Therapy* (Atlanta, GA: Scholars Press, 1992).

Mays, Benjamin E., *The Negro's God as Reflected in His Literature* (1938; reprint, New York: Atheneum, 1968).

Miller, Floyd J., *The Search for a Black Nationality: Black Emigration and Colonization, 1787–1863* (Urbana: University of Illinois Press, 1975).

Mitchell, W. T. J., *Picture Theory: Essays on Verbal and Visual Representation* (Chicago: University of Chicago Press, 1994), 183–207.

Moses, Wilson Jeremiah, *Alexander Crummell: A Study of Civilization and Discontent* (New York: Oxford University Press, 1989).

————, "Cambridge Platonism in West Africa: Alexander Crummell's Theory of Development and Culture Transfer," *New England Journal of Black Studies* 3 (1983): 60–77.

————, *The Golden Age of Black Nationalism, 1850–1925* (Hamden, CT: Archon Books, 1978).

Myrdal, Gunnar, et al., *An American Dilemma: The Negro Problem and Modern Democracy,* 2 vols. (1944; reprint, New York: Pantheon Books, 1972).

Neusch, Marcel, *The Sources of Modern Atheism: One Hundred Years of Debate over God,* trans. Matthew J. O'Connell (New York: Paulist Press, 1982).

Newman, John Henry, *An Essay in Aid of a Grammar of Assent* (reprint, Notre Dame, IN: University of Notre Dame Press, 1979).

Niebuhr, H. Richard, *The Kingdom of God in America* (1937; reprint, New York: Harper & Row, Publishers, 1959).

————, *Radical Monotheism and Western Culture* (New York: Harper, 1960).

Offley, Greenburg W., *A Narrative of the Life and Labor of the Rev. G. W. Offley, A Colored Man, and Local Preacher* (Hartford: n.p., 1860), 14–16.

Owens, Sharynn L., *Moving into Its Second Century: Mount Zion Baptist Church* (White Plains, NY: Monarch, 1975).

Patterson, Orlando, *Slavery and Social Death* (Cambridge, MA: Harvard University Press, 1982).

Pennington, James William Charles, introduction to *Essays: Including Biographies and Miscellaneous Pieces in Prose and Poetry,* ed. Ann Plato (Hartford: n.p., 1841), xviii.

Plato, *The Republic of Plato,* trans. Allan Bloom (New York: Basic Books, Inc., 1968), sections 514a–517b.

Preminger, Alex, T. V. F. Brogan, et al., eds., *The New Princeton Encyclopedia of Poetry and Poetics* (Princeton, NJ: Princeton University Press, 1993), 1230–1233.

Proudfoot, Merrill, *Diary of A Sit-In,* 2nd ed. (1962; reprint, Urbana: University of Illinois Press, 1990).

Raboteau, Albert J., *Slave Religion: The Invisible Institution in the Antebellum South* (New York: Oxford University Press, 1978).

Rahner, Karl, "Anonymous Christians," in vol. 6, *Concerning Vatican Council II,* trans. Karl-H. and Boniface Kruger, of *Theological Investigations* (Baltimore: Helicon Press, 1969), 390–398.

————, "Anonymous Christianity and the Missionary Task of the Church" in vol. 12, *Confrontation,* trans. David Bourke, of *Theological Investigations* (New York: Seabury Press, 1974), 161–178.

————, "Observations on the Problem of the 'Anonymous Christian' " in vol. 14, *Ecclesiology, Questions in the Church, the Church in the World,* trans. David Bourke, of *Theological Investigations* (New York: Seabury Press, 1976), 280–294.

Redekop, John Harold, *The American Far Right: A Case Study of Billy James Hargis and Christian Crusade* (Grand Rapids, MI: William B. Eerdmans Publishing Company, 1968).

Rich, Adrienne Cecile, *A Wild Patience Has Taken Me This Far: Poems, 1978–1981* (New York: W. W. Norton, 1982).

Ricoeur, Paul, *Freud and Philosophy: An Essay on Interpretation*, trans. Denis Savage (New Haven: Yale University Press, 1970), esp. 390–418.

———, *Interpretation Theory: Discourse and the Surplus of Meaning* (Fort Worth, TX: Texas Christian University Press, 1976).

———, *The Symbolism of Evil,* trans. Emerson Buchanan (Boston: Beacon Press, 1969).

Robinson, James H., *Road Without Turning: The Story of Reverend James H. Robinson* (New York: Farrar, Straus and Company, 1950).

Salter, John R., Jr., *Jackson, Mississippi: An American Chronicle of Struggle and Schism* (Hicksville, NY: Exposition Press, 1979).

Sartre, Jean-Paul, *Being and Nothingness: A Phenomenological Essay on Ontology,* trans. Hazel E. Barnes (New York: Washington Square Press, 1966), 252–302, esp. 259–260.

Schatzman, M., *Soul Murder: Persecution in the Family* (New York: Random House, 1973).

Schechter, William, *History of Negro Humor in America* (New York: Fleet Press Corp, 1970).

Shengold, Leonard, *Soul Murder: The Effects of Childhood Abuse and Deprivation* (New York: Fawcett Columbine, 1989).

Smith, Theophus H., *Conjuring Culture: Biblical Formations of Black America* (New York: Oxford University Press, 1994).

———, "The Spirituality of Afro-American Traditions" in *Christianity Spirituality,* vol. 18 of *World Spirituality: An Encyclopedic History of the Religious Quest,* eds. Louis Dupré and Don E. Saliers (New York: Crossroad Press, 1989).

Soskice, Janet Martin, *Metaphor and Religious Language* (1985; reprint, Oxford: Clarendon Press, 1989).

Storr, Anthony, ed., *The Essential Jung* (Princeton, NJ: Princeton University Press, 1983), 91–93.

Thurman, Howard, *Disciplines of the Spirit* (1963; reprint, Richmond, IN: Friends United Press, 1977), 22.

Thomas, Alexander, and Samuel Sillen, *Racism and Psychiatry* (Secaucus, NJ: Citadel Press, 1972).

Walker, David, *David Walker's Appeal, in Four Articles; Together With A Preamble, to the Coloured Citizens of the World, But in Particular, and Very Expressly, To Those of the United States of America* (1829; reprint, New York: Hill and Wang, 1965), 28.

Warnke, Georgia, "Ocularcentrism and Social Criticism" in *Modernity and the Hegemony of Vision,* ed. David Michael Levin (Berkeley, CA: University of California Press), 287–308.

Washington, James Melvin, *Frustrated Fellowship: The Black Baptist Quest for Social Power* (Macon, GA: Mercer University Press, 1986), 23–45.

———, "The Crisis in the Sanctity of Conscience in American Jurisprudence," *DePaul Law Review* 142 (Fall 1992): 11–60.

Watkins, Mel, *On the Real Side: Laughing, Lying, and Signifying—The Underground Tradition of African-American Humor* (New York: Simon & Schuster, 1994).

West, Cornel, *Prophesy Deliverance! An Afro-American Revolutionary Christianity* (Philadelphia: Westminster Press, 1982), 35.

———, *Race Matters* (Boston: Beacon Press, 1993), esp. 11–20.

Wittgenstein, Ludwig, *Blue and Brown Books: Preliminary Studies for the 'Philosophical Investigations'* (1958; reprint, New York: Harper Torchbooks, 1965), 77.

Young, Perry Deane, *God's Bullies: Native Reflections on Preachers and Politics* (New York: Holt, Rinehart, and Winston, 1982).

PRAYERS

Akers, Doris: "Lead Me, Guide Me" (1953)
The words of "Lead Me, Guide Me" are reprinted here as published in hymn no. 355 in *The New National Baptist Hymnal,* 4th ed. (Nashville, TN: National Baptist Publishing Board, 1978), and are used with the permission of Uni-Chappell, Inc., New York, NY.

[Alexander, Margaret Abigail Walker]: "Brother Ezekiel Prays Besides Hetta's Deathbed" (1966)
Both of Margaret Walker Alexander's prayers are taken from her poignant historical novel, *Jubilee,* which narrates the story of Vyry Dutton Ware Brown, the child of Hetta, an African slave, and John Morris Dutton, a white slave master. Vyry's story spans the turbulent

years from the 1850s through the 1870s. Brother Ezekiel's prayer is for the euthanasia of Hetta. See Margaret Walker, *Jubilee* (1966; reprint, New York: Bantam Books, 1988), 381.

————: "Vyry's Prayer in the Wilderness of Reconstruction" (1966)
Vyry utters this prayer after stopping Innis Brown, her second husband, from continuing his brutal beating of Harry, Innis's stepson. This incident reminds Vyry of the violence of her slave experience, as well as the bitter hatred and violent persecution of the ex-slaves since the rise of the Ku Klux Klan in 1866. See Walker, *Jubilee*, 10–11. Also see the preceding note.

Allen, Richard: "A Prayer for Faith" (1787–1830), "A Prayer for Hope" (1787–1830), and "A Prayer for Love" (1787–1830)
Richard Allen, *The Life, Experience, and Gospel Labors of the Rt. Rev. Richard Allen, To Which is Annexed The Rise and Progress of the African Methodist Episcopal Church in the United States of America* (1833; reprint, Philadelphia: F. Ford and M. A. Riply, 1880), 32, 29–30, 30–31. These prayers were written sometime during Allen's ministry but not published until shortly after he died in 1831 as part of a very small collection of his writings.

Anonymous: "Again and One More Time" (1895)
Southern Workman (April 1895): 60–61.

————: "A Deacon's Campmeeting Prayer" (1928)
Heard and transcribed by Andrew Polk Watson, "Primitive Religion Among Negroes in Tennessee" (M.A. thesis, Fisk University, 1932), 48–49. This prayer was reprinted, without attribution, in Langston Hughes and Arna Bontemps, eds., *The Book of Negro Folklore* (1958; reprint, New York: Dodd, Mead, 1983), 256.

————: "A Poor Negro's Prayer" (1864)
The editor apologizes for misplacing the source of this prayer, which was discovered in the course of his general research in African-American religious history.

————: "Prayer for Teacher" (1958)
See [Hughes, James Mercer Langston, and Arna Wendell Bontemps].

————: [A "Colored" Woman], "A Prayer for the Mourner's Bench" (1867)
This prayer was reported in *The Independent* (New York), 19 (30 May 1867): 2. The anonymous reporter introduced the prayer with these words: "A colored woman at Richmond made this quaint but genuine prayer."

————: "De Same God" (1928?)
See [Hughes, James Mercer Langston, and Arna Wendell Bontemps].

————: "A Slave Woman's Prayer" (1816)
See [Hays, Stephen].

————: "The Sun Done Rose" (1895)
Southern Workman (April 1895): 61.

————: "Sunday School Prayers" (1933).
See [Mays, Benjamin Elijah].

Baker, Benjamin Stanley: "A Benediction for a Church Ground Breaking Service" (1989)
Benjamin S. Baker, *Special Occasions in the Black Church* (Nashville, TN: Broadman Press, 1989), 68.

[Baldwin, James Arthur]: "The Prayer of Florence's Mother" (1952)
The background for this fictive prayer is separated from the prayer itself. See James Baldwin, *Go Tell It on the Mountain* (New York: Dell Publishing, 1952), 66–67, 68. These page numbers refer to the December 1985 printing of this classic novel.

Baldwin, James Arthur: "Trying to See the Light" (1989)
James Baldwin, *Gypsy and Other Poems,* with etched portraits by Leonard Baskin (South Hadley, MA: Gehenna Press, 1989). This poetic prayer was untitled. I have given it a title for stylistic consistency. Copyright ® 1989 by David Baldwin. Used here with permission.

Bibb, Eloise Alberta Veronica: "An Offering" (1895)
Eloise Bibb, *Poems* (Boston: Monthly Review Press, 1895), 107. Reprinted in Joan R. Sherman, ed., *Collected Black Women's Poetry,* vol. 4 (New York and Oxford: Oxford University Press, 1988).

Binga, Anthony, Jr.: "A Benediction for a Peaceful Soul" (1889)
Anthony Binga, Jr., *Sermons on Several Occasions,* vol. 1 (Richmond, VA [?]: n.p., 1889), 324.

Bontemps, Arna: See Hughes, James Mercer Langston.

[Botkin, Benjamin Albert]: "They Would Pray" (1945)
B. A. Botkin, ed., *Lay My Burden Down: A Folk History of Slavery* (Chicago: University of Chicago Press, 1945), 27.

Brawley, Benjamin Griffith: "Lord God, to Whom Our Fathers Prayed" (1899)
I am grateful to Quinton H. Dixie, my executive research associate and a Ph.D. candidate in church history at Union Theological Seminary, for

bringing this lost prayer to my attention, and for the invaluable assistance of Dr. Randall Burkett in securing a copy of it from Harvard University's Widener Library, which has a microform copy of the original. A first edition copy of this hymn is held by the Library of Congress and the Atlanta University Library.

Brooks, Walter Henderson: "Holy Spirit, Come!" (1940), "In This Hour" (1941), "The Inward Conflict" (1932), "One Thing I Crave" (1945), "A Prayer for the Nations" (1918)
Walter Henderson Brooks, *The Pastor's Voice: A Collection of Poems* (Washington, DC: Associated Publishers, 1945), 66, 94, 80–81, 57, 79.

Brown, Diana: "I Ask You, Jesus, to Take Care of Me" (1949)
Lorenzo Dow Turner, *Africanisms in the Gullah Dialect* (1949; reprint, Ann Arbor, MI: University of Michigan Press, 1973), 269, 271. For further information about the recording and transcription of this prayer see Diana Brown and Lorenzo Dow Turner in "Contributors."

Brown, James: "You Know the Purpose of Our Gathering, Jesus" (1980)
Patricia Jones-Jackson recorded and transcribed this prayer during the Ushers' Anniversary worship service of the New Jerusalem African Methodist Episcopal Church in Wadmalaw, South Carolina, 13 July 1980. The spirited audible responses of different members of the congregation are indented and italicized here in strict conformity with Dr. Jones-Jackson's transcription. Dr. Jones-Jackson first published this transcription as part of "Oral Tradition of Prayer in Gullah," *Journal of Religious Thought* 39 (Spring–Summer 1982): 21–33. The prayer itself can be found on pages 27–33. She also included it in her fine book *When Roots Die: Endangered Traditions on the Sea Islands* (Athens and London: University of Georgia Press, 1987), 82–87.

[Cameron, James]: "O Lord, Have Mercy!" (1930)
In August 1930, sixteen-year-old James Cameron, along with two other black teenagers, was arrested on the suspicion of raping a white woman and killing a white man. A white mob abducted Cameron, Thomas Shipp, and Abram Smith, from their jail cells and lynched them. According to Cameron, "With the noose around my neck and death in my brain, I waited for the end." But someone hushed the mob's macabre ritual and saved Cameron's life with these words: "Take this boy back. He had nothing to do with any raping or killing!" Cameron spent time in prison anyway. See James Cameron, *A Time of Terror* (Baltimore: Black Classic Press, 1982), 16–17, 19. The quotations in this note are from page 74.

Campbell, Lucie Mae: "Touch Me, Lord Jesus" (1941)
The musical score for this famous hymn can be found in most hymnals used by African-American congregations. See Jon Michael Spencer, *Black Hymnody: A Hymnological History of the African-American Church* (Knoxville, TN: University of Tennessee Press, 1992), for a useful analysis of these hymnals. For a first-rate analysis of Campbell's hymnody, and the place of "Touch Me, Lord Jesus" in her sacred compositions, see the essays by Horace Clarence Boyer, Luvenia A. George, and Charles Walker in Bernice Johnson Reagon, ed., *We'll Understand It Better By and By: Pioneering African American Gospel Composers* (Washington and London: Smithsonian Institution Press, 1992), 81–138. The words for "Touch Me, Lord Jesus" are reprinted here as published in hymn no. 336 in *The New National Baptist Hymnal,* 4th ed. (Nashville, TN: National Baptist Publishing Board, 1978).

Cleage, Albert B., Jr.: "A Prayer for African American Peoplehood" (1968)
Albert B. Cleage, Jr., *The Black Messiah* (New York: Sheed & Ward, 1969), 170.

Cleveland, James: "Lord, Help Me to Hold Out" (1974)
The words and music for this hymn can be found in several African-American hymnals, for example, *Lead Me, Guide Me: The African American Catholic Hymnal* (Chicago: G.I.A. Publications, 1987), hymn no. 229.

[Cobbins, Otho B.]: "A Child's Prayer" (1966)
Otho B. Cobbins, ed., *The History of Church of Christ (Holiness) U.S.A., 1895–1865* (New York: Vantage Press, 1966), 79.

Coker, Daniel: "Prayers from a Pilgrim's Journal" (1820)
Daniel Coker, *Journal of Daniel Coker, A Descendant of Africa, From the Time of Leaving New York, in the Ship Elizabeth, Capt. Sebor, on A Voyage for Sherbro, in Africa, in Company with Three Agents and About Ninety Persons of Colour. The Rev. Samuel Bacon, John B. Bankson, Samuel S. Crozer, Agents* (Baltimore: Edward J. Coale, 1820), 12, 15–16, 17, 31, 38–39.

Colemon, Johnnie: "A Peace and Affirmation Prayer" (1989)
Frank B. Jones, *Psalms in Black: A Study of Black Prayer in Three Diverse Contexts* (Ann Arbor, MI: University Microfilms, 1989), 300–305. I have made changes in brackets to further refine Dr. Jones's transcription. His transcription is punctuated to approximate, as much as possible, the way this prayer was uttered. His purpose was anthropological; my changes seek literary consistency.

Corbett, Maurice N.: "Appeal to Heaven" (1914), "Lord, Your Weak Servants Bow" (1914)
Maurice N. Corbett, *The Harp of Ethiopia* (1914; reprint, Freeport, NY: Books for Libraries Press, 1971), 77–80.

Costen, Melva W.: "The Classic African-American Prayer" (1981)
This is Professor Costen's richly textured recollection of the classic African-American folk prayer that she heard "in the black Presbyterian church of her youth." Versions of this prayer are still being heard in African-American churches of various denominations in the 1980s and 1990s. See Melva W. Costen, "The Prayer Tradition of Black Americans," *Reformed Liturgy and Music* 15 (Spring 1981): 87–88.

Crummell, Alexander: "We Bless God" (1888)
This prayer is an excerpt from a transcription by Professor Wilson Jeremiah Moses of MS.C. 315 in the Schomburg Research Center, New York Public Library. See Alexander Crummell, *Destiny and Race: Selected Writings, 1840–1898,* ed. with intro. Wilson Jeremiah Moses (Amherst, MA: University of Massachusetts Press, 1992), 244.

Crutcher, William Townsend: "Thank You for Each One of Them" (1984)
Papers of William Townsend Crutcher, Mount Olive Baptist Church, Knoxville, TN. This prayer was transcribed and edited by the editor from a recording of one of the January 1984 Sunday morning services of the Mount Olive Baptist Church.

Cullen, Countée Porter: "Pagan Prayer" (1925), "The Shroud of Color" (1925)
Countée Cullen, *Color* (New York and London: Harper & Brothers, 1925), 20–21, 26–35.

Dabney, Elizabeth J.: "Dear God, Thank You for the Morning Light" (1945), "O My God, Please Close This War" (1945), "Please Send Our Boys Back Home" (1945), "What It Means to Pray Through" (1945)
Elizabeth J. Dabney, *What It Means to Pray Through* (1945; reprint, Memphis, TN: COGIC [Church of God in Christ] Publishing Board, 1991), 21, 86, 59–60, 16–17.

Dandridge, Raymond Garfield: "Cleave Us Way, O Lord" (1920)
Raymond Garfield Dandridge, *The Poet and Other Poems* (Cincinnati: n.p., 1920), 31.

Davis, Leroy: "I Call upon Your Name, Lord Jesus" (1993)
Brother Leroy Davis offered this prayer as part of an eleven-thirty Sunday morning worship service at the St. John Progressive Baptist Church (Austin, TX). See Walter F. Pitts, Jr., *Old Ship of Zion: The*

Afro-Baptist Ritual in the African Diaspora (New York and London: Oxford University Press, 1993), 16–17. See "Contributors" for further information on Leroy Davis and Walter F. Pitts. This prayer is used with the permission of the publisher, Oxford University Press.

[Dett, Robert Nathaniel]: "Keep Me from Sinkin' Down" (1927)
According to Dett, "This song was found on a fragment of a page of an old book of Negro songs. It is to be regretted that the complete book was not available in order that credit might be given to the original transcriber." This statement is a footnote to the musical composition for this "hymn of tribulation." See Robert Nathaniel Dett, ed., *Religious Folk-Songs of the Negro as Sung at Hampton Institute* (Hampton, VA: Hampton Institute Press, 1927), appendix 12.

Dorsey, Thomas Andrew: "Precious Lord, Take My Hand" (1932)
Dorsey wrote the words to this song shortly after his wife, Nettie, and son, Thomas, Jr., died during childbirth. Thomas A. Dorsey, *Precious Lord, Take My Hand* (Chicago: Hill & Range Songs, 1938). © Copyright 1938 by Hill & Range Songs, Inc. Copyright renewed, assigned to Uni-Chappell Music, Inc., New York, NY. Belinda Music, Publisher. Used by permission.

Douglass, Frederick: "O God, Save Me" (1893)
Frederick Douglass, *The Life and Times of Frederick Douglass Written by Himself* (1893; reprint, with notes by Henry Louis Gates, New York: Literary Classics of the United States, 1994), 572–573.

Douroux, Margaret Pleasant: "Give Me a Clean Heart" (1970)
The words and music for this hymn can be found in several African-American hymnals, for example, *Lift Every Voice and Sing II: An African American Hymnal* (New York: Church Hymnal Corporation, 1993), hymn no. 124.

[Drake, J. G. St. Clair]: "A Familiar Prayer" (1940)
J. G. St. Clair Drake, *Churches and Voluntary Associations in the Chicago Negro Community: Report of Official Project 465-54-3-386 Conducted Under the Auspices of the Works Projects Administration* (Chicago: n.p., 1940), 355, 356, 357.

Du Bois, William Edward Burghardt: "Give Us Grace" (1909–1910)
Herbert Aptheker, ed., *Prayers for Dark People* (Anherst, MA: University of Massachusetts Press, 1980), 21.

———: "A Litany of Atlanta" (1906)
Independent 61 (11 October 1906), 856–858. Reprinted in William

E. B. Du Bois, *Darkwater: Voices from Within the Veil* (1920; reprint, New York: Schocken Books, 1969), 25–28.

————: "A Prayer for Endurance" (1909–1910) and "A Prayer for Vision and Thought" (1909–1910)
Aptheker, ed., *Prayers for Dark People*, 27, 50.

————: "The Prayers of God" (1914)
Dr. W. E. B. Du Bois first published this poignant protest prayer as an unsigned poem under the title "The Christmas Prayers of God." See *Crisis* 9/2 (December 1914): 83–84. Several drafts in the microfilm version of the W. E. B. Du Bois Papers verify how difficult it was for Du Bois to write this prayer. His keen regard for theological subtlety is also evident. It was later published in his *Darkwater*, 249–252.

Dunbar, Paul Laurence: "Lead Gently, Lord" (1895), "The Warrior's Prayer" (1895), "When Storms Arise" (1895)
Paul Laurence Dunbar, *The Complete Poems of Paul Laurence Dunbar* (1895; reprint, New York: Dodd, Mead, 1930), 98, 123, 66.

Ellison, John Malcus: "Bless Those Who Teach" (1961) and "Rekindle Our Sense of Wonder" (1961)
John Malcus Ellison, *They Sang Through the Crisis: Dealing with Life's Most Critical Issues* (Valley Forge, PA, and Chicago: Judson Press, 1961), 126, 93.

Ferrill, London: "A Pastor's Last Prayer for His People" (1854)
This prayer was quoted in a biographical sketch of Pastor Ferrill in William J. Simmons, *Men of Mark: Eminent, Progressive and Rising* (1887; reprint, Chicago: Johnson Publishing Company, 1970), 208; see also John Wilson Townsend, *Lore of the Meadowland* (Lexington, KY: J. L. Richardson, 1911).

Forbes, James Alexander, Jr.: "Help Me, Lord, to Stand for the Kingdom" (1978)
This prayer was offered in the Duke University Chapel on 24 October 1978. It is used here with the permission of the author as transcribed in O. Richard Bowyer, Betty L. Hart, and Charlotte A. Meade, *Prayer in the Black Tradition* (Nashville, TN: Upper Room, 1986), 40–41. With the permission of the author, changes in punctuation, as well as a few other emendations, have been made.

Forbes, James Alexander, Jr.: "O God of Love, Power and Justice" (1990)
This prayer was offered at New York City Hall on the occasion of Mayor David Dinkins's celebration of the Martin Luther King, Jr., Holiday, 15 January 1990. The original copy is in the personal papers of

James Alexander Forbes, Jr., and is used here with the permission of the author.

Gilbert, Ralph Mark: "God Speed the Day" (1941), "Look Thou with Compassion upon Every Heart" (1941), "O Shepard Divine" (1941), "Our Need for Thee" (1941), "We Need Thy Way" (1941)
Typescripts of "The Negro at Church, a weekly [radio] presentation emanating from the lecture room of the First African Baptist Church, of Savannah, Ga., Dr. Ralph Mark Gilbert, Pastor." This radio program was broadcast by the Savannah Broadcasting Company, Station WTOC, on 4 August 1941. This typescript is taken from the papers of Ralph Mark Gilbert, 1899–1956, and is published here by the courtesy of Mrs. Eloria S. Gilbert.

Hammon, Jupiter: "Penitential Cries to God" (1760)
Jupiter Hammon, *An Evening Thought, Salvation by Christ, with Penitential Cries: Composed by Jupiter Hammon, A Negro belonging to Mr. Lloyd, of Queen's Village, on Long Island, the 25th of December, 1760.* Reprinted in Dorothy Porter, [comp.], *Early Negro Writing, 1760–1837* (Boston: Beacon Press, 1971), 529–531.

Hawkins, Walter: "Dear Jesus, I Love You" (1976)
This song became a gospel "hit" when it was released in 1976. Used by special permission of Libris Music BMI. All rights reserved.

Haynes, Lemuel: "A Prayer for New Birth" (1776)
Lemuel Haynes, "A Sermon on John 3:3," in Richard Newman, ed., *Black Preacher to White America: The Collected Writings of Lemuel Haynes, 1774–1833* (Brooklyn, NY: Carlson Publishing, 1990), 37–38.

[Hays, Stephen]: "A Slave Woman's Prayer" (1816)
Stephen Hays reported this prayer by an anonymous slave woman in his *The Praying African,* tract no. 92 in *Publications of the American Tract Society,* vol. 3 (New York: American Tract Society, [1832?]), 390. The date is based on internal evidence in Hays's tract.

Haywood, Garfield Thomas: "Draw Me, Dear Jesus" (1928)
G. T. Haywood, comp., *The Bridegroom Songs: Bethlehem Temple Edition* (Detroit, MI: Voice in the Wilderness, n.d.), 7. This prayer is the words for hymn no. 7, "Draw Me, Dear Jesus." The hymn carries the copyright date 1928. Psalm 63:8 and Song of Solomon 1:4 (KJV) are cited as its inspiration.

Heard, Josephine Delphine Henderson: "Doxology" (1890), "I Will Look Up" (1890), "Matin Hymn" (1890), "Thou Lovest Me" (1890), "Unuttered Prayer" (1890)

Josephine Delphine Henderson Heard, *Morning Glories* (Philadelphia: n.p., 1890), 108, 51–53, 62–63, 39. Reprinted in Joan R. Sherman, ed., *Collected Black Women's Poetry,* vol. 4 (New York and Oxford: Oxford University Press, 1988).

Henton, Richard Daniel: "A Prayer for Healing" (1983)
Frank B. Jones, *Psalms in Black: A Study of Black Prayer in Three Diverse Contexts* (Ann Arbor, MI: University Microfilms, 1989), 189–198. I have made changes in brackets to further refine Dr. Jones's transcription. His transcription is punctuated to approximate, as much as possible, the way this prayer was uttered. His purpose was anthropological; my changes seek literary consistency.

Holly, James Theodore: "A Prayer at Westminster Abbey" (1878)
Alonzo Potter Burgess Holly, *God and the Negro: Synopsis of God and the Negro or the Biblical Record of the Race of Ham* (Nashville, TN: National Baptist Publishing Board, 1937), 150–151.

[Hughes, James Mercer Langston, and Arna Wendell Bontemps]: "De Same God" (1928?) and "Prayer for Teacher" (1958)
Langston Hughes and Arna Bontemps, eds., *The Book of Negro Folklore* (1958; reprint, New York: Dodd, Mead, 1983), 257, 257–258.

Imes, William Lloyd: "A Prayer for a College Woman" (1956)
William Lloyd Imes, *The Black Pastures, an American Pilgrimage in Two Centuries: Essays and Sermons* (Nashville, TN: Hemphill Press, 1957), 28–29.

Jackson, Jesse Louis: "The Prayers of Our Grandmothers" (1977)
Jesse L. Jackson, *Straight from the Heart,* ed. Roger Hatch and Frank E. Watkins (Philadelphia: Fortress Press, 1987), 118–119.

Jackson, Rebecca Cox: "Instructions in the Midst of Prayer" (1843)
Jean McMahon Humez, ed., *Gifts of Power: The Writings of Rebecca Jackson, Black Visionary, Shaker Eldress* (Amherst, MA: University of Massachusetts Press, 1981), 189–190.

[Jacobs, Harriet A.]: "A Piteous Prayer to a Hidden God" (1861)
Harriet A. Jacobs, *Incidents in the Life of a Slave Girl Written by Herself* (1861; rev. ed., ed. Jean Fagan Yellin, Cambridge, MA, and London: Harvard University Press, 1987), 70.

Jea, John: "A Desire to Know Our Characters" (1816) and "For the Morning" (1816)
[John Jea], *A Collection of Hymns Compiled and Selected by John Jea, African Preacher of the Gospel* (Portsea, [England]: n.p., 1816), hymn nos.

290, 293. Although the only copy of this hymnal is in the Bodleian Library of Oxford University, a critical selection from it can be found in Graham Russell Hodges's excellent anthology *Black Itinerants of the Gospel: The Narratives of John Jea and George White* (Madison, WI: Madison House, 1993), pp. 171, 172.

Johnson, James Weldon: "God of Our Weary Years" (1921)
This prayer is the third verse of Johnson's (1871–1938) famous poem titled "The Negro National Anthem." The poem was set to music by his brother, J. Rosamond Johnson (1873–1954), and published under the title "Lift Every Voice and Sing."

Jones, Absalom: "A Thanksgiving Prayer for the Abolition of the African Slave Trade" (1808)
Absalom Jones, *A Thanksgiving Sermon, Preached January 1, 1808, in St. Thomas's, or the African Episcopal Church, Philadelphia: On Account of the Abolition of the African Slave Trade, on That Day, by the Congress of the United States* (Philadelphia: Fry and Kammerer, 1808). This entire sermon has been reprinted in Dorothy Porter, [comp.], *Early Negro Writing, 1760–1837* (Boston, Beacon Press, 1971), 335–342. The prayer itself is at the end of Jones's sermon. In Porter's anthology, it is on pages 341–342.

Jones, Charles Price: "As I Am Running" (1906)
The words of this prayer are taken from hymn no. 310, with the same title, in *His Fullness Songs*, rev. ed. (Jackson, MS: National Publishing Board of the Church of Christ (Holiness), U.S.A., 1977). The first edition of *His Fullness Songs* was published in 1906. Few of Jones's many hymns in this important hymnal were dated; I am using 1906 as the probable time of publication. Since Jones lived such a long life, it could have been written later. Jones usually cited a biblical passage as the inspiration for his hymnody. In "As I Am Running," he cited Hebrews 12:1–3.

———: "Lord, Rebuke Thy Servant Not" (1906)
The words of this prayer are taken from hymn no. 329, with the same title, in *His Fullness Songs*. Jones was inspired by Psalm 6, and literally incorporated several parts of this ancient psalm into this prayer.

———: "Prayer for Consecration" (1906)
The words of this prayer are taken from hymn no. 322, with the same title, in *His Fullness Songs*. Jones cited Hebrews 12:1–3 as his inspiration for this prayer.

————: "A Prayer for Spiritual Assurance" (1894)
Otho B. Cobbins, ed., *History of Church of Christ (Holiness) U.S.A., 1895–1865* (New York: Vantage Press, 1966), 24–25.

Jones, Singleton Thomas Webster: "A Bishop's Benediction" (1892)
Singleton T. Jones, *Sermons and Addresses of the Late Rev. Bishop Singleton T. Jones, D.D., of the African M.E. Zion Church, with A Memoir of His Life and Character Written by Rev. J. W. Smith* (York, PA: P. Anstadt & Sons, 1892), 81.

Jordan, Lewis Garnett: "A Marriage Prayer" (1929)
L. G. Jordan, *The Baptist Standard Church Directory and Busy Pastor's Guide* (Nashville, TN: Sunday School Publishing Board of the National Baptist Convention, U.S.A., 1929), 101.

King, Martin Luther, Jr.: "A Pastoral Prayer" (1956)
Harold Carter, *The Prayer Tradition of Black People* (Valley Forge, PA: Judson Press, 1976), 109–110.

Lawrence, George: "A Prayer for the Abolition of Slavery" (1813)
George Lawrence, *Oration on the Abolition of the Slave Trade, Delivered on the First Day of January, 1813, in the African Methodist Episcopal Church* (New York: Hardcastle and Van Pelt, 1813). This address has been reprinted in Dorothy Porter, [comp.], *Early Negro Writing, 1760–1837* (Boston: Beacon Press, 1971), 374–382. Lawrence's prayer is the last paragraph of his address. In Porter's anthology, it is on page 382.

Lawson, Robert C.: "Prayer for Freedom from Race Prejudice" (1925)
R. C. Lawson, *The Anthropology of Jesus Christ Our Kinsman* (New York: Church of Christ Publishing Company, 1925?), 42.

Lee, Jarena: "A Prayer for Sanctification" (1808?)
Jarena Lee, *Religious Experience and Journal of Mrs. Jarena Lee, Giving An Account of Her Call to Preach the Gospel* (1849; reprint, with an intro. by Sue M. Houchins, New York and London: Oxford University Press, 1988), 8–10.

Lincoln, Charles Eric: "The Eighth Psalm" (1958) and "Return, O Lord" (1944)
C. Eric Lincoln, ed., *This Road Since Freedom: Collected Poems* (Durham, NC: Carolina Wren Press, 1989), 58, 59.

————: "A Prayer for Love" (1958)
See Lincoln, ed., *This Road*, 57. Both the words and music for this hymn can be found in *Songs of Zion: Supplemental Worship Resources 12* (Nashville, TN: Abingdon Press, 1981), hymn no. 70. This prayer is reprinted here with the permission of the author.

Lofton, Fred C.: "Pray for the Christian Family" (1978)
Fred C. Lofton, *When We Pray* (Elgin, IL: Progressive Baptist Publishing House, 1978), 117–119.

————: "We Need Thee, Lord Jesus, As Never Before" (1993)
Fred C. Lofton, *A Crying Shepard: A Therapy of Tears, Altar Prayers Delivered at the Metropolitan Baptist Church, Memphis, Tennessee* (Winter Park, FL: Four-G Publishers, 1993), 145–147.

McGirt, James Ephraim: "The Century Prayer" (1901)
James Ephraim McGirt, *Some Simple Songs and a Few More Ambitious Attempts* (Philadelphia: George F. Lasher, 1901). This poem can more readily be found in Joan R. Sherman, ed., *African-American Poetry of the Nineteenth Century: An Anthology* (Urbana and Chicago: University of Illinois Press, 1992), 460.

McGuire, George Alexander: "A Prayer for Good Friday" (1923)
Negro Churchman 2/8 (August 1924): 1.

————: "A Prayer for the Synod" (1924)
Negro Churchman, 1/4 (April 1923): 3–4.

McNeil, Genna Rae: "Lord, I'm Willing" (1989)
This prayer is the lyrics of a hymn written by Professor McNeil, music by Joseph Joubert. Correspondence of Genna Rae McNeil to James Melvin Washington, Durham, NC, 14 February 1994.

McNeil, Jesse Jai: "We Cast Ourselves upon Thee" (1961)
Jesse Jai McNeil, *Minister's Service Book for Pulpit and Parish* (1961; reprint, Grand Rapids, MI: William B. Eerdmans, 1993), 195–196.

Mason, Charles Harrison: "An Exhortative Invocation" (1919)
German Ross, J. O. Patterson, and Julia Atkins, comp., *The History and Formative Years of the Church of God in Christ . . .* (Memphis, TN: Church of God in Christ Publishing House, 1969), 32–33.

————: "A Vision at the Great Azusa Prayer Meetings" (1907)
C. F. Range, Jr., ed., *Official Manual with the Doctrines and Discipline of the Church of God in Christ, 1973* (Memphis, TN: Church of God in Christ Publishing House, 1973), xxvii–xxviii.

Massie, William: "A Thanksgiving Prayer" (1935)
This prayer was featured on the cover page of *Negro Journal of Religion* 3/10 (November 1937): 1.

[Mays, Benjamin Elijah]: "Sunday School Prayers" (1933)
These prayers were found in "a group of stenographic reports" of African-American Sunday school worship services and were published

and analyzed by Benjamin Elijah Mays and Joseph William Nicholson, *The Negro's Church* (1933; reprint, New York: Arno Press, 1969), 141–148.

Nichols, Lewis Ruffin: "The Soul's Thirst" (1895)
Christian Recorder (16 May 1895). This prayer was written in Georgetown, SC, on 10 April 1895.

[Nicholson, Joseph William]: See [Mays, Benjamin Elijah].

Payne, Daniel Alexander: "The Hour of Prayer" (1837)
The Colored American (July 1837)

————: "Prayer for Dedication of a Church Edifice" (1848)
Daniel A. Payne, *The Semi-centenary and the Retrospection of the African Methodist Episcopal Church in the United States of America* (1866; reprint, Freeport, NY: Books for Libraries Press, 1972), 82–84.

————: "A Sacred Ode: A Prayer for the Consecration of a Pulpit" (1866)
Bishop Payne "composed" this poetic prayer "in the pulpit of Bethel Church, Philadelphia, immediately after its consecration." *Semi-centenary,* 47–49.

Phillips, Charles Henry: "A Poetic Prayer for a New Day" (1870)
C. H. Phillips, *The History of the Colored Methodist Episcopal Church in America: Comprising Its Organization, Subsequent Development, and Present Status* (1898; reprint, New York: Arno Press, 1972), 184.

[Pipes, William H.]: "Send It Now, Lord" (1951), "Thank Thee for Everything" (1951), "Thou Have Widen the Way for Us" (1951)
William H. Pipes, *Say Amen, Brother! Old-time Negro Preaching: A Study in American Frustration* (1951; reprint, Detroit: Wayne State University Press, 1992), 114–115, 9, 114.

Plato, Ann: "A Teacher's Prayer" (1841)
Ann Plato, *Essays; Including Biographies and Miscellaneous Pieces in Prose and Poetry* (Hartford: n.p., 1841), 94.

Popel, Esther: "Grant Me Strength" (1934)
Esther Popel, *A Forest Pool* (Washington, DC: n.p., 1934), 11.

Powell, Raphael Philemon: "A Prayer for Freedom" (1957)
R. H. Powell, *A Prayer for Freedom* (New York: n.p., 1957). This sermonic prayer was published by the author in booklet form and deposited in the Schomburg Research Center, New York Public Library. It is used here with the permission of the author, who resides in New York City.

Ransome, William Lee: "Benediction" (1973)
Harold Carter, *The Prayer Tradition of Black People* (Valley Forge, PA: Judson Press, 1976), 61–62.

Reid, Frank Madison, III: "A Prayer for Liberation That Leads to Liberating Love" (1994)
Personal Papers of Frank Madison Reid III (1951–).

Samuels-Belboder, John Nathaniel: "A Prayer of Contrition" (1935)
Negro Journal of Religion 1/2 (March 1935): 2.

Shackelford, Theodore Henry: "Thou Hast Supplied My Every Need" (1916–1918)
Theodore Henry Shackelford, *My Country and Other Poems* (Philadelphia: Press of I. W. Klapp Company, 1916–1918), 175.

Smalls, John B.: "Elijah's Stay" (1898) and "A Prayer for the Human Heart" (1898)
John B. Smalls, *The Human Heart Illustrated by Nine Figures of the Heart* (n.p.: York Dispatch, 1898), 78, 54.

Smith, Amanda: "A Conversation with the Lord" (1893)
Amanda Smith, *An Autobiography: The Story of the Lord's Dealings with Mrs. Amanda Smith, the Colored Evangelist* (Chicago: Meyer & Brother, 1893), 132–133.

Smith, J. Alfred, Sr.: "A Plea for Divine Presence" (1989)
J. Alfred Smith, Sr., *A Prayer Wheel Turning: Selected Pastoral Prayers* (Morristown, NJ: Aaron Press, 1989), 62–63.

Smith, Sallie: "A Slave Mother's Prayer" (1890) and "Some Prayers of Slave Children" (1890)
Octavia V. Rogers Albert, *The House of Bondage Or Charlotte Brooks and Other Slaves* (1890; reprint with an intro. by Frances Smith Foster, New York and Oxford: Oxford University Press, 1988), 90–91, 96–97.

Stetson, Jeff: "Why, Jesus?!" Unpublished play. Used here by courtesy of the author.

Stewart, Maria W.: "And Now What Wait We For?" (1835), "A Prayer for Divine Companionship" (1835), "A Prayer for Holy Zeal" (1835), "A Prayer for Purification" (1835), "A Prayer for the Children of Africa in America" (1835), "A Prayer for Vision" (1835), "O God, This Great Work Is Thine" (1835), "Purge Us from All Our Dross" (1835)
Maria Stewart, *Productions of Mrs. Maria W. Stewart, Presented to the First African Baptist Church & Society, of the City of Boston* (1835; reprint, with

an intro. by Sue E. Houchins, New York and Oxford: Oxford University Press, 1988), 45–47, 48–49, 36–37, 27, 10–11, 34–35, 42–43, 30–31.

Stone, Orrin: "A Prayer for Power" (1889)
The Good Shepherd (Charleston, SC: n.p., 1889). This prayer was reprinted in an abbreviated form in Henry D. Spalding, *Encyclopedia of Black Folklore and Humor* (Middle Village, NY: Jonathan David Publishers, 1990), 211.

Stroyer, Jacob: "A Slave Father's Prayer" (1898)
Jacob Stroyer, *My Life in the South,* new and enlarged ed. (Salem, MA: Newcomb & Gauss, 1898), 21–22.

Sullivan, Leon H.: "A Prayer for a Positive Attitude" (1972)
Leon H. Sullivan, *Alternatives to Despair* (Valley Forge, PA: Judson Press, 1972), 29.

Tanner, Benjamin Tucker: "Ah, Tender Soul" (1899)
Christian Recorder (30 November 1899).

————: "Hidden Grief" (1895)
Christian Recorder (7 November 1895)

————: "Our Plea" (1894)
Christian Recorder (20 December 1894).

————: "Who?" (1895)
Christian Recorder (10 January 1895).

Taylor, Gardner Calvin: "A Prayer Before the Everlasting Fountain" (1980)
Gardner C. Taylor, *The Scarlet Thread: Nineteen Sermons* (Elgin, IL: Progressive Baptist Publishing House, 1981), 91–92.

Terrell, Lloyd Preston: "A Pastor's Prayer for a Son on Drugs" (1993) and "A Pastor's Prayer for Those in Prison" (1993)
Lloyd Preston Terrell, *Pray, Pastor, Pray!* (Columbus, GA: Brentwood Christian Press, 1993), 25, 60. Both of Pastor Terrell's prayers are used here with his permission.

Thomas, George: "O God, Slow Us Down" (1983)
Leo S. Thorne, ed., *Prayers from Riverside* (New York: Pilgrim Press, 1983), 70.

Thompson, Clara Ann: "I'll Follow Thee" (1908), "Out of the Deep: A Prayer" (1908), and "Storm-Beaten" (1908)
Clara Ann Thompson, *Songs from the Wayside* (Rossmoyne, OH: n.p., 1908), 9, 47–48, 77. Reprinted in Joan R. Sherman, ed., *Collected Black*

Women's Poetry, vol. 2 (New York and Oxford: Oxford University Press, 1988).

Thompson, Priscilla Jane: "A Hymn" (1900)
Priscilla Jane Thompson, *Ethiope Lays* (Rossmoyne, OH: n.p., 1900), 74. Reprinted in Joan R. Sherman, ed., *Collected Black Women's Poetry,* vol. 2 (New York and Oxford: Oxford University Press, 1988).

————: "A Prayer" (1907)
Priscilla Jane Thompson, *Gleaning of Quiet Hours* (Rossmoyne, OH: n.p., 1907), 9. Reprinted in Sherman, ed., *Collected Black Women's Poetry*, vol. 2.

Thurman, Howard: "The Hasty Word" (1969), "We Don't Know How" (1969)
Howard Thurman, *The Centering Moment* (New York and London: Harper & Row, 1969), 104–105, 103.

————: "I Let Go of My Accumulations" (1951) and "O God, I Need Thee" (1951)
Howard Thurman, *Deep Is the Hunger: Meditations for Apostles of Sensitiveness* (New York: Harper & Brothers, 1951), 201–202, 203–205.

Tillman, Katherine Davis Chapman: "A Hymn of Praise" (1902)
Katherine Davis Chapman Tillman, *Recitations* (Philadelphia: A.M.E. Book Concern, 1902). This poetic prayer can also be found in Claudia Tate, ed., *The Words of Katherine Davis Chapman Tillman* (New York and Oxford: Oxford University Press, 1991), 154–155.

————: "A Psalm of the Soul" (1896)
Katherine Davis Chapman Tillman, *Christian Recorder* (9 January 1896): 1. Also in Tate, ed., 141–142.

Tindley, Charles Albert: "Stand by Me" (1905)
The musical score for this famous hymn can be found in most hymnals used in African-American congregations. See Jon Michael Spencer, *Black Hymnody: A Hymnological History of the African-American Church* (Knoxville, TN: University of Tennessee Press, 1992), for a useful analysis of these hymnals. For a first-rate analysis of Tindley's hymnody, and the place of "Stand by Me" in his sacred compositions, see the essays by Bernice Johnson Reagon and Horace Clarence Boyer in Bernice Johnson Reagon, ed., *We'll Understand It Better By and By: Pioneering African American Gospel Composers* (Washington and London: Smithsonian Institution Press, 1992), 37–78. "Stand by Me" itself is reprinted in its original 1905 form on pages 72–73 of *We'll Understand It Better.*

————: "We Are Fully in Thy Sight" (1924)
Quoted in O. Richard Bowyer, Betty L. Hart, and Charlotte A. Meade, *Prayer in the Black Tradition* (Nashville, TN: Upper Room, 1986), 44–45.

Truth, Sojourner: "Always Pray" (1878)
Sojourner Truth, *Narrative of Sojourner Truth; A Bondswoman of Olden Time, Emancipated by the New York Legislature in the Early Part of the Present Century; with A History of Her Labors and Correspondence Drawn from Her "Book of Life"* (1878; reprint, Salem, NH: Ayer Company, 1990), 69–70.

[Walker, Alice]: "The Plea of a Raped Woman" (1982)
Alice Walker, *The Color Purple* (New York: Washington Square Press, 1982), 13.

Walker, David: "A Prophet's Plea to God" (1829)
David Walker, *Walker's Appeal in Four Articles; Together with A Preamble, to the Coloured Citizens of the World, but in Particular, and Very Expressly to Those of the United States of America,* 3d ed. (Boston: D. Walker, 1830). A reprint of this famous pamphlet was edited and introduced by Charles M. Wiltse (New York: Hill & Wang, [1965]). This ejaculatory prayer can be found on pages 73–74 of the reprint.

[Walker, Wyatt Tee]: "Lord, We Didn't Come Here to Stay" (1984)
Wyatt Tee Walker, *The Soul of Black Worship: A Trilogy: Preaching, Praying, Singing* (New York: Martin Luther King, Jr., Fellows Press, 1984), 37–38.

Watley, Matthew L.: "Dear God, if You Please" (1992), "Death" (1992)
William D. Watley and Matthew L. Watley, *Poems of a Son, Prayers of a Father* (Valley Forge, PA: Judson Press, 1992), 20, 84.

Watley, William Donnel: "Dear God, My Son Prays" (1992) "O God, Death Is All Around" (1992), and "O God, I Get So Tired of Racism Wherever I Go" (1992)
Watley and Watley, *Poems of a Son,* 21, 85, 81.

Westfield, Nancy Lynne: "I Must Tell Jesus" (1993)
This pastoral prayer was offered on 28 November 1993 in the sanctuary of Riverside Church in New York. It is printed here by permission of the author.

Weston, M. Moran: "Good Friday Declarations of Awareness" (1972)
M. Moran Weston, *Who Is This Jesus!* (New York: Columbia University Press, 1973), 65, 66, 67, 68.

Wheatley, Phillis: "A Mother's Prayer for the Child in Her Womb" (1779)
The anonymous transcriber of this prayer penned the following note at the bottom of the first page of the two-page transcription: "The words in brackets I supplied as indirectly belonging to the text." All words or punctuation bracketed thusly, [ ] are emendations to the transcription. For example, I changed the spelling of *brot* to *brought,* consistent with modern spelling. See Phillis Wheatley, "Prayer of Phillis's accidentally discovered in her bible," 30 June 1779, typed transcription with bracketed editorial insertions (microfilm, Schomburg Research Center, New York Public Library). A critical edition of Wheatley's writing can be found in William H. Robinson, *Phillis Wheatley and Her Writings* (New York and London: Garland Publishing, 1984), esp. pp. 55–56, where he transcribes and comments on this prayer.

Williams, Peter, Jr.: "A Prayer for Africa's Children" (1808)
Peter Williams, Jr., *An Oration on the Abolition of the Slave Trade; Delivered in the African Church, in the City of New York, January 1, 1808* (New York: Samuel Wood, 1808). This address has been reprinted in Dorothy Porter, [comp.], *Early Negro Writing, 1760–1837* (Boston: Beacon Press, 1971), 374–382. "A Prayer for Africa's Children" is on pages 349–350.

———: "A Prayer for Trust" (1817)
Peter Williams, Jr., *A Discourse, Delivered on the Death of Capt. Paul Cuffe, Before the New York African Institution in the African Methodist Episcopal Church, Oct. 21, 1817* (New York: B. Young and Co., 1817), 15.

Williams, Smallwood Edmond: "Memorial Prayer at Howard University in Memory of Dr. Martin Luther King" (1970)
Smallwood Edmond Williams, *Significant Sermons* (Washington, DC: Bible Way Church, 1970), 121–122.

Woods, Fannie: "A Slave Mother's Doleful Prayer" (1858?)
William H. Robinson recalled this prayer in his autobiography, *From Log Cabin to Pulpit, or Fifteen Years in Slavery,* 3d ed. (Eau Claire, WI: James Tifft, 1913), 43–44.

Wright, Jeremiah, Jr.: "An Altar Prayer" (1989)
Frank B. Jones, *Psalms in Black: A Study of Black Prayer in Three Diverse Contexts* (Ann Arbor, MI: University Microfilms, 1989), 248–255. I have made changes in brackets to further refine Dr. Jones's transcriptions of this prayer. His transcription is punctuated to approximate, as much as possible, the way this prayer was uttered. His purpose was anthropological; my changes seek literary consistency.

Wright, Obie, Jr.: "A Lenten Prayer" (1994)

Personal Papers of Obie Wright, Jr. (Olney, MD), printed here with permission of the author.

[Wright, Richard]: "A Mother's Desperate Plea" (1939)

Richard Wright, *Native Son* (1940; reprint, with notes by Arnold Rampersad, New York: Library of America, 1991), 725–726. Although *Native Son* was published in 1940, Rampersad discovered and restored significant deletions. To emphasize this, I use 1939, when Wright submitted his final manuscript to his publisher, as the date for this fictive prayer.

Index of Authors and Titles